Making a Life

Working by Hand and Discovering the Life You Are Meant to Live

✕

Melanie Falick

PHOTOGRAPHS BY RINNE ALLEN

ARTISAN | NEW YORK

Cover photograph: Mandy Pattullo's studio (see page 296)

Copyright © 2019 by Melanie Falick
Photographs copyright © 2019 by Rinne Allen,
except on the pages noted below:

Christine Ashburn, 320; Center for Furniture Craftsmanship, 146;
Alex Devol, 248 (top left); Melanie Falick, 12, 15 (right), 68 (right), 71
(top right), 135 (top), 139 (center), 141 (right), 178 (center), 179 (top
left), 318 (left); Jenny Hallengren, 175 (top left, center & bottom right);
Parker Keyes, 159 (bottom), 160 (top left), 163 (bottom right), 164 (top),
165 (top right & bottom); Vero Kherian, 237 (bottom); Anna Killian, 283
(center left & bottom left), 284 (top right); Nathalie Lété (from In the
Garden of My Dreams © 2017), 289 (right); Nikki McClure, 202 (bottom
left and right), 207 (center); Jane Merritt, 283 (bottom right), 284 (top left
& bottom left and right); Laurence Mouton, 11, 135 (bottom), 136–37, 139
(top left and right & bottom left and right), 140, 141 (left); Helynn Ospina,
241; Peter Prato, 314; William Rosenblatt, 149 (bottom); Tiina Tahvanainen,
16 (left), 171, 178 (top and bottom left), 179 (top right, center & bottom
left and right); Kristine Vejar, 102 (bottom left); and Elysa Weitala, 100, 101
(bottom), 103.

Library of Congress Cataloging-in-Publication Data

Names: Falick, Melanie, author. | Allen, Rinne, 1973–
photographer.
Title: Making a life / Melanie Falick ; photographs
by Rinne Allen.
Description: New York, NY : Artisan, a division
of Workman Publishing Co., Inc., 2019.
Identifiers: LCCN 2019016973 | ISBN
9781579657444 (hardcover : alk. paper)
Subjects: LCSH: Artisans—Biography. |
Handicraft—Philosophy. | Creation
   (Literary, artistic, etc.)—Philosophy. | Meaning
(Philosophy)
Classification: LCC TT139 .F35 2019 | DDC
745.5—dc23
LC record available at https://lccn.loc.
gov/2019016973

Design by Nina Simoneaux
Cover and interior lettering by June Park

Artisan books are available at special discounts when purchased
in bulk for premiums and sales promotions as well as for fund-raising or
educational use. Special editions or book excerpts also can be created to
specification. For details, contact the Special Sales Director at the address
below, or send an e-mail to specialmarkets@workman.com.

For speaking engagements, contact speakersbureau@workman.com.

Published by Artisan
A division of Workman Publishing Co., Inc.
225 Varick Street
New York, NY 10014-4381
artisanbooks.com

Artisan is a registered trademark of Workman Publishing Co., Inc.

Published simultaneously in Canada by Thomas Allen & Son, Limited

Printed in China
First printing, October 2019

10 9 8 7 6 5 4 3 2 1

Making a Life

How we spend
our days is, of
course, how we
spend our lives.

—Annie Dillard

For Chris, Ben, Mom, Dad, Arthur,
Jeff, Gina, Auntie Lee, and Uncle
Elliott—for believing in this idea
and in me, always

CONTENTS

Introduction

Keep Looking at
Your Hands

IN THE SUMMER of 2012, I attended the Yale Publishing Course, a one-week professional workshop on the school's campus in New Haven, Connecticut. At the time, I had already been working in the book industry for more than two decades and was the publishing director for STC Craft / Melanie Falick Books, an imprint of the New York publishing house Abrams. In this role, I focused on subjects I enjoyed and valued, such as knitting, sewing, quilting, printing, pottery, and other forms of creativity. I took great pride in my work and, having written five books myself, was in the somewhat unique position of genuinely understanding many of the challenges my authors faced when transforming the seed of an idea into a physical object to present to the world.

When I heard about the Yale program, which was billed as five days of lectures and discussions on the future of book publishing in the new global and digital landscape, I was intrigued. Once I arrived, however, I quickly realized that the emphasis would be more on the financial side of the business than the creative, leaving me feeling a bit like a square peg in a round hole.

Late one afternoon, I was relieved when Nigel Holmes entered our amphitheater-style classroom and gave an energetic presentation about his career as a graphic designer, art director, and illustrator. Holmes is internationally renowned for his work in information graphics (distilling complex data and ideas into appealing, easy-to-understand visual forms), and he began and ended his lecture by holding up a simple wooden boat that he had carved for his grandson. With that small handmade object, he reminded us to never let the lure of technology or business overshadow the value we place on working with our own hands. I left the classroom, walked straight to the bathroom, looked down at my hands, and started to cry.

Before going to sleep that evening, I wrote an email to Nigel to thank him. Early the next morning, I was happy to wake to a response:

What a nice message . . . thank you very much for taking the time to write (and at such a late hour!). Like you, I feel a bit lost at conferences such as this one, and I know that I should really attend all the sessions as a participant (not as a nervous presenter, just waiting for the one before mine to end), but I have generally gone through life using intuition more than focused reasoning, and it seems to have supported me so far. I very much like the feel of the books I can see on your site . . . you seem to be making beautiful books that encourage the kind of lifestyle that I was advocating last night: Technology is a great tool, but it will never be a substitute for human work and ideas. Keep looking at your hands.

Just shy of three years later, I left my full-time job at Abrams without a definitive plan for what I would do next, feeling sure I was making the right decision—and also excited and a little nervous. Looking back now, I realize that it was in the bathroom at Yale, after Nigel's lecture, that I began to accept that it was time for me to move on professionally. I was in tears because he had broken through the mental facade I had built to protect myself from confronting the scary reality that I was in a job that had, for a long time, been ideal but that would not suit me much longer. Although I was making a good living, I was no longer making a good life. I was so caught up in emails, deadlines, profit-and-loss statements, sales reports, social media stats, and worries about being financially prepared for retirement that I wasn't enjoying the present. Although I was publishing books about creativity, personally, I felt stuck—stressed and disconnected from my own dreams and values. I knew that if I didn't make a change, I would come to regret it.

My ideas for the future were vague: Aside from part-time freelance work I had lined up to cover bills, a two-week intensive graphic design course that I'd been talking about enrolling in for years, some family obligations, and an intention to spend more time in the garden, I didn't know what I wanted to do next. I just knew that I needed time to be quiet and let my mind wander. I recognized that after working for fifteen years within a corporate structure, I needed to set myself free of certain conventional dialogues about what was and wasn't possible, plausible, dreamable, so that instead of feeling trapped, I could reignite my passion and identify the opportunities that I knew had to exist but that I could not yet see.

Not surprisingly, given the calm and satisfaction that handwork brings me—a realization I came to when I became an avid knitter in my twenties (and then quickly decided to meld my interest in it with my burgeoning career in publishing)—over the next few months, I spent many hours making things. Most of my endeavors were easy and small but required that I try something new. I did some shibori dyeing with indigo, carved stamps, lattice-laced my sneakers, and dyed socks with madder root. I learned to use a strap cutter and a beveler

to make leather bracelets, and I inserted my first zipper when I hand-stitched a pencil case out of repurposed Tyvek. Together with a woodworker friend, I built a bed swing for my porch. To my surprise, the most enlightening project was the simplest and seemingly most mundane: a box I created by strategically folding an ordinary piece of paper. Transforming that commonplace material, in just a few minutes, into a receptacle in which I could store something felt magical. It was so basic—almost primal. It was a skill that, like making my own clothing and growing my own vegetables, could have helped me survive if I had lived a very long time ago. In that box, I might have safeguarded seeds, small tools, or precious stones.

As I held my box in my hands, I realized that, in a circuitous way, during the last few

months, I had been attempting to connect to my own survival. Even though I didn't need to make my own clothing, boxes, or bed—or much of anything—to stay alive, I needed that bond to feel whole, competent and grounded, connected to my heart and soul, to my community, to my ancestors, and to the natural world around me. And, as a result of giving myself time to wander and to make, I no longer felt lost: I understood myself better and had found a new course. For starters, I would meld my personal and professional interests by writing another book of my own, one investigating and celebrating the role making by hand can play in making a good life. As an editor, I always told prospective authors that I was interested in the ideas that were bubbling out of them—the books that they couldn't imagine *not* writing. That is what *Making a Life* became for me.

In Bagru, India, I watched as Dheeraj Chhipa submerged cloth block-printed using a mud-resist technique called *dabu* into a twelve-foot-deep indigo vat that his family has been dyeing in for more than twenty-five years. Dheeraj and his father, Rambabu, then spread the cloth on the road to dry. *Chhipa* means "printers" in Hindi. The Chhipa family have been block printers in India—and before that, Pakistan—for more generations than they can count.

OPPOSITE, TOP RIGHT

In a factory near Delhi, India, these women were assembling thousands of heart-shaped felt wreaths for an American big-box store.

THE JOURNEY I took to write this book was idiosyncratic, guided mostly by my following leads from one person and place to the next. I explored, I listened intently, I took notes, I made things, I overcame fears and challenges. In the process, I felt true to myself and fully engaged. For practical reasons, I focused most of my attention on makers in the United States, but I couldn't pass up the opportunity to travel abroad at least some of the time. I love learning about how people around the world live, especially by way of their making traditions, and I know that one of the best ways to begin to understand one's own culture is to see it through the lens of another.

It seems like a miracle to me now that early on in the development of this book, more by happenstance than meticulous planning, I ended up in Jaipur and New Delhi, India, and soon thereafter in Oaxaca, Mexico. These trips helped me hone my perspective on what it means to make by hand and start to comprehend how it relates to economic development and globalization. I traveled to India with a team from an American homewares company. I accompanied them first to Bagru, in Jaipur, where we met Dheeraj Chhipa, who studied art at the Indian Institute of Crafts and Design and is trying to maintain his family's multigenerational block-printing legacy by modernizing their traditional aesthetic, improving the quality of their base fabric, and reaching out to the international luxury market. Next we went to factories where textile products are made, often by hand, on a much larger scale. I quickly saw that the weaving, tufting, and braiding of rugs,

stitching of pillows, and screen-printing of cloth for mass consumption that the workers there were doing is very different from the kind of textile-making I do at home, where I am able to choose what I want to make based on my own needs and tastes and then produce it from start to finish according to my schedule and whims. In these factories, in most cases, each worker was a member of a team responsible for one step of a process (such as winding yarn, warping looms, hemming, correcting errors, or even folding). I hope that the workers felt pride in what they created together, but I suspect they were there more for a paycheck with which to support their families than for the satisfaction of seeing a pile of their products being loaded onto a truck so they could be shipped abroad for consumption—or for the kind of existential satisfaction many makers experience when they are working with their hands for the sheer pleasure of it.

Of course, India's economy is unique to its own history, culture, and political climate, so Indians are approaching making by hand and by machine in their own way. The government as well as many businesses there are eager to lure

To make the pottery they fire in their courtyard, the Mateos first gather clay from the nearby landscape. Among the tools they then use to make their vessels are a corncob for forming and shaping the bodies, a river stone for burnishing the clay surfaces, and a scrap of leather for giving form to the rims.

manufacturing work to their shores, while in the United States, we are sending so much of ours abroad. And even though Indians are increasingly pursuing higher education and seeking the better-paying jobs subsequently available to them, there is still a large population ready and willing to work in factories, some from families that have been doing handwork for generations. But much of the factory work is different from their traditional handwork, as it is designed for large-scale commerce, not to maintain or safeguard their skills or heritage.

Not long after my trip to India, I departed for the state of Oaxaca in Mexico, another country with long-standing and exquisite handmaking traditions that are being challenged by social and economic changes. I was there to participate in a one-week program focused on creativity and making as an expression of culture, hosted by the Pocoapoco residency. One of the highlights of my experience was a visit to the village of San Marcos Tlapazola, where I met the Mateo family—eight sisters, in-laws, and nieces for whom pottery is a way of life. In the large central courtyard of the bright pink house they share, they make pottery following the age-old traditions passed down to them by their parents and grandparents.

What struck me most as I watched these women was how organic and immediate their process was—they dig clay nearby, from a cornfield and the Sierra Sur mountains, and they fire it in the open air with dried agave leaves and other brush, corncobs, and donkey manure that they store on their roof and then toss down into the courtyard when they need it. Though they make some vessels in nontraditional shapes to meet demand from foreign customers as well as Mexicans, most pieces are still based upon the local culinary traditions: flat plates that are perfect for the corn tortillas that accompany almost every meal, a large *comal* (or griddle) for cooking those tortillas, a deep olla for boiling beans. The Mateo family, who are Zapotec (one of the sixteen indigenous groups in the state of Oaxaca), literally hold the history of their craft and culture in their hands.

MAKING BY HAND, it helps to remember, goes back to the beginning of human history and has developed in its own unique way in every culture. It is, in fact, our hands, especially our opposable thumbs (which allow us to make and use tools)—as well as our abilities to stand upright and make fire—that differentiate us most profoundly from our ape forebears. For hundreds of thousands of years, every object in the world that didn't occur in nature was made by hand—vessels like the ones the Mateo family still make, tools, cloth, shelters, wagons, ships, musical instruments, and on and on. Hands and human ingenuity assured survival. The purpose of each day was to do what was necessary to stay alive, which meant many hours of handwork.

It wasn't until the eighteenth century, when the industrial revolution began in parts of Europe and North America, that water and steam power and then electricity began to mechanize, and thus speed up, production, in turn reducing the necessity for human touch and increasing the ease of acquisition (and subsequent dispensability) of material possessions. And then the twentieth century saw the emergence of the digital revolution. Over the course of just a couple of hundred years in the so-called developed world, we have become passive consumers of products, services, and information rather than active makers, fixers, and even thinkers. Most of the time, what we buy is made somewhere else, by a machine or by people we'll never meet, sometimes working in conditions we would not accept for ourselves.

Given these circumstances, it's not surprising that some of us are discomfited and feel a need for a grounding counterforce. Just as the mechanization and mass production of the industrial revolution led to the Arts and Crafts movement (a late 1800s revival of interest in skilled handwork, craftsmanship, and refined design), the speed and anonymity of the digital revolution and the profit-driven globalization it fast-forwarded have led to what I call a DIY renaissance: a renewal of attention paid to the value of handwork

OPPOSITE, LEFT

Alice from Saudi Arabia
(by way of Belgium),
Maria from the United
States, Gillian from
Ireland, and I take
a break during our
printing workshop with
Lotta Anderson (see
page 170) on Åland in
the Baltic Sea.

OPPOSITE, TOP RIGHT

That's me under the
gray protective helmet,
welding with assistance
from Dan Dyer in Austin
(see page 158).

OPPOSITE, BOTTOM RIGHT

Dolores Swift (see page
306) and I hard at work
on our leather bags.

THIS PAGE

Elsa Mora (see page
150) and I take a walk
on her property in New
York's Hudson Valley.

as well as a concern about how what we
consume is affecting our health and the
environment. No longer required to make
with our hands in order to assure our
survival or make a living, more and more
of us now do so by choice. What was once
a necessity has become, for many, a joy,
a privilege, and a call to action. The DIY
renaissance is part of the same impulse that
continues to drive the slow fashion, slow
design, and slow food movements.

I believe that impulse to use our hands
to make things and, in the process, to
make them beautiful, is our evolutionary
birthright. It is this concept that scholar
Ellen Dissanayake has spent her life
studying, and it is with a conversation with
Ellen on the following pages that I invite
you to join me on this journey. From there,
I hope that you will enjoy reading about
the lives of the many makers I met and
spent time with during this extraordinary
adventure. I've loosely organized their
stories into five chapters—Remembering,
Slowing Down, Joining Hands, Making a
Home, and Finding a Voice—each one an

answer to the question of what it is we stand
to gain when we make things by hand.

All the people featured on these pages
are, without a doubt, very talented; however,
I chose them not because they are "the
best" but because the way they are leading
their lives is both relatable and inspiring.
For some, making by hand is a way of
earning a living—but more important for
each of them, it is a way of taking agency
over their own lives. They have shown me
what their version of a good life looks like.
I, in turn, am sharing their stories—and my
own—with you.

We all make many choices in our lives,
more than we sometimes recognize. I hope
that reading this book motivates you to carve
out some space in your routine to listen to
what your inner voice, your soul, is telling
you about what matters to you most; to tune
in to the small decisions you make each day
that determine how you spend your time
and, ultimately, shape the life you lead.

And, of course, I hope you will keep
looking at your hands. They may hold more
answers than you realize.

Making the Ordinary Extraordinary

WHEN I BEGAN working on my first book, *Knitting in America*, which was published in 1996, I remember pondering two questions: Why do we want to make things with our hands, and why do we want to make them beautiful? Although those questions were continually on my mind as I traveled around the country interviewing knitters, I never addressed them directly in the book. I simply stated matter-of-factly that making by hand and making things beautiful are innate desires. I came to that conclusion based on my own experiences, conversations with other makers, and talking to scholar Ellen Dissanayake and reading her seminal article "The Pleasure and Meaning of Making," which was originally published in *American Craft* magazine (and is now available on academia.edu).

When I began working on *this* book, I found myself asking the same questions but this time exploring them more deeply. My sister-in-law, who is an artist—and, coincidentally, once attended a dinner party with Ellen—reminded me about Ellen's writings, so I reached out to her again all these years later. Fortunately, she greeted my inquiry with kindness and generosity and offered to help me in any way she could.

Meeting Ellen in person about six months later in her book-and-art-filled one-bedroom apartment in the Capitol Hill neighborhood of Seattle was a highlight of this project. She had just had her eightieth birthday and was healthy and still passionate about studying and sharing her ideas. A self-motivated and mostly self-taught scholar with a bachelor's degree in music and philosophy from Washington State University and a master's degree in art history from the University of Maryland, she has devoted much of the last fifty years to pursuing her interests in art and evolution (questions of how and why art originated and evolved) and how they relate to such subject areas as evolutionary biology, psychology, neuroscience, anthropology, and paleoarchaeology. Today she is considered a global authority. When I was with her, she had just completed her fourth book, *Early Rock Art of the American West* (with coauthor Ekkehart Malotki), and was preparing to give a lecture on animal and human behavior at a conference in Portugal.

In many ways, Ellen's writings about art and making and her conviction that both are universal biological impulses inherited from our hunter-gatherer ancestors have helped me appreciate my own desires and choices. Recognizing that these impulses are literally wired into me genetically has helped me understand who I am, prioritize the role of making in my life, and trust that my efforts to encourage other makers—as a writer, editor, occasional teacher, and friend—are useful and worthy. I include this conversation with Ellen in hopes that her ideas will similarly comfort, challenge, and enlighten all who read it.

OPPOSITE

Ellen in her Seattle home.

"The fact that it feels good to make things with our hands harkens back to our hunter-gatherer nature, which lives on in our psychology."

Ellen and I talked for hours about our mutual fascination with the human impulse to make ordinary things extraordinary.

What compelled you to study the relationship between human evolution and art and making?

I started out as a pianist, then was a housewife in two thirteen-year marriages. During this time, I was able to travel a lot in non-Western countries like Madagascar, India, Nigeria, and Papua New Guinea and to live in Sri Lanka for fifteen years. I wondered why the arts were so omnipresent and emotionally moving everywhere in the world. Because my interests were so multidisciplinary, I didn't fit into any academic track, and I had to pursue my research on my own. Gradually, I began to publish my writings in the mid-1970s. I have traced what modern and postmodern societies call "art" (and "craft") back to the toolmaking and ceremonial practices of our human ancestors.

In your first book, *What Is Art For?*, published in 1988, you presented a new definition of art.

It was less a new definition than a new approach—the idea of treating art as a *behavior*, something that people do, rather than as a thing or a quality or a label that museum curators give or that critics write about. I gradually came to the conclusion that in its most simple sense, art (as a verbal noun that I now call "artifying" or "artification") is the act of making ordinary things extraordinary. It is a uniquely human impulse.

So you believe that artifying is an inherent, universal trait of the human species?

Yes. I believe that artifying is as normal and natural as language, sex, sociability, aggression, or any other characteristics of human nature. One could say that the general behavior of artifying (making things one cares about special) underlies all the arts.

You coined the term *joie de faire*—an inherent joy in making—and in "The Pleasure and Meaning of Making," you wrote that "there is something important, even urgent, to be said about the sheer enjoyment of making something exist that didn't exist before, of using one's own agency, dexterity, feelings, and judgment to mold, form, touch, hold, and craft physical materials, apart from anticipating the fact of its eventual beauty, uniqueness, or usefulness." From an evolutionary perspective, why is pleasure in making important?

The pleasure in handling is inherent in human nature for good reason: It predisposes us to be tool users and makers. We have this very unusual dexterous hand with an opposable thumb and flexible, sensitive fingers. Our *Australopithecus* predecessors made crude stone tools two and a half million years ago. I hypothesize that if their descendants didn't like (or were unable) to use their hands, they would not have survived and prospered as well as those who did.

The earliest hunter-gatherers had to be makers of everything they needed for their lives. In *The Raw and the Cooked*, distinguished French anthropologist Claude Lévi-Strauss wrote about a point at which our early human ancestors began to transform nature into culture. They took raw food and cooked it and made pots from clay. Later, they wove raw fibers into cloth. Art historian Herbert Cole elaborated on Lévi-Strauss's ideas and talked about the raw, the cooked, and the *gourmet*. He said that sometimes just cooking food is not enough:

You want to make it special. You don't just simply make a clay pot—on special occasions, you incise or paint it with stripes and other geometrics. In *Early Rock Art of the American West*, my coauthor, Ekkehart Malotki, and I cite the making of cupules (small cup-shaped marks pounded into rock surfaces) two hundred thousand years ago at Sai Island in present-day Sudan as the first evidence of artifying (to date). But it is quite likely that there was body decorating, as well as dancing and singing (in other words, making ordinary body movements and gestures and vocal sounds extraordinary) much earlier. These behaviors don't leave traces behind, but they seem quite natural to our species as they occur very early and easily in small children.

You have emphasized in your work other aspects of human nature that derive from our remote hunter-gatherer past.

In *Art and Intimacy*, I sorted the emotional needs of all humans into five categories that originated in our hunter-gatherer ancestors. The first I called hands-on competence (the ability to do the things required of men and women in society), which of course for hundreds of thousands of years required using one's hands. Another I called elaboration, or making special. Meeting these needs is as important today as it was back then. Modern-day makers might choose to create pottery or sew clothing not because they have to but because they feel the urge, even need, to do it. The fact that it feels good to make things with our hands harkens back to our hunter-gatherer nature, which lives on in our psychology.

In a traditional society, hands-on competence, learning to do what is expected of adult men and women, is what growing up is about.

Yes. Girls were taught to prepare food, boys to make animal traps and fishing nets. In some groups, only females or only males made pots or wove baskets. All these skills were acquired as a matter of course by watching and interacting with others, and the skills were within the capability of all normal people. Today, although they have the "freedom" to choose their own paths to satisfying work, not all young people can figure out their own place in the larger world, where it is difficult to acquire the skills that will bring the money and prestige that have become the measure of success. In traditional societies, a material object that one made was tangible evidence that one had accomplished something, even though it might not have been "the best." Participation was the important thing.

Besides hands-on competence and elaboration, what are the other three needs of our hunter-gatherer nature that you identified?

Mutuality, belonging, and meaning. *Mutuality* is having a close, intimate relationship with another person or people, beginning from the first moment after birth and continuing throughout a lifetime. *Belonging* is being an unquestioned part of a like-minded group. Believing what other people in your group believe (what we call "myths" when we encounter them in tribal societies) provides assurance that life has *meaning* and purpose. And making special

(or elaborating) demonstrates that one cares about what one has made and reinforces the beliefs that give life meaning.

If making with our hands and making special are part of our inheritance from our hunter-gatherer ancestors, what do you think happens when we are not satisfying those needs?

In small-scale societies, life as lived satisfies the five fundamental needs—there is a kind of unity or wholeness of belief and behavior that is shared by everyone. In modern pluralistic societies that extol the individual, we have more opportunities and choices, but we forfeit the security of being in a group that supports our beliefs and accepts who we are. Each person has to find their own way of satisfying the basic emotional needs that were laid down in the way of life of our hunter-gatherer ancestors. I think a lot of modern people's ennui, or feelings of depression or meaninglessness, comes from the fact that although our physical and material needs are met, we are not satisfying these psychological or emotional needs of our hunter-gatherer nature.

Today, we model consuming more than making (and replacing rather than repairing). What happens if we don't model making for our children?

Young children inherently want to use their hands. First, they learn to pick up, then to place down, to drop, to hammer. Then they start manipulating and playing with everything they encounter. Later, they begin (often spontaneously, without being taught) to dance, sing, dress up and

TOP

Ellen's living room shelves are filled with mementos from the more than two decades she spent living in Sri Lanka, traveling in Nigeria, and teaching at the National Arts School in Papua, New Guinea.

BOTTOM

Ellen's multidisciplinary approach to the study of art and evolution is reflected in the carefully organized reference materials in her office.

play make-believe, perform, and so forth. When they are young and in preschool or kindergarten, many are encouraged to make things—paper snowflakes and jack-o'-lanterns, clay bookends—but as they get older, making things isn't usually considered a priority. If we don't foster making, many children's natural drive to do it will atrophy. In premodern societies, the infant's and child's pleasure in handling and then using objects evolved naturally into making them—implements, vessels, homes, regalia. Today, for many reasons, we buy things rather than make them. Although this is convenient, we forfeit our evolved birthright of being makers, and may not even discover it.

Do you think making and making special could actually be less important today than they were in the past?

A child's impulse to handle and make and the tradition among individuals and societies to make significant things and occasions special are ongoing. Though making may not be important in a practical sense anymore, I don't think it is less critical today than it was a quarter of a million years ago. I have said that the psychological losses of not artifying can be likened to a vitamin deficiency. You may not know that you have it, but once you learn that you do and rectify it, you feel so much better.

I believe that using my hands to make things and generally being competent with my hands are essential to my happiness. I would even say essential to my emotional wellness.

All makers seem to feel that way and wonder why everyone else doesn't. Maybe everyone finds some essential thing they can do. I play the piano. My son likes to work on his car and to rehab houses. My daughter makes quilts. My grandfather was a cabinetmaker. There are people who sing all the time. They might wonder why other people don't. I would guess that everyone has the need to make the ordinary extraordinary, to artify in some way. I have a few friends who, when they send something in a real envelope (rare these days), artify the envelope with colored pencils and fancy lettering, framing the address with scrolls or other designs. Artifying includes setting a table with flowers or, if you're going to a party, wearing something special.

I've met a lot of people, especially women, who know that their handwork is important to them on a deep level but play it down or trivialize it. Or, even worse, people around them trivialize it.

In a society that considers the arts to be something to do in your spare time, it is hard to justify doing it—especially when others consider it only a pastime, a "frill."

That's why finding even two or three like-minded (and -handed) makers can be inspirational. Also, if it is pointed out that working for money is a very recent development, at least people might be able to see themselves as being in a line of makers and elaborators that goes back two hundred thousand years or more. At one time, making was crucial to our individual and species survival and, certainly compared to passively ingesting entertainment, probably still is. Neglecting the fundamental emotional needs of humans may result in seriously dysfunctional individuals and societies.

What do you think will happen if we continue to allow machines to replace our hands for so many tasks? Beyond not making our own clothes, some of us don't even chop vegetables anymore but instead buy them precut. And, of course, cars that drive themselves are imminent.

Evolution works so slowly that it is hard to point out the deleterious effects of *not* making, since so many people seem to get along well without doing it. Although a few people eat a paleo diet, those who don't are still surviving. The rave concerts with audience participation are a kind of ceremonial ritual full of artifications—one

could say it is an atavistic attempt to get back to those satisfactions. My own opinion is that we are neglecting at our peril what neuroscience has revealed are "right hemisphere" functions (paying attention to our surroundings, empathy, intuition, metaphor, emotional expression, aesthetic decisions and appreciation, and so forth— aspects of the arts that we have no words for because the right hemisphere lacks "propositional" or "rational" language). We have made a world that requires "left hemisphere" skills (analysis, detachment, sequential argument) in order to survive.

It sounds depressing to say that we are psychologically and emotionally really badly off, especially in modern society, because we neglect those five basic needs. We are rich in material comforts that our ancestors did not have but poor in the emotional satisfactions they had by virtue of their lifestyle. It is a big mismatch. Simply using our hands—or dancing and singing and other artifying—is not going to stop that. However, in individual lives, and in the lives of the children we raise or can influence, I think we can be aware that active making, and making special, contributes to satisfactions (fulfillment of basic emotional needs) that cannot come any other way.

ONE

Remembering

JESSICA GREEN

A Weaver's Prayer

Melanie: As a child, what did you want to be when you grew up?

Jessica: This. It was born in the third grade when I read *Little House in the Big Woods*. I wanted to be Laura.

AND SO BEGINS my interview with Jessica Green, in some ways a modern-day Laura Ingalls Wilder. We are not in a log cabin deep in the Wisconsin woods, where the Little House stories of mid-nineteenth-century American homesteading begin, but rather in a shingled, tin-roofed cabin in southern Appalachia, in Sandy Mush, North Carolina, where the Great Smoky and Blue Ridge Mountains meet. While the location is not remote, I did pass a sign with the words Beaten Path printed on it during my forty-minute drive here, northwest from the Asheville airport—and we are definitely off it. The sign was posted on a winding road right around the spot where I began to wonder if I was going to lose my cellular service, which would deactivate the navigational app I was relying on to reach the steep dirt lane that would lead me up past the apple trees to Jessica's house.

Jessica is a weaver—of cloth, yes, and also of ideas and lives. This reveals itself as soon as we start talking and is confirmed a few hours later when her friends begin to arrive on her deck for their weekly Sunday supper.

Trevor is an arborist. Lottie is a farmer. Nathalie runs an urban-homesteading supply business. Alex is an architect who is here only temporarily while retrofitting a school bus that he plans to travel and live in as he moves around the country from one design/build work site to the next. Emma is a masseuse, and Zanni is a social worker. I ask them how they know one another, and one of them says, "Jessica brings people together." And they all agree. A few of them were at Bennington College in Vermont at the same time in the early 2000s, then they each went their separate ways but have now reconvened on a road in rural North Carolina with a vision of weaving a new kind of life together. At once pragmatic and idealistic, they aspire to create a version of communal living that they are calling a village, one in which each of them maintains independence but is also committed to the well-being of the others and the importance of their bonds.

"In our culture, all our limbs have been cut off because we don't have a relationship to each other that is based in collective power," Jessica begins. "What is considered a high-class way of me relating to you is to ask you how you are doing. You tell me; I say that sounds great or so hard. We drink our tea. I ask if you have a good therapist. We don't have a relationship based on doing. I don't come and work in your garden

Jessica weaving in her studio, wearing one of her beloved nana's dresses—and a pair of very well worn socks.

OPPOSITE, RIGHT

Jessica knitting in her living room. She describes the time she spends knitting as a little gift to herself: a chance to relax and recalibrate.

"Who do
I become
as I fully
engage in
a series
of simple
repeatable
tasks?"

—From Jessica's
handout, *Tension &
Release: A Weaver's
Notebook Journal Zine
for Gracefully Treadling
Between Dualities*

The Cabbage School, Jessica says, "is about being together and doing something that contributes to our survival." At an inaugural event, three classes were offered to thirty students: Weaving and Embodiment (taught by Jessica and a friend with a doctorate in performance and philosophy), Mapping and Anti-Mapping (co-taught by a philosopher, an interior designer, and an architecture professor), and Library (co-taught by an archivist, a fine woodworker, and the owner of an urban homesteading supply store).

Jessica's Appalachian cabin was built by a college friend, who sold it and twenty-three acres of land to her in 2011. A few years later, when a neighbor put the adjoining seventeen acres and a house on the property up for sale, Jessica's mother immediately envisioned a school there and bought the real estate to support that possibility.

Jessica loves to use the cloths she weaves in her home, and she hopes that others will do the same.

with you. We don't actually figure out how to build a structure so that when your kid comes home from school, he or she has a place to be. We're not actively engaged in each other's lives."

But what could a new reality look like? That is the question that Jessica and her community are exploring. During Sunday supper, they talk about the Cabbage School, the alternative educational center they are establishing in an old house on the property. They also recall their recent work digging a French drain at Nathalie's place, and the afternoon they spent together making healthful tinctures and bitters using plants they had foraged from the land and grown in their gardens. Jessica had recently butchered her four pigs, and she reminded Trevor to pick up a share of pork from the freezer. When her three cows (two Dexters and one Dexter-Jersey mix) are producing, there is milk, butter, and cream to distribute. Jessica also raises Cormo sheep, whose wool a neighbor shears for her. Jessica uses it in her weaving, sometimes spinning it herself and dyeing it with plants she grows or forages.

It is important to everyone in the community that they integrate not only with one another but also with the people who settled on this land before them. When Jessica was weaving a series of ten-inch "everyday cloths" to send off to the Bradbury Art Museum in Arkansas, where they would be exhibited like paintings on a wall in a show called *Quiet Work*, she decided that she would first lend them to neighbors to use however they wanted in their everyday lives. Mr. Reeves, who is eighty-nine, got one. ("He's a gem," she says. "Mostly we talk about pork.") And so did some locals whom Jessica had not yet formally met. "It was a sweet and easy way to approach them," she recalls. "I had this little veil, a reason to sit down and say, 'Hi. I see you all the time, and I'm working on this project.'"

Jessica came to weaving by chance in her twenties. After graduating from college with a concentration in anthropology and performance art, she moved to Colorado to be an attendant to a Tibetan lama at a monastery and retreat center for about eighteen months. Next she headed to New York City, where she lived with friends and supported herself by working a series of odd jobs, including managing a tattoo shop and babysitting. Through a series of random connections, she ended up building an indoor raised garden bed for growing marigolds as part of an installation for textile artist Tali Weinberg. Tali's loom was the first one Jessica recalls ever encountering in person, and when she sat down at it, in front of a cloth of marigold-yellow ombré, it felt to her like a homecoming. "All of a sudden, I felt connected to this different lineage flow, a lineage of weavers," Jessica remembers.

After being required to
read *Little House in the
Big Woods* in her third-
grade class and then
to hand-dip candles
and make punched-can
votives in conjunction
with the text, Jessica
was hooked on both
the Little House series
and on crafting. She
devoured the rest of
the books in the series
and, from that point on,
dreamed of living a life
closely connected to
the land and to her own
survival. "I have reread
these books so many
times," Jessica tells me.
"They're like candy."

Before even raising a thread or throwing
a shuttle, Jessica knew she had to learn
to weave, which she began to do at the
Penland School of Craft in North Carolina
the following summer. Her teacher, Suzie
Liles, owner of the Eugene Textile Center,
was so impressed by Jessica's natural affinity
that she invited her to Oregon to study and
work with her. Jessica made the move a
year later, and there she met more teachers,
including Judith MacKenzie (see page 56).
"It was like she was born to weave," Judith
says of her now dear friend. "The loom is
a natural extension of what her mind and
body are doing."

"I connect with her deeply," responds
Jessica. "She is the truest teacher I have
ever encountered, a treasure, someone I
strive to be like."

In the early days, Jessica's focus was
on American Colonial coverlets, which
appealed to her as a way of connecting to
her own heritage (some of her ancestors
emigrated to the Colonies from Sweden in
the eighteenth century) and also because
of the history of American women weaving
their own cloth to assert independence
from the British during the Revolutionary
War. Around that work, she built a business
called A Little Weather and sold her textiles
to high-end shops like ABC Carpet &
Home in New York City, by commission,
and directly from her website. Since then,
her work has become more intimate as she
has begun to explore warps and wefts in
an increasingly improvisational manner,
often within a series of small, finely woven
squares of cloth. This shift is leading her
out of the so-called craft world and into the
realms of art and design.

"I encountered weaving as an anti-art,
as a way of creating something useful
without a complicated relationship to the
craft-art-design question. I just wanted to
be making," Jessica explains. But she is
slowly realizing that by letting go of her
own preference for functionality (which
was landing her in the craft realm) and
presenting her work within art and design
realms (for example, exhibiting at the
International Contemporary Furniture
Fair and the Architectural Digest Design
Show), she is able to charge prices that more
realistically reflect the hours she puts into
the pieces. Customers sometimes purchase
her work as "art" to put on display, while
others see her work in this setting but then
commission her to create cloth they intend
to put to practical use, such as place mats or
bedcovers. Either way, she has found that
the context within which a customer first
encounters her textiles determines their
expectations about cost.

While preparing to teach a weaving
class at Penland (just eight years after she
wove for the first time in the very same

TOP LEFT

Raising animals, Jessica explains, lends rhythm and meaning to her days. About her flock of Cormo sheep, she says, "They teach me about approach: how to hold a calm joy in my heart and my whole body. I have to be confident yet open. Any stress or anxiety in my step or my face or the flick of my wrist will send them running."

TOP RIGHT

Beans, peaches, mead, pear butter, and wild rose petal honey are among the many provisions Jessica preserves from her summer gardening and foraging—a delicious reminder of the earth's bounty, especially during the winter months.

Jessica wove the cloth on her bed with cotton and linen yarn she dyed with indigo, homegrown weld, foraged sumac, and iron. To create the watercolor effect, she dyed the yarn for the weft as she progressed, coordinating it with the warp. The pillow covers are her riff on Colonial coverlets, part of an earlier body of work.

OPPOSITE, BOTTOM LEFT

Skeins of cotton, linen, and wool dyed with indigo, madder, and black walnut.

OPPOSITE, RIGHT

Jessica has woven several series of small (about ten-inch square) cloths, which she calls Quiet Cloths, Farm Journals, and Prayers for Imperfection. Each cloth, she says, is an experiment in weaving as time telling and holds the power of a moment of quiet attention.

studio), Jessica compiled a photocopied collection of writings, drawings, and songs for her students titled *Tension & Release: A Weaver's Notebook Journal Zine for Gracefully Treadling Between Dualities*. Jessica's ability to gracefully navigate dualities—whether the question of art vs. craft, individualism vs. socialism, success vs. failure, idealism vs. pragmatism, or practicing artist-maker vs. teacher—impresses me. The seeds of this grace seem to have been planted in her childhood.

Jessica grew up in Austin, Texas, with her parents, both lapsed Mormons, and two brothers. From grades six through twelve, she attended a small independent school with students from around the world, where she was, in many ways, encouraged to design her own education. "My confidence in being able to be a pioneer came from this school," she states assuredly. It also has roots in her close relationship with her extended Mormon family and the connection she felt for a long time to early Mormon mysticism and the Mormon history of homesteading. "I learned early on that if I asked my relatives to teach me things, they wouldn't try to convert me." From them she learned everything from sewing garments to cross-stitch and embroidery to gardening, all of which she loved.

Most influential was her maternal grandmother, whom she describes as "an adamant crusader for joy" and central to who Jessica is. "She lived in a fantasy world, and if you were willing to go there with her, it could be nothing but magical all the time," Jessica lovingly recalls. "We made a whole world around us all the time. We made Pilgrim costumes with little

bonnets, we made full shadow-puppet shows of *Sylvester and the Magic Pebble*, my favorite book. She tap-danced at my college graduation. Everything felt like an escapade." And everything felt possible. From her, Jessica inherited what she calls "an unshakable joy" and "faith in the impossible," which bring her to the present day and her quest to manifest a new type of village life rooted in indigenous joy and mutual empowerment that reverberate outward to others.

"I desperately want to incite a cultural shift, and just because it is impossible doesn't mean it's not something to strive for," Jessica tells me as we settle down in a cozy corner of her studio near a woodstove and a window-side claw-foot bathtub. The ideal she strives for—and toward which real progress can certainly be made—is one that brings people in touch with their own authority, their ability to sustain their lives within a community that doesn't depend on often-broken political and social structures and where equality and respect for the environment are endemic. Weaving is, for her, part of the solution, not just metaphorically in terms of weaving together ideas and lives, but literally: The simple repeatable task—the raising and lowering of sheds, the throwing of the shuttle, the making of cloth to protect and warm the body or clean up messes or elevate the ordinary—this, for her, is a union of the mythic and the mundane; it is holy; it goes back to the beginnings of humanity and is a prayer that holds seeds of potential for a better world. And then she looks directly into my eyes and says, "What better prayer is there than that?"

OPPOSITE, TOP LEFT

Within her studio, Jessica has five looms so she can both teach classes there and, when needed, bring in assistants to help her with orders.

OPPOSITE, TOP RIGHT

Jessica preparing her warp threads for weaving. On her hand is a tattoo of sumac, one of several tattoos she has gotten to represent plants that are important to her.

OPPOSITE, BOTTOM

Watching Jessica as she raises and lowers sheds, throws a shuttle, then pulls the beater, all the while treadling with her feet, I understand her description of weaving as a "wholly embodied practice— performance art."

TOP

Jessica walking through the pasture that stretches between her house and the studio.

BOTTOM LEFT

A friend built this studio for Jessica to replace a dilapidated barn whose foundation was crumbling. Some of the boards from the original structure were incorporated into the new one, while others were repurposed for a sauna on the property and for her friends Emma and Zanni's new house down the road.

BOTTOM RIGHT

Jessica loves bathtubs, even in unexpected places. About the one in her studio, she says, "I use it to wash wool and aid in my natural dye practice, for personal bathing, as a sweet way for folks to inhabit the space and come visit me for self-care, as a cool refresher when folks are working in the fields here."

Agnes Martin: You can ask me for my
definition of art if you want.

Interviewer: OK, I will, what is it, please

AM: Art is the concrete representation
of our most subtle feelings.
That is the end.

36

TENSION & RELEASE

a weaver's notebook journal zine
for gracefully treadling between dualities

SWEETNESS + CHARM
Personal Areas — hang work   WARPS: 12"
- Cardboard Pile
- Free yarns back to...   SMOOTH ROUGH   TANGLE
- TOOLS back!
- YARN CHECKED IN
- Trash to dumpster...   COLOR
- recycling to dumpster
- dye kitchen   PATTERN
- SWEEPING

weaving lessons

As a teacher, Jessica strives to create what she calls a "mini-finite utopia," where students let go of expectation, comparison, and judgment; encounter their own authority; and learn to feel comfortable making their own decisions and solving their own problems rather than waiting to be told what to do. When they return home, she hopes they will be able to apply these lessons not only in the cloth they weave but also, more broadly, in the lives they lead. These photos were taken during a two-week workshop at Penland School of Craft in Penland, North Carolina. Jessica also teaches at Warren Wilson College in Swannanoa, North Carolina; at the Cabbage School; and in her studio.

The Spiral of Our Galaxy

THE FIRST TIME I encounter Renate Hiller, it is by way of a four-and-a-half-minute video on YouTube. I see a graceful, gray-haired woman using a stone spindle to transform locks of white wool roving into fine, strong yarn. She sets her rustic, homemade tool (a stone and a stick tied together, an ancient innovation) into a circular motion with the flick of her long fingers, then lets its momentum create the strength-giving twist in the raw wool she is releasing from above.

As she works, she speaks with a poetic practicality, in an elegant German-accented English, about why spinning and other fiber crafts are important even in today's machine-driven world. She likens the spiral formed when spinning to the spiral of our galaxy as seen from outer space and to the spiral of hair on top of our heads. She describes spinning as "a cosmic gesture of creation"—that is, an activity that brings us closer to the divine and at the same time allows us to experience beauty and utility. She speaks about the way children learn, by grasping first with their hands, then with their minds. She suggests that when we "conveniently" buy our sweaters pre-knitted, our vegetables pre-chopped, or our bread pre-baked—that is to say, when we stop knowing how to use our hands to meet our most basic needs—we become estranged from nature, from the value and meaning of things, and from the empathy that we need to care for one another and our world.

When, through a series of coincidences, I find myself in Renate's living room in Chestnut Ridge, New York, a few years later, I am starstruck. Just like, I suspect, many of the more than one hundred thousand people who have watched her video online, I have elevated her in my mind to a near-mythic status for her ability to put words to the yearning I feel inside. With sureness and simplicity, she articulates why the innate flexibility and dexterity of our hands are gifts we should not ignore, despite the seeming practicality of machines designed to replace them and technology designed to distract us.

When the video was filmed in 2010, Renate was the codirector of the Fiber Craft Studio, an educational center in Chestnut Ridge linked to Sunbridge Institute (a training center for Waldorf school teachers), the Green Meadow Waldorf School, and several other institutions situated on the same parcel of land that was settled by a group of social progressives in the 1920s. Renate first learned about Waldorf education in 1976 as a young mother in Germany in search of a kindergarten for her son. She and her husband and their two children (their three-year-old son and a six-month-old daughter) had moved from New

OPPOSITE

Archaeologists believe that humans may have been spinning with a stone spindle, like this one that Renate made herself, as far back as thirty thousand years ago. When you work with a spindle, Renate points out, it orbits. "You hold it between heaven and earth. When you look at yarn, it is a spiral. Our galaxy seen from outer space is a spiral."

York to their homeland for her husband's job and would stay there for six years. During that time, both children would attend Waldorf schools and Renate would join a parent handwork group and be introduced to the school's philosophy of anthroposophy, which is rooted in a belief in an innate, symbiotic relationship between one's physical and spiritual beings. "I connected with it right away. It made so much sense," Renate recalls, and it has in many ways influenced her life's path ever since.

Waldorf school and anthroposophy founder Rudolf Steiner was an Austrian philosopher, scientist, and visionary who lived from 1861 to 1925 and whose ideas about human development, education, architecture, ethical banking, organic farming, and myriad other subjects are still reverberating around the world today. Within the Waldorf curriculum, students ranging from preschoolers to high schoolers are taught to engage all their senses to learn academic and intuitive ways of working and

develop into clear-thinking, compassionate, responsible adults. Handwork and other sensory experiences are key in this process of inner and outer development, and knitting, sewing, crochet, woodworking, and other forms of purposeful activity are integrated into lessons throughout all grades.

In Germany, as part of that Waldorf parent group, Renate sewed fabric dolls and knitted garter-stitch lambs for a new kindergarten classroom. "When I knitted the first lamb and it was done, I couldn't believe how beautiful it was," she says. "It was such a simple design and caught the essence of 'lamb-ness.'" Renate was already quite accomplished at needlework, having learned from her mother and grandmother as well as from a favorite teacher at school (in fact, as a young girl, she had fantasized about becoming a handwork teacher, and during my first visit, she showed me pristine examples of complex sewing, embroidery, and lace crochet that she had executed as a child). But, she says, when she encountered

OPPOSITE, LEFT

Two Waldorf dolls sewn by Renate as an adult. In the kindergartens, the children are given hand-sewn dolls (often made by members of the parent handwork group) with which to play and learn. Older students make their own dolls.

OPPOSITE, RIGHT

Renate came to handwork as a child growing up in Germany. Naturally gifted, she fondly recalls learning from her mother and grandmother and also a favorite grade-school teacher. When I visited, she brought out pristine examples of early work, including those shown here. Even she is in awe of the preciseness of the stitches she made as a girl.

Waldorf-inspired handwork, "a whole new chapter began."

That chapter included enrolling her children in the Green Meadow Waldorf School when the family returned to the States in 1985 and eventually becoming so deeply involved in handcrafts at the school, as well as in the study of anthroposophy and the community in general, that she was asked to become an instructor in the teacher training program at Sunbridge College. By 1992, her work there was consuming so much of her attention that she decided to give up a career in publishing to devote herself full-time to both teaching and taking courses at Sunbridge, then to helping develop their Applied Arts program specifically for handcraft-teacher training. And that, in turn, led to her becoming one of the founding members of the Fiber Crafts Studio, which was originally part of Sunbridge and is now a related but independent entity that offers Waldorf teacher education as well as public programming.

A turning point for Renate came in 1986, when she was spotted by Grete Fröhlich at a parent handwork meeting. Fröhlich, in her eighties at the time, had studied with a student of Rudolf Steiner's in Germany and was a pioneer of Waldorf education in the United States. She was attending the meeting to teach the group how to sew undershirts for Waldorf dolls, which are an essential toy in early-childhood classrooms. Renate recalls Grete saying, "I can see you have used your hands," then telling her she wanted to work with her. "I thought about it," Renate says, "and I knew that destiny had spoken, that I had to go and work with Grete and that it would be until the end of her life or mine. I knew that somehow with deep knowledge." This elderly lady, who handled scissors "with absolute certainty and made the most simple and beautiful pattern without drawing anything and was so agile in her mind," Renate recalls, became Renate's teacher and role model. Nearly until Grete's death at the age of one hundred, Renate visited her weekly at the Fellowship, an assisted-living center housed on the Waldorf campus.

Together, Renate and Grete worked through the handwork section of the Waldorf curriculum, both the underlying pedagogy and the hands-on practice. Much of the emphasis, Renate explains, is on observing and appreciating the qualities of things, ultimately to elevate one's level of consciousness or, one could say, to connect to a spiritual layer of being. For example, when you look at two different yellows—one reddish, one more green—the reddish yellow feels warm, and the greenish one cool, not through touch but through an intuitive sense experience. The same is true with forms: A shape that is wide at the bottom, like a pyramid, might feel static and heavy, while a balloon form might transmit a sense of buoyancy.

Renate and Grete sometimes took walks, sometimes made things, and sometimes explored art history. Renate recalls a particular day when, to demonstrate a lesson, Grete drew the basic layouts of an ancient Egyptian temple and Romanesque and Gothic churches on the back of a used envelope and asked, "What is expressed through these forms based on the consciousness of the times?" Through such questions, Grete helped Renate develop and deepen her perceptive sensibility; that is, the ability to simultaneously perceive an object's physical and spiritual presence and articulate one's ideas in a way that is clarifying to oneself and others.

So when I ask Renate to elaborate on what she meant when she suggested in the YouTube video that spinning can be a way to connect to the divine, I am not surprised that she is able to explain her thoughts clearly and succinctly: "When one also considers the beautiful spiral forms that are so prevalent in nature (such as the nautilus shell and pinecones) and in art through the ages and in all cultures, one cannot but become convinced that there is a common source to all this, a higher divine consciousness. And maybe through the meditative working with the spindle, we might, for moments, be able to connect with, or tune in to, this higher

consciousness, which you could also call the divine in us and in the world."

Although Renate retired from her position as the director of the Fiber Craft Studio in 2012, she continues to inspire its members, serve on the advisory circle, and share with them her fiber explorations. When I visit her, she is working on a new sweater design using wool yarn she plant dyed and spun herself, a design that she hopes will be part of a published book someday. She and Mikae Toma, a longtime associate and codirector at the Fiber Craft Studio, have already completed much of the work on this labor of love, in which they demonstrate how joyful and nurturing it can be to design and create one's own clothing based on organic shapes. When we talk about photography for this book, she insists that we take at least some of our photos up the road at the Fiber Craft Studio and include her friends and cocreators there. Along with her family, that space and the people within it are a lifeline, a support system, and a continual source of creative energy.

Like her mentor Grete Fröhlich, Renate is sure that it is through handwork that she is meant to serve. When I ask her why we want and need to make things with our hands, and to make them beautiful, she responds with eloquence: "It has to do with the fact that there is more to being a human being than the physical body and the movements we make. There is a longing in us, in soul and spirit, to reconnect with the divine. When we are engaged in creating beauty ourselves, we are in our own way doing just that."

LEFT

Renate still treasures the time she spends with her friends at the Fiber Craft Studio. Here she is joined by member Miho Suzuki, current director Chris Marlow, and volunteer Janet Gomez.

RIGHT

A photo of Grete Fröhlich, Renate's mentor. "She was still knitting, making animals without patterns, practically to the end of her life," Renate tells me. "She would say, 'The reason I am still at home up here'—pointing to her head—'is because I have been doing this work with my hands.'"

"So much handwork has to do with reawakening ourselves to the wonders of the natural world."

OPPOSITE, TOP & BOTTOM RIGHT

Renate uses all her senses to experience this fresh Jacob fleece. "The living quality of the fibers is amazing," she says as she immerses herself in it. "So much handwork has to do with reawakening ourselves to the wonders of the natural world."

OPPOSITE, BOTTOM LEFT

Two sweaters Renate designed and knitted, along with her notes. When we are following someone else's pattern, she says, we are mostly stuck in our heads: thinking, counting, reading. When we are figuring out a design for ourselves, we are feeling, asking questions, observing, and making decisions, connecting to the process and the metamorphosis of the work on a deeper level.

TOP

Renate spinning at Orchard House, home of the Fiber Craft Studio.

BOTTOM

Renate in the Fiber Craft Studio's dye garden. She played an integral role in introducing plant dyeing into the modern Waldorf curriculum.

SARAH JERATH

Playing in the Mud

I FEEL HONORED when Sarah Jerath offers to take me up Hunters Hill during my springtime visit to Parbold, her small village (population about 2,600) in northwestern England. It's a short drive from her narrow, two-story house, which was the village pub back in the seventeenth century, to the bottom of the hill, then a ten-minute walk up a dirt path to the spot where she decides we should stop first. Once part of a stone quarry, the hill is, in fact, where many of Sarah's most vivid and happy memories were born (and also the source of both the stone with which her house was built and many of the aggregates she now uses in her ceramics). It was her playground when she was a child, she explains, the place where she and her siblings and the family dog spent countless hours "making dens, walking up and down streams, getting in muddy places, exploring." And, together, we do more or less the same. Using both clay we carried with us and some we dig from the hill and mix in, we form small, primitive bowls, bury them in the earth and, after a couple of minutes, pull them out to see what sorts of stones and leafy detritus they might have gathered. Next we walk across a grassy field, following the curve of a stone wall into the hilly woods, ransoms and bluebells at our feet. Sarah scuttles down toward a stream, then hurls a slab of clay against a tree trunk to see what kind

of texture the trunk might imprint. As we make our way back across the field and to the car, Sarah stops and takes in the scene with a deep breath. "When I come up here, I feel so free," she says. "I love listening to the birds and smelling the freshness. It makes me feel well and energized."

In these modern times, when many people feel compelled to share—even overshare—Sarah keeps a low profile. Instagram is the only social media platform she engages with, and even there she remains mysterious. Her bio reads "ceramics" and is without a link to a website. Somewhat regularly she posts moody still lifes of her work—plates and bowls, and some sculptural pieces, in natural tones—mostly taken close-up on a worn wooden surface (which, I discover, is a table in her small kitchen). Now and then there is a shot of tree roots or wood ash or, once, a video of a flock of starlings against a cloudy sky. Captions, if they exist at all, tend to be minimal—"indigenous," "rhythm," "murmuration"—although she will make exceptions and write in more detail occasionally, such as when directing her followers to an auction of artworks to raise funds for refugees.

Sarah's ceramics, made of porcelain and stoneware, look simultaneously primitive and modern: Shapes are organic; colors and textures hint at the wood ash and sandstone

TOP LEFT

While grinding wood ash to use in a glaze, Sarah is reminded of grinding spices with her Indian grandfather's large stone mortar and pestle. She enjoys exploring the colors she can achieve with different types of wood and firings.

TOP RIGHT

As a child, Sarah marveled at the different stones on the hill and how they glistened and changed colors when they were carried downward in streams during heavy rains. Today she strives to bring that same sense of awe about color to her ceramics, by working with stones and other aggregates from that same landscape.

CENTER LEFT & RIGHT

Sarah's creations are the antithesis of machine-made precision, a pure celebration of the earth's natural resources combined with the sensitivity of the human hand. "When I'm making," she says, "It's like I'm playing an instrument. I don't hear songs in my head; it's a song I'm creating."

BOTTOM LEFT

To make this tool (her own version of a *hakeme* brush), Sarah gathered haircap moss from the hill and from her mother's garden and bound it to a twig with string. She uses it to add texture and also to layer natural materials onto her work.

BOTTOM RIGHT

One of Sarah's mugs. Like much of her work, it somehow looks both primitive and modern.

with which she tints and texturizes them and the stones and botanicals (pine needles or flower heads, for example) she sometimes imprints on their surfaces. Her creative motivation is to connect with the intrinsic beauty and rhythm of the earth's natural resources in a sustainable way. "The earth doesn't belong to people," she says. "It belongs to itself." To meet the practical challenge of making a living, she sells her work to individuals (many of whom she meets through Instagram), to a couple of galleries, and to restaurants of Michelin chefs, mostly in the United Kingdom but also in Europe and Asia. For some restaurants, she scouts the landscape on-site or where their ingredients are grown to find aggregate clay or other natural materials to incorporate into their collections.

It is this type of direct connection to the land, as well as to fellow artisans whose work has evolved around their local culture and terrain, that excites her. In fact, even before she found her way to clay, when she was studying for an undergraduate degree in economics and politics at the University of Leeds in the early 1990s, she was absorbed in environmentalism. It was nearly a decade later that Sarah (by then the mother of a five-year-old daughter) began exploring visual arts at the University of Central Lancashire, eventually landing in their ceramics department, where she began the research into sustainable ceramics and natural glazes that continues to this day.

The pieces in her final show before graduation—large, polished forms made using molds with custom-blended clay, natural aggregates, and crushed by-products of industry like brick and glass—were well received, but she remembers them with a mixture of pride and disappointment. "The work wasn't expressive or immediate enough for me. There was precision, and it required too many industrial tools," Sarah recalls. "I just wanted to go back to the land and see what color the different sandstones from the hill would fire to."

And that is, essentially, what she did. With a graduation gift of five hundred pounds from her grandmother, a hand-me-down kiln from her mother (who had toyed with pottery years earlier), and her father's help transforming a storage area at the back of her house (once a stable for horses and carriages) into a studio with running water and electricity, she set to work, getting her first break when an artist representative with connections in the restaurant world spotted her pinch bowls in her friend Dolores Swift's shop (see page 306) and reached out to her.

"I wanted to work from home and sell my pottery in the village where I'd grown up. I didn't want to be displaced from my land to do a job," Sarah explains. She also wanted to establish a healthy practice, one free of chemicals (to which she is extremely sensitive). Sarah dreams of a future that is in some ways more like the past, when communities in places like Parbold were more vibrant and centralized, when social bonds were stronger, when people worked in harmony with the cycles of nature and respected the environment rather than feeling enslaved by machines running 24/7. In the meantime, she continues to delve deeper and deeper into her own instinctive process, collecting inspiration and materials from the hill—and playing in the mud.

"My goal isn't just to be putting plates on tables for people," Sarah clarifies. "I'm an artist, and I'm still on my journey. Everybody's soul is attuned to something different. If you honor that within yourself, you fulfill who you are meant to be."

r&d on the hill

Temporarily burying a bowl in the ground and throwing a piece of clay against a tree to see what happens are among the playful ways in which Sarah seeks inspiration on the hill. Back at the studio, she might take a slightly more deliberate path, embedding natural materials into clay or rolling clay across a piece of bark. Sarah hopes that as her work evolves, it will become increasingly expressive, "not so contrived or thought through." The "research and development" on the hill is key to that process.

"When I'm making, it's like I'm playing an instrument. I don't hear songs in my head; it's a song I'm creating."

OPPOSITE, TOP

Sarah wove silver birch from the hill around the perimeter of this large ceramic bowl.

OPPOSITE, BOTTOM

Sarah displays some of her work, along with found objects, in her living room. During the winter, she likes to relax by making pinch pots in front of the woodstove. She also uses the stove to burn different kinds of wood to create the ash she incorporates into her glazes.

THIS PAGE

Sarah uses the dishes she makes every day and hopes that others will as well. "I want them to be used and loved, not to just be an aesthetic thing on display," she says.

JUDITH MacKENZIE

Harnessing the
Power of the Wind

WHEN I WAS saying good-bye to Nikki McClure and Jay T Scott (see page 196) in Olympia, Washington, and heading northeast to Forks to meet Judith MacKenzie, they suggested a couple of places I might enjoy checking out along the way. It was rainy and chilly, and I wanted to get to Forks before nightfall, but I did manage to break up the three-hour drive with a short hike in the Quinault Valley in Olympic National Park. From there, I posted a photo on Instagram of what I described as "Cousin Itt–style moss or maybe lichen," a hairy vine that hung from massive tree branches in thick, cobwebby strands. I showed the photo to Judith soon after I arrived, while she was preparing our dinner, and she identified it immediately: It was a lichen called usnea that can be used as a dye—it creates a mustardy yellow color—and also medicinally for inflammation. Judith took a break from chopping vegetables and pulled a glass plate holding dried usnea, lungwort, parmelia, and a few other local lichens from the opposite end of the wooden table we were standing at. Not only did she have the answer to my question, she also had specimens she had foraged to illustrate her point, plus an eight-hundred-plus-page book on the subject called *Lichens of North America*. Judith, it turns out, has been dyeing with lichens since childhood and, as a teen, studied them

while working at Garibaldi Provincial Park in British Columbia, among some of the greatest botanists of that time.

A crone, in prehistoric matriarchal societies, was a wise, powerful, mature, and respected woman—a healer and wayshower. That is how I think of Judith, one of the most knowledgeable and revered contemporary teachers of spinning, weaving, and dyeing, practices that date back millennia. "Spinning thread," Judith tells me in her soft, confident voice that seems made for telling bedtime stories, "is what got us out of the cave. Without thread, we would have starved because we couldn't trap or pull things." The sails on Christopher Columbus's ship were hand-spun and handwoven, as were Elizabeth I's dresses, and all the amazing silver and gold threads, silk brocades, and pile carpets of the Ottoman Empire. Humans have probably been spinning for over twenty thousand years, and weaving for nearly as long. Threads have been made by machine only since the late 1700s.

Judith spun for the first time as a child growing up in Squamish, British Columbia, in the 1950s. At the time, the mountain-ringed town, at the head of Howe Sound and midway between Whistler and Vancouver, was a remote outpost accessible only by a once-a-week boat. Each evening, after washing and putting away the dinner

Judith says that most of her good ideas come to her when she is walking. Here she is on the beach in Forks, which, she explains, is as far west as anyone can go before heading east. (If one were to get in a boat and sail on, the next stop would be Japan.) She calls this spot the end of the earth, then points out that the Makah, an indigenous tribe that has inhabited this landscape for thousands of years, describe it as the beginning of the world.

By removing all the non–load-bearing walls inside a double-wide trailer, Judith has given her home the look of an open-plan ranch house meets textile laboratory. At the far end of the kitchen, opposite the front entry, is a portable stainless-steel catering table, fitted with three vats and a countertop work space, which she uses for immersion dyeing. At the far end of the living room is the woodstove she relies on for heat. Near the sliding door at the back porch are a loom and her electric carder.

BOTTOM LEFT

Vintage and antique knitting needles are among the many interesting textile tools Judith has collected over the years.

BOTTOM RIGHT

Standing with her on the timber-strewn beach, watching the waves rumble, crash, and retreat before our eyes (see page 57), and then returning to her house and seeing her splitting wood out back so she can heat her home, I can imagine Judith living a long time ago, at a time when hand-spinning and hand-weaving as well as dyeing with lichens were commonplace and necessary, before machinery took over and was deemed "better." Judith counters: "When we lose our ability to make things with our hands, we lose part of our humanness."

Judith learned to knit from her mother, a socialite turned wild child who left her family to pursue a career as a singer and then married Judith's father, a labor organizer, but Judith didn't take to knitting in the same way. Then, as now, she favored creating the yarn over stitching it into garments. Weaving entered Judith's life many years later, when she was living in a communal home in Vancouver, a single mother of two children, and began taking classes at the nearby Handcraft House and at the University of British Columbia. Among her teachers was the internationally acclaimed artist Joanna Staniszkis, whose exploration of new techniques and unconventional materials resonated with Judith.

"When I first learned to weave, I couldn't sleep," Judith recalls. "It was like being on fire. I would dream about it and wake up threading a loom or treadling. It is a physical motion that is like dancing. You move your feet and your hands in different rhythms. It was magical to see cloth grow. I never got over it. I am still not over it."

From that point on, Judith was determined to make a living doing what she loved. In the 1970s, she mainly sold her weavings and hand-spun yarn. Then, late in that decade, she hit upon a new trend, spinning an unusual, multicolored and -textured yarn that was the diametric opposite of the conventional, solid-colored single- and two-ply yarns that were common at the time. Today it would be called art or novelty yarn, but back then, Judith dubbed it wolf yarn because "it kept the wolf from the door"—that is, it paid the bills. In fact, in its heyday, Judith employed ten people

dishes, eight-year-old Judith would grab an empty jug and head down to a neighbor's homestead to collect fresh milk.

"Mrs. Axen wore handwoven dresses and beautiful shawls," Judith vividly recalls. "She had baskets she made herself, and she would sell hand-spun and hand-knitted socks and honey from the bees she raised to the fishermen. I was smitten. I have no idea why. That's the magic of it all. When I would go down and get milk, I'd stare at the spinning wheel. She finally asked me if I wanted to try to spin. I can't tell you how happy that made me." From then on, young Judith would spend as many evenings as she could with Mrs. Axen, a Norwegian intellectual who had left politically unstable Europe with her husband in the 1920s in order to, as Judith remembers, "find someplace on the edge of the world to raise their kids in peace."

"In an unspoken way, my grandmother taught me that plants had secrets that some people knew and others ignored, that we had abandoned skills that had worked well for thousands of years but had been forgotten."

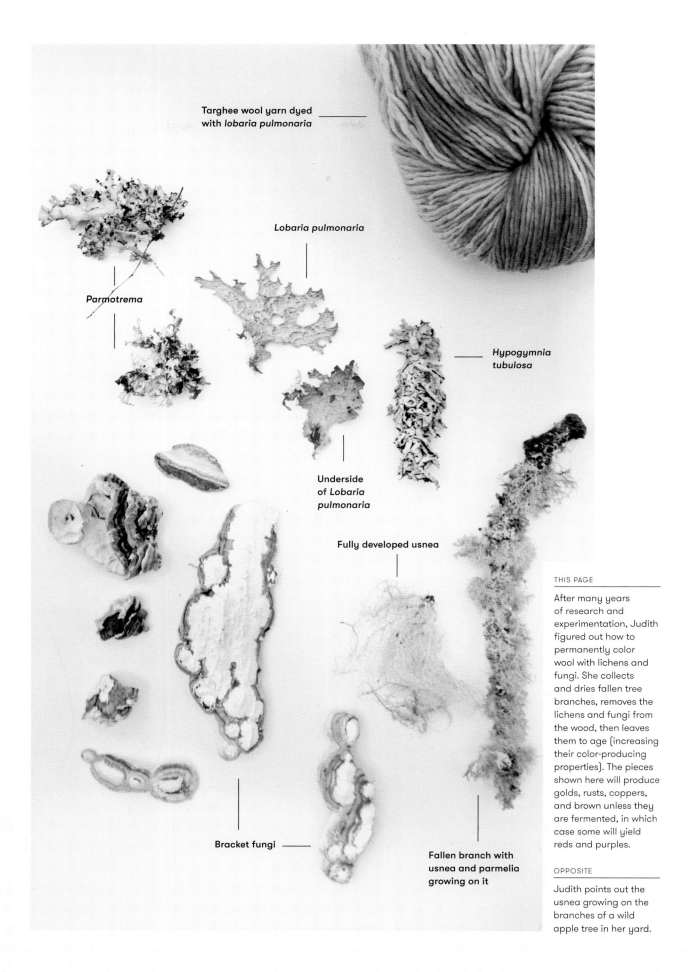

Targhee wool yarn dyed with *lobaria pulmonaria*

Parmotrema

Lobaria pulmonaria

Hypogymnia tubulosa

Underside of *Lobaria pulmonaria*

Fully developed usnea

Bracket fungi

Fallen branch with usnea and parmelia growing on it

THIS PAGE

After many years of research and experimentation, Judith figured out how to permanently color wool with lichens and fungi. She collects and dries fallen tree branches, removes the lichens and fungi from the wood, then leaves them to age (increasing their color-producing properties). The pieces shown here will produce golds, rusts, coppers, and brown unless they are fermented, in which case some will yield reds and purples.

OPPOSITE

Judith points out the usnea growing on the branches of a wild apple tree in her yard.

Judith uses a tabletop electric carder of her own design (made with a lathe motor, spare bicycle parts, a carding cloth, and wood) to create multicolored batts that she sells to spinners. Because she layers the fiber onto the carder with great care—"It's fun, like painting," she says—the many colors remain distinct rather than merging and muddying. Spinning with it is full of surprises as the colors and textures shift.

A sampling of Judith's handspun and naturally dyed yarns. Clockwise from top left: lichen-dyed fawn brown wool overdyed in an indigo exhaust bath; natural white mohair dyed with cochineal; natural white wool dyed with archiled rock tripe; natural gray wool dyed with walnut hulls; and natural white wool dyed with walnut hulls.

Judith has been spinning since childhood. "I can spin the fiber thin so I can sew with it or thicker so I can weave with it; I can put a slub in it if I want—that's my choice," Judith says as she demonstrates at her wheel in front of a kitchen window.

to meet demand for the yarn and garments made from it. By the time that market dried up in the 1990s (when the trend switched back to fine, smooth yarns), Judith had established a name for herself as a teacher and as a judge at fiber festivals, as a custom dyer of exotic fibers, and as a designer of machine-spun yarns that she would have produced at small mills and wholesale to yarn stores. The most successful of her own yarns was a lace-weight bison yarn she sold under the name Buffalo Gals.

Between 1995 and 2009, Judith split her time between a ranch in Montana and teaching on the road, writing articles for textile magazines and authoring a few how-to-spin books along the way. In Montana, she and her second husband ran a sheep-shearing business that took them around the state and into Wyoming and Oregon. Her husband and his team would shear more than a thousand sheep a day, and Judith would class all the fleeces (evaluate their quality based on cleanliness, length, strength, color, and consistency to determine their value at market) before packing them.

In 2009, after Judith and her husband decided to divorce, Judith moved to Forks, where she had been teaching classes for many years and where she has resided ever since. A small town on the westernmost edge of the United States, five hours from the closest airport, might not seem like an obvious choice for a woman who is on the road teaching about two weeks out of every month, but for Judith, it works. "I understand this landscape," she says. The ocean is less than two miles from her doorstep, and the glaciated peaks of the Olympics surround her. To incentivize her to move to the town, the City of Forks gave her a large studio in a historic building plus artist-in-residence status. Judith bought 6 acres and a double-wide trailer on a 720-acre property that served as a US military base for a short time in the 1940s and is now inhabited by only fifteen other households. "People who want to be alone live here," Judith points out. "It's peaceful and quiet. I hear the ocean waves instead of the freeway, and I see deer and elk, plus hawks, ravens, peregrines, and blue jays right out my window."

While Judith's journey has taken many twists and turns (including her Forks studio burning to the ground in 2012; she has since found a space in Port Townsend that she uses for teaching), when I visit her and we talk late into the night, I understand that fortitude, curiosity, and optimism are among the keys to her good life. "It's an amazing thing to love what you do and to also be good at it," she tells me.

Her passion for textiles and, in particular, the lichen dyeing we talked about upon my arrival harkens back, she believes, to

BOTTOM RIGHT

An assortment of Judith's treasured handmade tools, including a pre-Columbian beater (center), which she—like the generations of weavers who possessed it before her—uses to push weft threads into place on her loom. As humans, we are, by definition, tool makers, Judith points out. Our brains and our hands allow us to make tools and, in turn, the way we use those tools changes our brains.

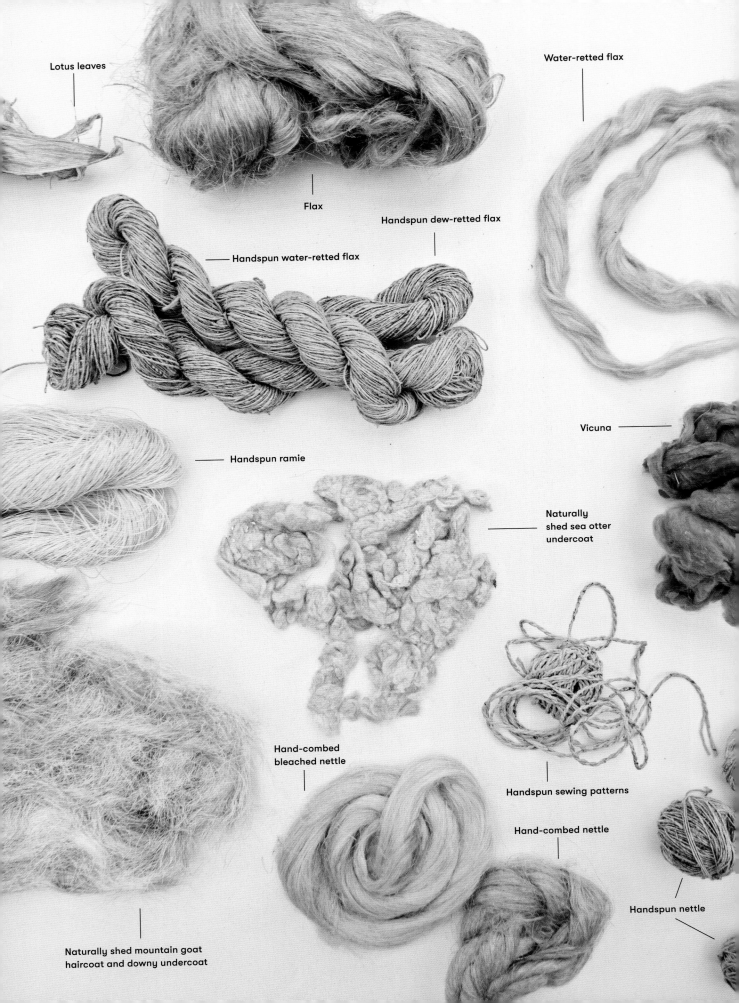

Lotus leaves

Flax

Water-retted flax

Handspun water-retted flax

Handspun dew-retted flax

Vicuna

Handspun ramie

Naturally
shed sea otter
undercoat

Hand-combed
bleached nettle

Handspun sewing patterns

Hand-combed nettle

Handspun nettle

Naturally shed mountain goat
haircoat and downy undercoat

"Hello, Melanie. Hope I'm not too late to fit into your schedule. Had an offer to look at some muskoxen I just couldn't refuse. What you are writing about is meaningful to me. In many ways, my life has been a gamble that being an artisan, working with my hands, could provide a model for a successful life. I have found it a very capable way to make a living, and now that I am well past the spring chicken stage and perhaps quite a bit further into the winter chicken part, I do feel sometimes a little bit scared (what will I do when I can't feel the fibers move through my fingers well enough?) and a little bit smug (that I have been able to have such a life). But mostly I just feel more than a little bit on fire to see what will happen next in my work."

—An email from Judith, after I wrote to her about planning a visit

her ancestors who immigrated to North America from Inverness and the Isle of Skye in Scotland. When Judith was a child, her grandmother regaled her with tales of Scottish fairies who crept into cottages at night and dyed and wove and did chores for the families, and she took her on long walks through the back streets of Vancouver to forage for herbs, fruits, and armloads of flowers that grew out into the alleys. "I learned to love plants—wild and cultivated—from her," Judith explains. "In an unspoken way, my grandmother taught me that plants had secrets that some people knew and others ignored, that we had abandoned skills that had worked well for thousands of years but had been forgotten."

It is skills at risk of abandonment that Judith has made a career of teaching. "When we lose our ability to make things with our hands, we lose part of our humanness," she laments. Her students, she believes, attend her classes because they are seeking competence, community, and creative expression, ideals that may not be adequately met in their everyday lives. Suzanne Pedersen, the creator of the celebrated Madrona Fiber Arts retreat in Tacoma, Washington, first met Judith in

weaving class in 1994 and taught classes with her for the next twenty-five years. Of her dear friend, she says, "Judith teaches like no one else. She creates a community of learning in every class and demystifies every fiber and process, then brings them alive with history and backstory."

For Judith, of course, making with her hands is the most natural way of being. As she sits at her wheel treadling with her feet, her fingers gently easing twist into the fiber, transforming a puff of wool into durable thread, she elaborates: "We are drawn to transforming; it is one of our most defining acts. Whether a potter with clay, a weaver with thread, a musician with sound, or a writer with words, we take raw materials and create new forms. It's as natural to us as a tulip bulb making a tulip. I can take this fiber and, with will and intent, I can spin it forty different ways. It is up to me to decide what it's going to do and shape it accordingly. Before your eyes, I can take something that is formless and not able to be used in any true way and make it into a sail that you could sail across the Atlantic with. To be able to harness the power of the wind to move you across water, that's pretty amazing."

Drawing a Line

"I LIKE HOW you can draw a line with the willow," Annemarie O'Sullivan says as we stand in her willow plot near the village of Horam, in the south of England, and she bends a straight stem that is taller than both of us into a gentle curve. To get here, we walked from a small parking lot, past a lake, and through hilly woodlands blanketed with ramsons and bluebells. The site is a former brickworks made available to local artists and small-scale farmers by its owner (a biodynamic land trust) under the umbrella of a program called Sacred Earth.

Annemarie makes baskets as well as large installations and site-specific work out of willow, which is why she began growing twenty-plus varieties in long rows on her half-acre allotment here in 2011. We are visiting in May. Over the course of several weeks during the previous winter, her husband, Tom McWalter, cut, sorted, bundled, and labeled about three truckloads of three- to ten-foot or longer stems (or rods), and gradually hauled them back to their home in Isfield, twenty minutes away. There he left them to dry under cover for six months to a year, ready and waiting for Annemarie to select, prepare, and weave them one by one into her desired forms. Annemarie typically joins him for the harvest, but this season she was too occupied filling orders for the New Craftsmen, the London gallery that

represents her, and for customers who order directly from her website. Though the work of the harvest is cold, wet, and physically demanding, Annemarie would have preferred to have been part of it. "We *are* nature," she tells me, and living in sync with nature's resources and cycles—growing willow, making baskets, being outdoors—is how Annemarie finds peace.

Regarded as one of the United Kingdom's top basket makers, Annemarie is, in fact, relatively new to the medium. On a whim in 2004, needing even a brief respite from mothering a two-year-old boy while pregnant with another child, she enrolled in a one-day course in nearby Brighton. Immediately she felt drawn to the materials, motions, and rhythm of basket making—and to the practicality of creating a utilitarian object. Within six months, she had given birth to her second son, resigned from her teaching job at a Buddhist-based primary school, and enrolled in a part-time comprehensive basketry program at City Lit, an adult-education institute in London. For the next five years, she commuted back and forth to London one day each week for her on-site coursework, all the while feeling like she was doing exactly what she ought to be doing even though, at the time, the likelihood of making a living as a basket maker seemed remote at best. In many ways, it ran completely counter to what

Annemarie shows me the beautiful lines she can draw with a single willow rod in the field.

OPPOSITE, BOTTOM

Annemarie's baskets are in high demand, and she doesn't keep many of them around. "The day a basket is made, it goes out," she explains. "The joy is in the making, and letting go isn't hard." Here she is carrying greens from the garden in a cyntell (a traditional Welsh agricultural basket) that she made for her own use.

"I absolutely
have to live in
this creative
way to be sane.
It is how the
world makes
sense to me."

When Annemarie (here with photographer Rinne Allen) began working with willow, she had access to only a couple of varieties. "They would arrive sprayed with chemicals and wrapped in plastic. I just felt like there was something inherently wrong," she recalls. By sourcing cuttings from basket makers in England and Ireland, as well as some from beds in Lewes that she traced back to the sixteenth century, she is now able to grow nearly fifteen hundred plants in twenty-plus varieties without any pesticides. "Mine are much wonkier and more colorful than any commercially available," she says. They range in color from gray to light pink to red to black, varying a bit depending on the growing conditions each year. When the plants are ready to be harvested in late winter, they are between three and ten feet tall, depending on the variety. Annemarie and her husband, Tom, cut them down and, over the course of a few weeks, haul them away.

she was raised to believe possible. But, she says today, "I absolutely have to live in this creative way to be sane. It is how the world makes sense to me."

Annemarie grew up in Ireland, on the outskirts of a village in County Meath, about forty miles north of Dublin. "I was brought up in a religious, fear-driven, and controlled environment," Annemarie recalls. "And I was very well behaved for the wrong reasons." The youngest of five children, she was good at art but was told by her parents that she couldn't pursue it because it wouldn't lead anywhere worthwhile. "I was academic, so the idea was that I could do something much 'better,'" she remembers. Annemarie always found refuge being underwater and swimming and, at fifteen years old, in 1987, was Ireland's national backstroke champion, though her athletic aspirations were halted when she injured her shoulder the following year. She went on to earn a degree in sports science as well as a primary-school teaching certificate from Loughborough University in England.

Spending time in the water, however, remains an integral part of Annemarie's life, and she tries to make time for a dip in a pool, river, or the sea daily. Her affinities for both swimming and basket making are, she says, closely related. She cites the rhythm and repetition and the meditative state they evoke, the connection to the natural world, the full-body physicality required, and the way both forms of movement entail, at their essence, making lines. "When I'm making and in my state of flow," she explains, "I'm repeatedly drawing a line with my hand. And when I swim, I always see that same hand going into the water and drawing a

line. That for me is incredibly peaceful. Drawing a line over and over. That is the right place for me."

When I ask Annemarie about sources of inspiration for her work, she starts with the expected—the rich history of basket makers and their wares—then detours to Picasso's very simple line drawings and to skeletal forms that don't necessarily need to be filled in. She is, as we speak, completing the circular base of a large harvest basket. Rods of willow are radiating several feet outward from the center. She lifts and gathers them together, then contains them within a circular hoop that Tom has steam bent for her out of local sweet chestnut wood. Next she will begin the weaving, around and around, and the basket will start to take shape. "It is chaotic for a while, then it all becomes more ordered. Then we trim it, and it becomes this neat, quite small and restrained object. I love the rules of this, but I love making my own rules, too," she says. Her intention is to reach such a high level of technical mastery that she can then relax and become playful without sacrificing quality. "It's important to me that my work is well crafted, that it isn't just an art piece. It needs to be strong," she explains.

Annemarie's desire for playfulness is perhaps most evident in her site-specific work, such as *Cluster*, a series of spherical forms so large that they could easily be walked in and out of and that she and a team of volunteers wove out of sweet chestnut for an interactive installation at a former church turned art gallery in Brighton. Or a quartet of willow fish traps, or putchers, she and Tom wove and suspended on sweet chestnut posts over a lake at Forde Abbey, a historic estate in Somerset.

Tom studied product design at university, then worked building stage sets and artist studios and as a landscape designer. He has been collaborating with Annemarie full-time since 2017. He also handles, as Annemarie puts it, most family "shopping, cooking, and washing up, and gets the boys to wherever they need to be, all the socks in the right place." Their artistic and economic goals for the basket making are deeply intertwined with their family life and values, and Annemarie is sensitive to the inevitable impulse to work more. But, she says, "I don't want to grow into some big business. I want to be healthy, and I want the space and time to enjoy being here."

Annemarie strives to be present—both in the moment and literally here on this land and with her family. Together, she and Tom have been renovating their sixteenth-century house since they bought it in 2012; they grow much of their own food and heat their home with wood they chop themselves. When they do travel, either with their sons or on their own, their trips usually involve swimming, cycling, or hiking and also some sort of basketry. Together they have searched for hazel and sweet chestnut baskets in the French Pyrenees and learned a specialized frame basket technique from a maker in Northern Ireland. While Annemarie was visiting her sister in Queensland, Australia, she had the chance to meet an aboriginal family whose heritage includes some of the very first baskets in the world. "They are still

working with the same fibers, on the same land, making the same pieces of work that have been made for hundreds, if not thousands, of years," Annemarie recalls. The experience, she says, "was like gold dust, it is so rare. Lots of people dip into basket making like it's a sweeties shop, but these people have passed it from one generation to the next to the next. There is an unbroken lineage," she says, a line that reminds her that for tens of thousands of years, basket making was an essential skill used to make vessels of all sorts—to hold and transport everything from young children to berries to herring in Sussex where she lives today to the potatoes she remembers digging as a child in Ireland, and even the ammunition used in World War II.

By studying historic baskets, Annemarie is learning how people lived decades, centuries, and millennia ago. By copying their baskets, she is teaching herself skills. And by designing and making new baskets, she is drawing a line that connects her to them and to the present, to the here and now, to the natural universe to which we all belong.

TOP RIGHT

In 2012, Annemarie and Tom bought this sixteenth-century house, and they have been restoring it themselves ever since. About reworking some of the wattle-and-daub walls, Annemarie says, "To go outside, come in with a bunch of big willow, weave a wall panel, then go out and get some earth maybe with straw and some horse manure, mix it up, slap it on, and push it into the weave to make a wall—that feels amazing and really right." Her two teenage sons, she admits, "would like to live in a shiny new house with a big TV."

BOTTOM

On a wall above the kitchen and living room in the house, Annemarie displays her collection of baskets made by others.

the beginnings of a harvest basket

When Annemarie is ready to start a new piece, she chooses the rods she desires from the dried willow in storage, then submerges the willow in a long trough of water—one day per foot in length—to soften it; next it is left standing for another day to drain off excess water. To make a strong base, she cuts rods to her desired lengths, lays sticks out in a slath (or grid) underfoot, then "ties them in" with a pair of weavers. Through her art practice, Annemarie has found a way to grapple with and explore order and disorder—in basketry and in herself. There is a history (even a long-standing, rule-driven British guild system) to look back on, there are techniques to be learned (then riffed upon to drive unique creative expression), and there are natural materials to be respected and manipulated (but never completely tamed).

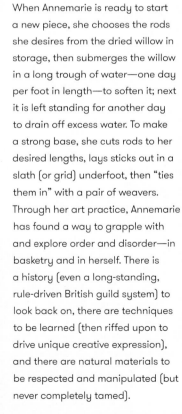

TWO

Slowing
Down

Balancing Motherhood and Art

THE STAGE WAS set for Maura Ambrose's swift rise from somewhat adrift art school grad to successful artist and entrepreneur when, in the summer of 2010, she and her husband, Chap, took off on a four-month road trip in their newly refurbished Volkswagen camper van, a journey mapped according to the dates and locations of four friends' weddings. Maura was tracking their backroads adventures through small-town America on Instagram, and when the then-young social-media site chose her feed to promote, tens of thousands of users began to follow along. In Savannah, Georgia, the couple's last stop before heading home, Maura stepped into a natural dye garden for the first time and found a new artistic path.

In quick succession, between 2011 and 2014, Maura launched a line of quilts made with her own naturally dyed fabrics under the company name Folk Fibers; fulfilled a seventeen-quilt commission for Levi's, then another, smaller one for Terrain; crisscrossed the country as part of a Levi's-sponsored maker-art project; and was among ten honorees at 2013's Martha Stewart American Made Awards. Topping off her run of impressive achievements was a commission from musician John Mayer for a quilt to be used as artwork for his single "XO," released in 2014. That same year, Maura gave birth to her daughter, Ada, and everything shifted again.

"Motherhood saved me in a way," Maura contends. "I would have burned out if I hadn't been forced to pause and stop." Then she counters, "What fulfills me beyond being a mom and wife is doing artwork and connecting with the people that brings me toward." It is now within this push and pull of motherhood, career, and art that she is navigating her way.

Maura started making quilts when she was a sophomore at the Savannah College of Art and Design (SCAD) in Georgia. A transplant from the furniture-making program, she never paid attention to the fibers department until one fateful day in 2004 when she wandered in and caught a glimpse of raw wool, spinning wheels, looms, and dye pots. "Finding it was the biggest rabbit hole I've ever gone down," Maura remembers. She immediately raced over to her adviser's office to lock down her classes for the upcoming semester.

First came Introduction to Fibers, a broad overview of surface, structure, and color techniques, and 3-D Design, which entailed basket weaving, felting, knitting, and crocheting, taught by Cayewah Easley, a young Native American teacher, who was fresh out of the Cranbrook Academy of Art's MFA program. "Cayewah said, 'In my family, we never used words to communicate emotions, but we used artwork,'" Maura recalls. Although Maura

Maura made this reverse-appliqué quilt for her daughter with hand-spun, handwoven khadi cotton she dyed with madder root, pecans, pomegranate, and Osage, plus wool batting. About Ada, Maura says: "The effervescence of life coming out of her is so inspiring."

OPPOSITE, TOP

Maura is ever enchanted by the colors she can achieve with natural dyes. Shown here are whole madder roots, chopped madder roots, fabric dyed a rust color with madder; curled Osage orange wood shavings that Maura gets from a woodworking school in Vermont, fabric dyed yellow with Osage; black walnuts, fabric dyed in two shades of tan with walnuts; and a pot of onion skins.

OPPOSITE, BOTTOM LEFT

Maura pulls a madder plant from her garden.

OPPOSITE, BOTTOM RIGHT

A piece of cloth dyed with madder hangs to dry above a bunch of dye pots in the yard.

grew up in a home that was more sporty than artsy, the idea of using art as a means of storytelling and intimate expression resonated with her immediately. "Cayewah's work was conceptual and deeply personal, so much her story," Maura remembers.

Next came the Art Quilt with Pamela Wiley. It was a ten-week course in which students explored conceptual quilt-making while practicing traditional techniques, such as four-patch and triangle piecing, backings, battings, and bindings. Then, just a few weeks before the term would end and a final project of each student's own design would be due, Denyse Schmidt showed up and gave a two-hour improv-piecing workshop that blew Maura's creativity wide open. Rather than carefully planning a pattern, cutting fabric, and then stitching a log-cabin block from the center out, Denyse instructed students to pull blindly from three scrap bags stuffed with small, medium, and large bits of fabric; stitch in multiple directions; and build wonky, beautiful blocks. "That exercise opened all these doors," Maura remembers of the fluid, playful approach, so much so that she decided to reimagine her final project for the course using Denyse's method and hand-quilt it with sashiko thread rather than run it through a sewing machine (Maura felt then—as she does today—that the machine is too hard on the fabric). Although she had sewn only minimally before college, Maura

intuitively understood the preciousness of textiles, especially those made with care.

Maura grew up with her parents and an older sister in a suburb near Orlando, Florida, and in Cary, North Carolina. Although sewing in the house was limited to what could be achieved on a frustrating machine that couldn't maintain proper tension, Maura's maternal grandmother and aunt had, in the 1950s and '60s, been avid and accomplished seamstresses, and her grandparents' attic was full of fabulous evidence. Prom dresses, bridal gowns, sports suits, shirts, skirts, in all the different stages, from yardage to cutout pieces pinned to tissue paper patterns to finished garments, were all stored there, along with notions and tools Maura treasures to this day. "The attic is where I would go when I visited my grandparents for a week every Christmas," she recalls. "My grandmother told me I should take a box every time I came, so I would go up and pull out my favorite stuff and sort it out and pack it." At home, Maura would carefully reexamine her treasures—which included bark cloth, patterned cotton sateens, and linens—but she rarely used them. "I was saving that fabric like a chipmunk saves its nuts," Maura says. "I didn't want to mess it up or cut into it when I wasn't ready. I would pull it out and lay it around and think about what to make with it. I didn't want to use it for something as temporary as a skirt I would outgrow. I

OPPOSITE, TOP LEFT

An assortment of pillows and pieced and whole-cloth quilts, all made with fabric Maura dyed with natural indigo and, for the striped quilt, pomegranate rind. Maura pays careful attention to subtle color nuances as she patchworks the pieces of her quilts together.

always folded it and put it back on my shelf and kept it." That was the routine until Maura's first quilt classes at SCAD. There she realized, "A blanket is where you use your special fabric. You never outgrow it; it lives longer in the home." This was where her "sentimental fabrics" were meant to be. "I finally made that connection: I knew what I was saving this all for," Maura adds. "When I came to quilting, I found my medium."

Although quilting remained Maura's focus throughout her SCAD years, it took her a while to figure out how to transform it into a viable business. Her postgraduation career path was winding and included a brief stint in the catalog department at Free People in Philadelphia—corporate life wasn't for Maura—and jobs as a preschool teacher and on organic farms in Philadelphia and Austin. When she and Chap, whom she met at SCAD and married in 2007, took off on their road trip in 2010, they knew they would be making their way from one wedding to another in Oklahoma, Wisconsin, North Carolina, and, finally, in their old stomping grounds in Georgia. While in Savannah,

Maura stopped by the SCAD fibers department to say hello and was faced with some questions about her current art practice that made her uncomfortable. Although she and friends had maintained a studio in Philadelphia and she had sold a few quilts since graduation, including that original one inspired by Denyse Schmidt's workshop to MTV for the set of *The Real World: Hollywood* and two more to go with it, she admittedly wasn't doing that much. When Maura was on her way out, the weaving teacher mentioned that the class was headed to a neighborhood garden where they were growing natural dyes. Maybe she would like to join them.

"It was a wake-up call," Maura says. Right away she connected with the idea of dyeing fabric with plants she grew herself and making quilts with it, so she immediately picked up a couple of books the students recommended to her (*Eco Colour* by India Flint and *Harvesting Color* by Rebecca Burgess) and began reading them in the van. Three weeks later, a few days after she and Chap pulled into their driveway

TOP RIGHT

Maura does all her hand-quilting with sashiko thread; she often stitches with it in its natural cream shade—as shown here on this whole-cloth quilt.

CENTER LEFT

Maura grows madder in her garden to use as a natural dye for her quilt fabric. While working on organic farms before starting Folk Fibers, she learned a lesson that she lives by today: "It's not about how much you are getting paid; it's about how much you love the work. That's the ticket to a good life, a happy life."

CENTER RIGHT

Maura stitched these pillows for her family room using linen she dyed with indigo, Osage, Osage with iron, madder, cutch, and walnuts.

BOTTOM LEFT

This close-up of a log-cabin quilt top shows the kaleidoscope of colors Maura can achieve with her natural dyes. She compares stitching with fabric she has dyed herself to "painting with the best palette."

BOTTOM RIGHT

Maura sells her machine-pieced, hand-quilted textiles in custom-made cedar boxes onto which her husband, Chap, laser etches the Folk Fibers logo. She likes to meet the people who buy her quilts so she can share the story of how she makes them.

A quilt idea has to be really strong for Maura to be willing to take time away from mothering her daughter, Ada. Here she and Ada play with one of the family's bunnies.

CENTER LEFT

For Easter, Maura and Ada color eggs with natural dyes like madder, turmeric, and cochineal.

CENTER RIGHT & BOTTOM

Maura creates dyes from a few different flowers that grow around her house, including marigolds, coreopsis, goldenrod, and, shown here, 'Arizona Sun' blanketflowers.

"It's not about how much you are getting paid; it's about how much you love the work. That's the ticket to a good life, a happy life."

in Austin, she sowed indigo seeds in the garden; on January 1, 2011, Maura launched Folk Fibers. Then, just a few months later, via Twitter, she reached out to Jay Carroll, a creative brand director at Levi's whose job it was to travel around the world, search out heritage craftsmanship, and highlight it in a cool fashion-oriented way. Rather than introduce herself to Jay directly, however, she used some social media savvy and tweeted to her many followers that they should head over to Jay's feed if they were interested in American heritage, crafts, and road trips. Before long, Jay had checked out the quilts on Maura's website, all of which incorporated fabrics from her grandmother's attic, and commissioned her to make a collection of quilts for Levi's using their repurposed denim. And that is how the three-year whirlwind during which Maura Ambrose became a bona fide It Girl of the DIY movement began.

Today Maura looks back on it all with a mixture of pride and gratitude, but she also acknowledges that the attention bestowed on her during that short period of time

bred a vulnerability that she was forced to grapple with once Ada appeared. "I was getting a lot of my confidence outwardly," Maura admits. When her daughter was born and the pace of her work—and the related adulation—inevitably slowed, she had to reconnect with her more important *inner* sense of self-worth. She also had to figure out how to balance her identity as a mother with her identity as an artist. "I totally put Ada before me for two years," Maura recalls. "I lost myself, for better or worse, and started to resent it a little bit. She was keeping me from me. For a while, it was painful, then it was a relief."

Now, she says, the quilts she is making are "dream quilts." With a limited amount of time available to work, she is picky about the projects she puts her energy into. "Everything is more sentimental now," Maura adds. "When I used to get the question 'Is it hard for you to sell your work?' I always said, 'I can't wait to sell it. It propels me forward. I sell the quilts to release them. They are love songs going out into the world.'" Now, instead, she begins each quilt with the idea that she is creating it for her own home and family. In the process, she may discover that the quilt she is making is, in fact, not meant to be kept. "I have to start in this deep place. I have to fake myself out," she explains.

With Ada by her side, she continues to explore natural dyeing, but not always with the goal of creating long-lasting fabric for quilts. Instead, they experiment with dyes

Two of Maura's quilt tops on display on the outdoor clothesline near her outdoor dyeing area. Although her initial passion for quilt making was ignited by an improv-piecing workshop taught by Denyse Schmidt, today Maura is also attracted to designs that require precise planning.

that are easily accessible but sometimes fugitive, meaning not color- and/or lightfast. They collect mushrooms, lichens, and acorns in the woods, flowers from a field in front of their house, rosemary from the garden around back, and avocado and onion skins left over from cooking, then dye with them either in a pot set on a cookstove or in a jar in the sun. Maura keeps fabric that she has premordanted (prepared to receive dye) on hand to quicken the process for her young daughter, but their projects are not limited to fabric. For Easter, they color eggs with cochineal, madder, and turmeric.

The studio for dyeing is conveniently located on and around a covered porch outside. Supplies that need to be kept dry are stored in an old wooden cupboard. A series of stockpots, strainers, and electric burners stand ready for any project (whether a spur-of-the-moment one with Ada or a carefully-thought-out one with heirloom potential). A clothesline is drawn

from one tree to another on the edge of the woodlands that ring most of the ten-acre property. They live in Bastrop now, about a forty-minute drive from downtown Austin, but Maura spends most of her days out here in the country—where, with fascination, she tracks the nature around her, including snakes, bobcats, and wild hogs.

Committed to Folk Fibers for the long term, she works on her quilts whenever she can. Sitting at a ten-foot-long wooden worktable in her studio, just steps away from the family room, she is surrounded by shelves of naturally dyed fabrics ready to be cut, racks hung with quilts and quilt tops in different stages of completion, a sewing machine (with reliable tension!), favorite books, a collection of cowboy hats, and perhaps most important, bits and bobs from her grandmother's attic, treasures that called out to her so long ago and led her to this time and place where, she says, "I'm doing this because it brings me joy."

A Slow Fashion Pioneer

WHEN I ARRIVED in Florence, in northwestern Alabama, and sat down to interview Natalie Chanin, founder and creative director of the fashion and lifestyle company Alabama Chanin, she had a stack of postcards on the table in front of her and was addressing them to her senators. She wanted to tell them how she was feeling about current events. Additional postcards were placed around the studio for her employees to access if desired and also at the entrance to the company's store and café for her customers' use. While she isn't prone to preaching her political views publicly, she does lead her company according to her values, which include respect for her environment, community, and customers. And sometimes that means writing to her senators and encouraging others to do the same.

A pioneer in the slow fashion movement, Natalie has been promoting the benefits of good, clean, and fair business, matched with elevated design and craftsmanship, since the early days of the twenty-first century, when slow fashion was quietly emerging as an offshoot of the slow food movement. Many of her peers in the industry questioned her judgment when, in the mid-2000s, she began writing a book to share instructions for making the hand-sewn and often intricately embellished organic cotton jersey garments on which Alabama

Chanin's success had been built, garments that were (and still are) made by local artisans being paid a living wage and that have been celebrated in the pages of *Vogue* and sold in stores like Bergdorf Goodman and Barneys in Manhattan and Tokyo. But Natalie was committed to publishing the information to make the clothing accessible to people who couldn't afford to buy it from her but who could make it less expensively themselves—or hire someone locally to make it for them instead. She also wanted to preserve and spread the handwork skills that making these garments required, many of them skills she learned as a child from her grandmothers, mother, and aunts. Fortunately, Natalie's good intentions paid off: Her first book, *Alabama Stitch Book*, published in 2008, was successful and not only launched a new division of her company for DIYers, now called the School of Making, but also led to four (and counting) subsequent titles: *Alabama Studio Style*, *Alabama Studio Sewing + Design*, *Alabama Studio Sewing Patterns*, and *The Geometry of Hand-Sewing*. Her customers for the finished garments were unfazed. If anything, the books helped broaden her brand's reach.

I was Natalie's editor for all those books, so I have had a front-row seat from which to watch her and her company evolve—as well as some peeks behind the scenes. I

"Cooking, repairing a car, or building a house—these are all skills we need for life. When we get to the point where we aren't able to make things with our hands and feel no mastery, we feel lost."

Natalie in her living room. To embellish the dresser behind her, she drilled a pattern of holes and backstitched through them with white cord.

Enamored with the
rich story of repair and
wear that its stitches
and seams appeared
to be telling, Natalie
purchased this corset
at a flea market in New
York City in 2000. "It
essentially inspired the
next two decades of my
life," says Natalie.

have also been hand-stitching and wearing this clothing ever since she handed me two layers of jersey, one with a leafy stencil pattern spray painted on it, and taught me how to "love my thread" and work reverse appliqué on the afternoon we met for the first time to discuss her proposal for *Alabama Stitch Book*.

Natalie came to making by hand as part of everyday life. She grew up in the 1960s and '70s in Florence, a small city that, at the time, relied on the cotton industry and, in particular, farms and factories, for much of its employment, and where many residents, including her grandparents, still regularly practiced what she calls the "living arts." They sewed their own clothing and quilts, grew and preserved their own fruits and vegetables, baked their own breads and pies, and watched out for their neighbors, all of which Natalie learned to do alongside them. But while today she reminisces fondly about those early days and strives to sustain and celebrate many aspects of them in both her business and personal affairs, like a lot of young people, she needed to leave and explore other lands before developing a genuine appreciation of her upbringing. For Natalie, that period of exploration lasted twenty-two years and included studying environmental design and textiles at the College of Design at North Carolina State University (where she became enthralled with the concise design theories of the Bauhaus movement, which

still guide her), working as a sportswear designer in New York (during which time she witnessed degrading working conditions in factories overseas and realized that she couldn't in good conscience be part of the mainstream fashion economy), and freelancing as a stylist for music videos, advertising, and magazines in Europe.

It was after returning from Europe and living temporarily at the Chelsea Hotel in New York City in 2000 that Natalie conjured the idea of designing and hand-stitching cotton jersey clothing. It began out of necessity—she needed something special to wear to a party and didn't have anything suitable in the backpack she was living out of. Recalling the beauty, mystery, and strength of the seams on a hand-sewn, oft-repaired and -resized vintage corset she had recently picked up at a neighborhood flea market, she cut apart an old T-shirt and refashioned it by hand-sewing it back together with seams and knotted thread ends exposed on the public side of the cloth.

The experience of both using her hands to make something, which she hadn't done in a long while, and wearing her creation and having people become so captivated by it that they would not only compliment her but also reach out to touch it was so interesting that Natalie came up with the idea of making more of these garments and selling them. But to achieve the scale she imagined—a few hundred one-of-a-kind T-shirts, to start—she realized that

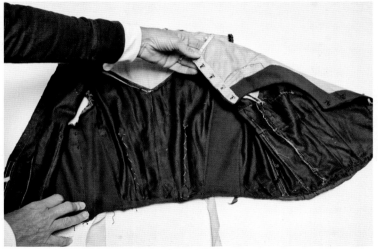

In a Bauhaus-inspired program at NC State College of Design, Natalie learned an essential way of approaching design, no matter the medium, that continues to serve her to this day. "If you look at the Bauhaus wheel of learning [a visual representation of the classic curriculum], you will find a lot of what we do," she says. Alabama Chanin's round, spoked logo (in Natalie's hands and on the piece of cloth shown here) is, in fact, reminiscent of that quintessential Bauhaus diagram (on the paper in the center).

Alabama Chanin garments tend to become heirlooms. They are made, Natalie says, "for this generation and the next and the next." Shown here is a hand-stitched organic cotton jersey dress from a 2015 collection. It is stenciled with the Large Paradise Flower pattern and embellished with appliqué, couching, and beading.

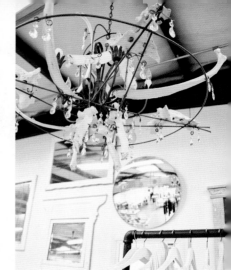

TOP LEFT

At the Factory, the floors are concrete, the ceilings are high and dotted with skylights, and—like the seams and knots on Natalie's first T-shirts—the ductwork for the heating, electric, and sprinkler systems is exposed. True to her Bauhaus training, Natalie focuses her design process on the nature of her materials and the desired function of the finished product.

BOTTOM

Natalie cutting out appliqué pieces to sew onto a Pansy swatch. She recalls spending hours as a child cutting flowers, butterflies, and other shapes out of fabric and adhering them to clothes and bags. Today she says she is happiest when she is fiddling with ideas on her own, whether that is figuring out how to best arrange appliqués on a swatch, writing a chapter in one of her books, reorganizing the Factory layout (all the furnishings are on wheels to make this easy), or developing a strategic five-year plan for the company.

she needed the help of the women back home in Alabama, many of whom she was sure had the skills required. She also knew they could use the work: Following the passage of the North American Free Trade Agreement in 1993, one by one, factories in Florence and the surrounding manufacturing communities began to close, creating an employment crisis.

Natalie's first venture gradually evolved into a series of couture collections made out of repurposed T-shirts that she presented at New York Fashion Week and then into a company called Project Alabama, which morphed into Alabama Chanin in 2006 when Natalie and an original business partner severed ties. Although the company now works mainly with domestic organic cotton jersey yardage rather than repurposed T-shirts and produces both hand-sewn and machine-sewn collections (as well as collections that merge the two techniques), the core of the hand-stitched line is still the straight stitch, the same stitch Natalie used to construct her first T-shirt at the Chelsea Hotel and that her grandmothers taught her when she was a child.

Today Alabama Chanin occupies about one-quarter of a 160,000-square-foot building that was once a cotton production facility in an industrial park on the outskirts of Florence. They call their facility, matter-of-factly, the Factory. While the location is unremarkable, once inside, visitors are transported into a world of design and production that feels both down-to-earth and elevated, welcoming and enterprising.

The first time I visited the Factory, it was for their Classic Studio Week workshop, a deep-dive into the Alabama Chanin philosophies and design and construction methodology—a dreamy five days of creativity, learning, hand-stitching, and camaraderie.

Our workshop began on a Monday morning with an exercise: Natalie asked each of us to write a vision statement in which we imagined how we wanted to feel about our experience at the end of the program. From there, we set out to actualize our aspirations with the help of a workshop leader and a master seamstress and with Natalie dipping in and out for inspiration and storytelling. We had the entire Alabama Chanin wardrobe to try on as we decided which of the DIY styles we wanted to make or riff upon as well as the company's complete library of fabric treatments to pore over as we debated our embellishments. Their garment styles are designed to be flattering, comfortable, and versatile. They can be unembellished, which in the Alabama Chanin nomenclature is called basic, or they can be lightly or heavily embellished, incorporating a mixture of stenciling, appliqué, reverse appliqué, beading, and embroidery.

Whether visitors arrive at the Factory to check out the shop, for a meal in the café, for one of the community stitch meetups, or for a two-hour, one-day, or weekend workshop or the intensive weeklong course, a highlight is paging through the white cotton jersey–covered binders that

showcase the hundreds of different fabric treatments the company has designed over the years. Most of them begin with a stencil design that is spray painted onto the top layer of a two-layered fabric and used as a guide for further embellishment. By mixing and matching colors of jersey and thread, the stencil and the shade of textile paint used to apply it, the stitching techniques (from basic straight stitch to more intricate embroidery), the bead placement, and the garment or other piece onto which the treatment is applied, Alabama Chanin has created a design language that they can continuously expand upon and that DIYers can follow precisely or use as a jumping-off point for their own unique explorations. Plans are under way to eventually move the swatch library, which already includes more than thirty volumes, to the Alabama Department of Archives and History in Montgomery. There it will be preserved for future generations to study alongside many other treasures from the state's rich history and culture.

While Natalie is often the focus of accolades about Alabama Chanin—she has been recognized by the Council of Fashion Designers of America and the Cooper-Hewitt, Smithsonian Design Museum, among others—she is quick to emphasize the strength of her team.

"They are the heart and soul of this business," she says. In recent years, she has been gradually delegating her responsibilities in order to eke out more private time and ensure that the business will be sustainable once she is ready to leave it. Despite her deceivingly extroverted public persona and her charismatic storytelling skills (an inheritance from her grandfather), she insists she is an introvert and loner at heart. "I could probably live in a convent," she says. Sitting quietly writing or reading, doing chores around her house, gardening, spending time with family—especially her daughter, who is in secondary school, and her son, who is grown and has a daughter of his own—these are the activities that she would like to slow down and make more time for.

With so many T-shirts and what she refers to as "miles of herringbone stitch" behind her, she says she no longer feels compelled to sew in the way that thousands of the School of Making customers do. While teaching a class, either in person or online, she easily demonstrates her mastery of the Alabama Chanin techniques, and when she sits for an interview, she is likely to pull a project from the company's communal workbasket (such as labels that need to be sewn onto garments or ponchos that

The Alabama Chanin fabric treatments are archived in swatch books so they can be studied by the design department as they evolve new work, as well as by customers considering ordering a custom item—say, a skirt, a wedding dress, or even upholstery—or a DIYer exploring their own ideas.

ALABAMA
CHANIN
#26382 Sylvan

Book 31
Alabama Chanin
#8293 Natalie's Dream

Book 27
Alabama Chanin
#0509 Embroidered Fern

TOP

Natalie reading on her porch with her dogs, Rowdy and Pree. She says she is most inspired when she has a lot of time to herself.

CENTER LEFT

Natalie uses a chair pad from an Alabama Chanin home collection in her kitchen.

CENTER RIGHT

Concrete castings of Natalie's daughter's shoes. "I like creating tiny monuments to a particular thing in my home," she says.

BOTTOM

An embroidered pillow from a collection inspired by the photographs of Charles Moore documenting the civil rights movement. In Natalie's handwriting, it reads, "Rethink, repair, revisit, resolve, replay, react, readjust, realize, reexamine, reverse, respond, recover, reconstruct, reconnect."

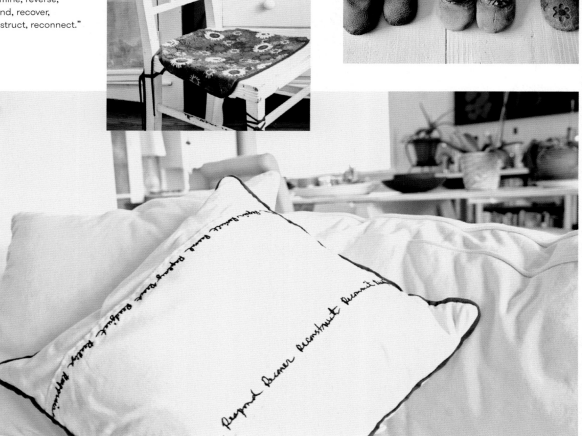

Natalie's daughter, Maggie, created this horse painting when she was four years old. It takes center stage in a home that is primarily white. In the foreground is the long surface that Natalie and Maggie call their crafting table because it is where they often get together to make things. Among the centerpieces is a tray of art supplies, including clay tools, paintbrushes, and ropes and yarns for basket making.

need to be seamed) to, she says, help her concentrate, but creatively, she feels drawn in other directions, to cooking, gardening, and—new to her—pottery. While teaching a stitching and stenciling class at the Penland School of Craft in Penland, North Carolina, she used some of her downtime to learn how to throw pots, and she discovered that she has an affinity for it. "Somehow I totally understand the structure of clay and how to use my hands to shape an object on a wheel," Natalie explains with wonder and excitement.

Reflecting on why making by hand is important in this day and age, she says, "Part of human happiness is being able to make and provide for ourselves. Cooking, repairing a car, or building a house—these are all skills we need for life. When we get to the point where we aren't able to make things with our hands and feel no mastery,

we feel lost. What about planting a garden so you could feed a hungry family, or sewing a dress that could clothe a freezing child? These may seem like small actions, but when multiplied by millions of people, those small actions are what resiliency looks like. If making by hand were a bigger part of our physical survival, the spiritual part might take care of itself."

Although I know that the relationship between self-sufficiency and wellness wasn't the subject of the postcards Natalie was writing to her senators when I arrived for our interview, I can't help but fantasize about a campaign on that very subject. Natalie's first book, *Alabama Stitch Book*, includes a cardstock postcard to pull out and instructions for embellishing it with stitching and beads before writing on it and mailing it. And then we can follow Natalie's lead and begin: "Dear Senator . . ."

Dyeing for a Better World

KRISTINE VEJAR IS on a mission to do her part to make the world a better place, one where all people are treated with respect and, in turn, treat the earth with respect— or, at the very least, she will spend her time trying. Her drive comes from two vastly different formative experiences: The first happened in the 1970s in rural Illinois, the second in 1999 and the early 2000s in Kutch, a remote desert region in the state of Gujarat in western India. Her mission is manifested at A Verb for Keeping Warm in Oakland, California, a retail store, classroom, dye studio, and gathering place for textile lovers and makers in the Bay Area—as well as a bucket list destination for creatives worldwide. The tools and materials for sale there, the teachers Kristine chooses to instruct there, and the sensitivity and social consciousness with which she puts Verb's program together reflect her drive to make a positive impact every day.

As a child, Kristine spent a month each summer in Sterling, Illinois, a tiny steel mill town where her mother was raised and where her grandparents still resided. Most days, she and her grandma Lorene would sit knitting and sewing along with Doris, who co-owned the Black Sheep yarn shop on the town square; Mary Jo; and an assortment of the other ladies in her grandmother's circle of friends. They would visit one another's homes to eat

lunch or dinner, to see quilts in progress, and sometimes so Kristine could choose a new outfit for her Barbie dolls. Laid out across a dining room table or a sideboard (or both!) would be intricately sewn Barbie wardrobes, created by some of the local women for extra income. From Lorene and her friends, Kristine learned how to knit, sew, and quilt, and, just as important to her, experience the value and joy of friendships forged though textiles. Kristine's time with these women also granted her a reprieve from a rocky home life in suburban Minnesota.

Kristine was an art history student at Mills College in Oakland, California, in 1999 when she decided to spend a semester in India. Though officially there to study art and architecture, she was immediately drawn to the vibrant textiles—this was her first time experiencing a culture in which the making of them was front and center. She wondered over long swaths of block-printed cloth and saris lying one after the other on riverbanks to dry. She was mesmerized by weavers walking out warps between trees to measure and organize their threads in preparation for the loom. She learned about Gandhi's call, in the early part of the twentieth century, for Indians to spin and weave their own cotton at home rather than buy cloth manufactured in British mills, part of a far-reaching program

"How does what we choose to consume affect others? How can we redistribute money to those whose work we believe in and who treat people, the earth, and their animals kindly? How can we work with our hands and be healthy and financially stable?"

—Questions Kristine hopes to raise among her customers at A Verb for Keeping Warm

These fabric swatches, pinned to a wall in the dye studio, are a section of a large installation/"shade card" that Kristine created during an extensive period of research and experimentation for her book, *The Modern Natural Dyer*.

A Verb for Keeping Warm refers to an ancient Uralian word. Kristine chose it as the name of her business, in part, as a way to generate conversation about how our lives have changed over time and the impact those changes have had on our social structures and the environment.

of nonviolent civil disobedience aimed at winning Indian independence. For a final research project, Kristine traveled by train from Jaipur to Ahmedabad, then by overnight bus to Kutch, landing her finally in a circle of women on the floor stitching. "It was like being with my grandma and her friends," Kristine remembers of her first experience in this remote desert. "I didn't need language to share an experience with them. I could share through stitching." These women were members of the Rabari, a seminomadic people known for their intricate appliqué and mirrored embroidery. "They were amazed," Kristine recalls, "that, as an American woman, I could cook or stitch." During that first, four-week trip, Kristine began recording the appliqué motifs that the Rabari incorporate into their textiles, motifs that reflect the world around them (flowers, birds, ant trails, and so on). She wrote a paper called "Threads of Light: Patterns of Change" in which she explored the ways in which Rabari women embed their histories in their stitches. Later, after graduating from college and being awarded a Fulbright grant, she would return to this region to continue her work with the Rabari as well as learn more about the natural dyeing, weaving, embroidery, and other forms of handwork that have been practiced in this area of India for centuries.

After a year and a half abroad, Kristine returned to the Bay Area in 2002 and, not unpredictably, felt troubled and lost. "The world was so big, and I had no idea who I was supposed to be in it," she recalls. "I could see all the problems but didn't know how to interface with them." The problems Kristine was grappling with ranged from socioeconomic and sexual inequality to the environmental toll of synthetic dyes, pesticides, and other chemicals used in the mass production of textiles to the lack of awareness among consumers of how and by whom textiles and other manufactured goods available in such profusion in stores are actually made. The slow food movement, centered on sustainably produced food and traditional cooking, was beginning to take hold in California, but slow fashion, a parallel awakening within the clothing economy, was still far behind. Not sure what to do, she took a well-paying job with an organic bedding company that demanded most of her time, and she tried to convince herself that she was satisfied. But by 2006, she had to face her truth. While struggling with debilitating panic attacks, which led to a fear of flying and then of crowded spaces and bridges, then to depression, Kristine began to understand, with the help of a therapist, that not seeking out and following her true passion was harming her. "I thought I could make a bunch of money and buy a house and be semi-happy," she says, reflecting on that time, but semi-happy wasn't cutting it; instead, she felt lonely and isolated, and her body was setting off an alarm.

Relying on savings originally set aside for a down payment on a home, Kristine left her job, unsure what to do next. She had already begun to sell cloth bags she sewed and hats and other accessories she knitted out of her hand-spun yarn, but she knew that investing more of her time in those ventures wasn't going to be fulfilling long term. Eventually, she recognized that her real passion was natural dyeing, and she gradually transformed her kitchen into her laboratory, using the knowledge she had gained in India as a starting point for a deeper exploration into this ancient art and science. First, Kristine sold her yarn at pop-up shops, then she opened a small storefront, and finally, in 2011, she moved to Verb's current location in Oakland, where she has been growing the business ever since.

Verb occupies 1,700 square feet of space on a quiet block of San Pablo Avenue bordering the city of Berkeley. Its name, a mystery to many, refers to a verb in an ancient Uralic language that meant "to keep warm." In the retail area of Verb, there is the store's own lines of yarn, dyed in the two studios on the premises, one indoor and one outdoor, plus a curated selection of natural yarns and fabrics from other companies with similar ethical ideals. Also for sale are tools and materials needed to sew, knit, embroider, and dye naturally; Verb's own lines of sewing patterns, which they wholesale to other shops as well; and project kits. For a product to make it into the store or an event to be scheduled there, Kristine prefers that it in some way supports the continuation of a hands-on tradition and is traceable to its source. For example, she stocks fabric made from naturally colored organic cotton grown at Sally Fox's farm in the Capay Valley, ninety miles northeast of the store. She runs a year-round schedule of trunk shows and classes with local and visiting instructors, ranging from Oakland resident Julie Weisenberger, who teaches her Cocoknits method of top-down knitting, to Maasaki Aoki of Tezomeya Natural Dyeing Studio in Kyoto, Japan, who teaches ancient Japanese natural dyeing methods. And she hosts an annual indigo dip (when anyone can come and use the Verb vat);

OPPOSITE

A display of three different lines of A Verb for Keeping Warm's yarns spun from local California fibers and dyed on site. By mixing and matching eight different natural dyes and the methods with which she handles them, Kristine has created a palette of about twenty colors that stay in these lines year-round. Other colors are added and taken away seasonally.

TOP

Kristine setting up a display at Verb, an experiential learning center where textile lovers can meet and connect with one another, expand their skills and understanding, and, Kristine hopes, develop empathy and appreciation for all the different people, past and present, who are part of the textile-making process.

BOTTOM

Dye studio production manager Sarah Ollikkala Jones (right) and Kristine working in Verb's indoor dye studio.

TOP

TOP

Adrienne Rodriguez handles operations at Verb and is also Kristine's life partner. Here she is checking on one of the indigo vats outside. After stirring, she will let the vat sit for about thirty minutes, then dip her fingers in to ascertain the liquid's viscosity (slipperiness). The viscosity tells her what she needs to know about the vat's pH level.

BOTTOM LEFT

The farmers at New Family Farm in Sebastapol, California, decided to grow these marigolds because they needed more pollinators in their fields. When they offered them to Kristine for natural dyeing, she happily accepted.

BOTTOM RIGHT

Linen eco-printed with marigolds grown in Verb's dye garden.

While Kristine tends to pots, Sarah sorts eucalyptus and ornamental plum they foraged from neighborhood trees to use for dyeing later.

book signings; a meetup for people who have pledged to make at least a quarter of their daily wardrobe themselves; and subscription programs that entitle mail-order customers to regularly scheduled deliveries of specially selected yarns, fabrics, raw fibers, and patterns.

By providing customers with the opportunity to learn how to create their own textiles and spend time with other makers, Kristine hopes to encourage important conversations. Among the questions she would like them (really, everyone) to consider and converse about: How does what we choose to consume affect others? How can we redistribute money to those whose work we believe in and who treat people, the earth, and their animals kindly? How can we work with our hands and be healthy and financially stable? And particularly relevant in the Bay Area, where

the computer companies of Silicon Valley so drastically impact the cost of living: Why are we willing to pay computer programmers millions of dollars but not the people who grow our food and fiber?

"Through Verb," Kristine says, "I reclaimed my normal life." By "normal," she is referring to the time she spent as a child with her grandparents in Sterling, to living in a comfortable, safe community where the residents know each other by name and care about one another and the quality of their environment, and where stitching is an integral part of the social structure.

Kristine learned from her grandmother and her friends in Sterling and from the Rabari in India that making textiles is a way to connect and share and tell one's story and, in the process, possibly make the world a better place. And that is exactly the normal life Kristine is striving to lead today.

For Kristine, indigo is endlessly fascinating—its history and legacy, complexities and magic. Always learning, she has worked with masters in Japan, Indonesia, India, and Mexico, and, of course, she dyes with it all the time at Verb. Shown here (clockwise from top left): different shades of indigo-dyed yarn, dried indigo, Kristine holding a piece of fabric that has just been pulled from the dye vat and is in the process of transitioning from green to blue as the oxygen hits it.

Japanese indigo treasures from the Verb textile library: a traditional drawstring rice bag, a large cloth mended with smaller scraps (top right), and a *kasuri* cloth (bottom left).

CLAIRE WELLESLEY-SMITH

Textiles in the Landscape

CLAIRE WELLESLEY-SMITH CREDITS her mother, a music teacher, and her father, a university librarian, for nurturing the curiosity around which she has built her unconventional career. "My parents brought me up to wonder and to really look at and notice details and relish those things," she says. Claire is a textile artist, author, leader of community-based arts projects, and PhD candidate researching how communal slow craft activities, especially textile handwork, impact individual and community resilience and well-being. She is also the single mother of four daughters.

I visit Claire at home in Shipley, a town in the northern English county of West Yorkshire that during the nineteenth century, along with its larger neighbor Bradford and much of the surrounding region, became an international hotbed of textile manufacturing and, to fill the many jobs, immigration. As I drive into town from the east and head down Saltaire Road, I cannot help but notice the massive Salts Mill, a defunct Italianate stone textile mill turned modern commercial center that, when it opened in 1851, was the largest industrial space in the world. Adjacent to the mill is Saltaire, a self-contained village where the millworkers and their families lived. "They are writ large," Claire explained to me when we spoke for the first time on the phone a

few months earlier. Their visual impact stands as a testament to the area's social and economic history, both its rise as a boomtown of the industrial revolution—thanks in part to the area's long-standing sheep population and the nearby railroad and waterways—and its eventual demise as mill work moved offshore starting in the mid-twentieth century. "There are literally textiles in the landscape," Claire tells me. And those textiles have become the actual and metaphorical fiber that holds together much of Claire's work. "What happens to the people in a community when the way of life that sustained them for a hundred years ends?" she asks. "And is there a way to use handwork and heritage as tools for recovery?"

Claire grew up east of Shipley in Leeds, another mill town that boomed during the industrial revolution. Some of her earliest memories are of her mother pinning out dress patterns on the dining room floor and her grandmother knitting her sweaters. "In my family, talking was mostly done when accompanied by making," Claire wrote in her 2015 book, *Slow Stitch: Mindful and Contemplative Textile Art*. Her first memory of making something herself goes back to a Sunday school class when she was six or seven and her teacher brought in small squares of floral cotton fabric and taught the children to hand-stitch patchwork pillow

Claire working[...] stitch journal, [...] practice that s[...] to meditation.

"What happens to the people in a community when the way of life that sustained them for a hundred years ends?"

Claire can step out
the back door of her
house (built in 1904)
into her small garden
and descend the steps
on the other side of
the gate to get to her
cavernous studio. The
mother of four children,
she appreciates the
flexibility that working
from home allows.

One of two battered
Edwardian leather
armchairs that Claire
found in the attic of
an old house she used
to live in, layered with
textiles, some of which
she made herself.
Although she began
this layering practice to
prevent further damage
to the chairs, over time
they have become
a sort of domestic
art installation in the
front parlor. The red
embroidery on the chair
back, a family heirloom
from Hungary, dates to
the nineteenth century.

covers. "I absolutely enjoyed it," Claire recalls. In primary school, she learned how to make bobbin lace, and in her early teens, she created lots of dangly beaded jewelry, but she suggests, "I probably enjoyed organizing the materials more than making stuff out of them."

At the University of Leeds, Claire continued with what she calls "haphazard" making: "I lived in a shared house with six other girls, all but one fine-arts students," she remembers. "We patched, mended, and adapted things we bought from jumble sales and charity shops, and swapped loads of our stuff all the time." Among her most vivid recollections are the 1960s-style minidresses that they'd alter to fit and wear to concerts, and a khaki army jacket, the back of which she embroidered with flowers growing from the hem up to the shoulder—"a labor of love" that she regretfully lost track of, she tells me.

Despite all the time she spent making and the pleasure she drew from it, surprisingly, not once did Claire consider taking an art class. Instead, she earned a degree in political science with supplemental studies in theology and sociology and then, in 1993, took a job helping nontraditional students find ways to finance a university education. She enjoyed her work and stuck with it until 2004, when she decided to stay home with her first three daughters, whom she gave birth to in quick succession in 1999, 2001, and 2003.

Leaving the structure of a fulfilling office job proved emotionally challenging for Claire. To help her out at an especially difficult time, her mom and dad offered to watch their granddaughters one afternoon a week so that she could enroll in a creative textiles class that intrigued her. "Attending the course offered me a quiet, creative space and some time away from the pressures of being at home with three very young children. I found working with textiles quite grounding," Claire remembers. She also made friendships that endure to this day and recognized how enriching and connecting conversations that happen through making can be. Over the next few years, Claire continued with the classes, which covered everything from embroidery to dyeing to printmaking, and created a new career for herself developing and running community arts projects while raising her children, including another daughter born in 2009. Busier than ever as a parent but with an unquenchable curiosity, in 2013 she decided to further develop—and, in her own mind, legitimize—her art practice by enrolling in a master's degree program in visual arts. Then in 2016, she began a PhD program to do more formal research on the benefits of craft-based engagement so that she would eventually be able to share her findings widely and make a positive difference in more people's lives.

Seeking a PhD implies a certain level of bookishness—indeed, Claire does engage in some heavy reading and deep thinking—but her daily life is very much that of a busy working mom. When I visit, we hang around the house until Claire's daughters are home from school and she is sure her youngest will be watched over by one of them. Then she leads me on a walk to Salts Mill and Saltaire, where she excitedly points out details that fascinate her, such as massive hooks attached to the sides of the buildings that, when the mill was active, were used to hoist bales of unspun fiber from the barges and deliver them to the spinning rooms on the top floor.

Next we head to Claire's personal garden allotment to see her many dye plants. Claire started the garden in 2010; since then, she has established four more as part of community projects in Yorkshire and Lancashire. Back at her studio, which is in the basement of her house, Claire shows me her textile work, which tends to be small and produced slowly, often with bits of repurposed fabric and lengths of thread that she dyes using plants she forages or grows at her allotment or in containers on her back porch. Each weekday morning, she tells me, she walks her youngest daughter to school. On the way, the two of them stop to look at a particular horse chestnut tree, paying attention to small changes. "These are the punctuation marks in the day," Claire says. "They can be really quite joyful, even if you notice just one thing, like a plant growing in the cracks of the sidewalk."

In all her work, Claire is inspired by provenance, or a local connection, always seeking to engage people by initiating dialogue about what exists within and around them. And she finds that when they are sitting alongside one another, slowly making textiles with their hands, the impact can be profound, no matter their life circumstances—whether the maker is an asylum seeker who only two months earlier had to flee her own country and now finds herself in one of Claire's community groups, learning patchwork techniques; a patient in a mental-health facility who is participating in a long-term seed-to-fabric project that includes learning about the history of the madder plant in the region, growing the plant, and then using the roots to dye woolen cloth; or one of the more privileged participants who sign up for the slow-stitching workshops she offers at her home studio and occasionally at other locations. "Textiles are universal even if our heritage stories are different," Claire says. Though the lives of her students can differ drastically, their receptivity to conversation while making textiles proves to be a common denominator. In fact, many of her

TOP

For *Resist*, a 2017 art exhibition, Claire marked the centenary of a local woman's peace march by covering cloth from an old woolen blanket with hundreds of running stitches using silk thread from one of Bradford's now-defunct mills, plus materials she found along the march's route (plants she used for dyes; fabric scraps to stitch the base; and random bits of metal, such as rusty nails, to create resist prints). Each stitch, Claire explains, was a mark of resistance, a commemoration of the local women's efforts to end to the ongoing carnage of war in 1917, as well as a nod to the women around the world who similarly marched in protests in 2017.

CENTER LEFT

A sampler Claire created using fabrics and threads she dyed with plants grown in her garden during a single year.

CENTER RIGHT

Teaching samples Claire uses to demonstrate ways of collaging and stitching naturally dyed and repurposed materials.

BOTTOM

Claire stores the many colors of thread she dyes on old wooden clothespins until she is ready to stitch with them.

OPPOSITE

The back of an English paper-pieced patchwork Claire made using fabrics she dyed with plants from a community allotment project. She recorded how she achieved each color on the papers.

groups continue to convene on their own even after the formal programming where they met has concluded.

"There's a huge amount of pleasure I get from working with textiles in a direct making sense," Claire tells me as she threads a needle with woad-dyed silk at her kitchen table and we sip cups of tea. "There are also the amazing, resonant stories they hold. You can look at a garment worn fifty or a hundred years ago and understand the shape of the person who wore it." Claire is working tiny blue flecks into her stitch journal, a length of repurposed curtain linen that she has been "journaling" on since 2013. For Claire, this daily practice resembles a moving meditation—each stitch like a breath, in and out.

Claire mentions the work of twentieth-century French American artist Louise Bourgeois, whose abstract cloth drawings— stitched-together fragments of personal clothing and household fabric—she first saw in an exhibition in London in 2010. Like Claire, Bourgeois believed that sewing could be a source of emotional repair, famously stating, "I have always had a fear of being separated and abandoned. The sewing is my attempt to keep things together and make things whole."

Claire's own artwork is, like Bourgeois's cloth drawings, small-scale, abstract, and poignant, a piecing of fiber, memories, and narrative. A work called *Resist* pays homage to the women who marched for peace in Bradford, England, in 1917 and the women (and men) around the world who marched again in 2017. An untitled piece incorporates fabrics dyed with plants Claire grew at her allotment during one growing season, evoking a poetic sense of time and place.

She says that "living a reflective life, living in a critical way, actually engaging with and questioning what is around us and looking at the reality of it" is her modus operandi. In Shipley, and in northwestern England in general, that often means questioning the impact of the industrial revolution and the subsequent deindustrialization on life there, for better and for worse. Claire reminds us that the existence of machinery that can produce yards of cloth in mere seconds does not negate the benefits of working on cloth by hand. Self-sufficiency, competence, empathy, periods of contemplation, and a closer connection to our history, our fellow makers, and the effect of mass consumption on the environment—all this is possible when we work one slow stitch at a time.

·THREE·

Joining Hands

Each One, Teach One

IT'S THE FIRST Saturday in April, and about fifteen members of the approximately one-hundred-member African American Quilt Guild of Oakland are gathered at the home of Marion Coleman in order to share their stories and their quilts with me. A couple of months earlier, Marion spread the word about my visit and graciously offered her home in Castro Valley for our get-together.

The guild has been meeting at the West Oakland Library on the fourth Saturday of every month except December since its founding in June 2000, so this is an extra event on their calendar. The agreement with the library is that they can convene in their meeting room monthly in exchange for hosting a community workshop and exhibit there every winter, which the guild carries out—proudly and happily—during Black History Month in February.

I first learned about AAQGO in the *New York Times*, where I read about their project Neighborhoods Coming Together: Quilts Around Oakland. This ambitious multiyear, grant-funded undertaking, the brainchild of Marion, included a citywide rotating exhibit of one hundred narrative quilts about life in Oakland, past and present, plus free workshops. The quilts, all stitched by guild members or community members who participated in the guild's workshops, were divided into groups and made their way through a circuit of exhibition spaces—

in places as diverse as the rotunda at city hall, an art gallery, a senior center, a library, elementary schools, and a women's cancer resource center.

We fill Marion's living room, and one by one, members speak about the role of quilting and the guild in their lives. Nearly everyone expresses their gratitude to Marion for inspiring them to explore their creativity—and their appreciation of the camaraderie, skill building, and community service that are key to the guild's mission. "I see my role as trying to empower people to know that they have talent. They can enjoy it and they can push themselves to try something different without being afraid, because it's all right to make mistakes," Marion says. Dolores Vitero Presley and Julia Vitero, founding members and sisters, have just finished teaching an elementary school of more than four hundred students how to quilt, visiting each classroom three times over the course of three weeks, waking at 6:00 a.m. to arrive for the morning bell and threading needles for the kids during lunch breaks. "We complain, but we love it," says Dolores. "Anything to do with kids, count me in. Teaching them is a way I can give back to the universe."

Niambi Kee taught herself to quilt from books at the Brooklyn Public Library after her now-grown daughters were born, and she joined the guild as soon as she

"I see my role as trying to empower people to know that they have talent. They can enjoy it and they can push themselves to try something different without being afraid, because it's all right to make mistakes."

—Marion Coleman

"It is very rewarding at my age to meet a group of ladies, all of whom are younger than me, with whom I have a lot in common."

—Frances Porter

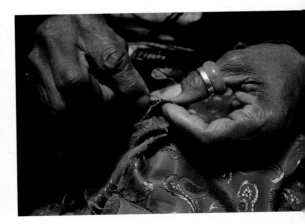

relocated from Brooklyn to California upon retirement. "I knew I would have an immediate family," she says. Today she likes combining commercial cloth with cloth she dyes herself to make quilts that reflect her ideas and experiences. She describes one she made in response to the Quincy Jones song "The Midnight Sun Will Never Set" and another she is planning based on the Maya Angelou quote "Try to be a rainbow in someone else's cloud."

Frances Porter, the guild's oldest member at ninety-two, began quilting about ten years ago and has been entering her quilts in the county fair ever since (the first year, her quilt was panned, she says with a laugh, but the second year, she took first prize). She has also donated quilts to her church and sorority and to schools for fund-raisers. Every year during Black History Month, she takes an Underground Railroad–themed quilt to local schools and reads a book about a runaway slave child using quilts as signs of safe houses along her route to freedom. About the guild, she says, "It is very rewarding at my age to meet a group of ladies, all of whom are younger than me, with whom I have a lot in common." "Each one, teach one" is a guild motto, she explains, and she enjoys sharing what she learns at the guild with others.

Although membership is open to all, the majority of members are African American women, many retired with grown children. For a long time, member La Quita Tummings belonged to a different guild, where she was one of only a few African American members. At the AAQGO, she feels more of a sisterhood, she says. "It's like having aunties and sisters. When we have a conversation, there are some things I don't have to explain because of our shared experiences as black women."

On the other hand, Ernestine Tril (who goes by Ernie) is Hispanic; about her guild "sisters," she says, "They get me." She joined AAQGO during a difficult time, after the death of her mother, when, she recalls, she was both working and drinking too much. "Quilting helped heal me," she says. "It took my mind off things. It gave me something else to do, an incentive." She is especially proud of her contribution to the Neighborhoods Coming Together project,

Barbara Fuston
specializes in
nontraditional quilts
featuring geometrics
and optical illusions.
These days she makes
her quilts two sided to
consolidate the bounty
of work she produces.

OPPOSITE, TOP RIGHT

After Zondra Martin
took a workshop with
members Dolores
Vitero Presley and
Julia Vitero at her
senior center as part
of the Neighborhoods
Coming Together
project, she decided to
join the AAQGO. Here
she is hand-stitching
a traditional gingham
quilt that she brought
to the meeting.

OPPOSITE, BOTTOM

One section of Marion's
Melody Makers quilt,
a celebration of the
integral role music
plays in African
American culture.

for which she created three quilts, and for her service on the guild's board, acting as the Northern California Quilt Council liaison. Marion got her involved. "I'm shy. If it weren't for Marion, I'd probably still be hiding away," she says. Marion has a knack for drawing people out, honed during the twenty-five years she spent working as a social worker. "I like it when people are able to realize how talented they are," she says modestly.

Marion learned to sew as a young child and started quilting as an adult when she discovered African-print fabrics and photo transfers that allowed her to make a memory quilt for her mother for her seventieth birthday. The walls of her home and her well-equipped studio bear witness to her ongoing dedication to the medium. With her quilts, she documents family memories, commemorates individuals and events in African American history and culture (such as the sole African American explorer on the Lewis and Clark expedition and the election of President Barack Obama), and comments on social issues like racism, homelessness, gun violence, and aging. She teaches and lectures widely, and in 2018, in recognition of her accomplishments and her commitment to keeping the tradition

of quilt making alive, she was named a National Endowment for the Arts National Heritage Fellow, a prestigious honor that began with a nomination by guild member Ora Clay. In the nomination letter, Ora, who was once an apprentice to Marion under an Alliance for California Traditional Arts program, wrote, "She is passionate in her belief that all of us should enjoy the beauty of art and our individual ability to explore our creative selves."

That guild-wide exploration is on display for me to see as each member reveals a quilt during our show-and-tell. Most of the projects the women unfold for me are wall quilts, as they tend to be smaller and easier to transport than bed quilts. Many of them would be identified as "art quilts" in the nomenclature of the quilt universe, as they do not rely on the classic patterns of what is commonly considered traditional American quilting, such as log cabins and flying geese. Instead, according to Marion, they draw upon "a long tradition of improvisational and narrative quilting within the African American community" to tell personal stories within a less uniform structure.

Ora Knowell's quilts tell important—albeit painful—stories, and they're not small. In fact, on this day she brought the

> "It's like having aunties and sisters. When we have a conversation, there are some things I don't have to explain because of our shared experiences as black women."
>
> —La Quita Tummings

TOP ROW, LEFT

From left to right, Dolores, Katie, and Rosita Thomas admiring a sampler quilt made with blocks stitched by various members. Part of the guild's mission is to donate quilts to worthy causes: this one went to Meals on Wheels.

TOP ROW, CENTER

Marion made *Hot Flash*, a self-portrait based on a photo she took of herself while she was going through menopause.

TOP ROW, RIGHT

Dolores (left) holding *Leaf One*, a paper-pieced quilt she made from a pattern by Judy Niemeyer. About the process, she says, "It was tedious, but it taught me to be patient." Next to her is her sister Julia, with a quilt she made based on an Ozark cobblestone pattern for which she found a faded clipping—a picture and two templates (but no instructions)—from a newspaper dated 1936. She stitched it by hand over the course of five years.

MIDDLE ROW, LEFT

Inspired by happy memories of growing up in Oakland, Ernestine Tril made this quilt for the guild's Neighborhoods Coming Together project. "All the kids—Hispanic, Anglo, African American, and Asian—would play together," she remembers, calling from their windows when they were ready to go outside to meet up.

MIDDLE ROW, CENTER

After our gathering, Marion headed to her studio to work on one of her quilts.

MIDDLE ROW, RIGHT

Niambi Kee combines commercial and hand-dyed fabrics in her quilts (and sometimes her clothing). The quilt shown here, called *Parenting Near Lake Manyara*, recounts a trip to Tanzania many years ago when, she says, "I had the privilege and honor to witness a herd of elephants going across the savanna. What especially impressed me then as a young parent was the way the babies were protectively tucked between the massive legs of the matriarchs."

BOTTOM ROW, LEFT

Carolyn made this quilt, called *We the Women of Color*, to represent "women of color in all their shapes and hues and personalities. It shows how beautiful we are inside and out," she says.

BOTTOM ROW, CENTER & RIGHT

Carolyn's *Spider Mandala* quilt uses all types of media, including string and tulle lamé, with a spirit figure on top.

largest quilt I have ever seen in person, at about two feet tall and more than sixty feet long. It is called *Homicide* and is composed of seventy panels, each one appliquéd with a human form to commemorate a person killed by gun violence. Ora learned to quilt as a child when homemade bedcoverings, patched together from worn-out wool and cotton clothing, were a necessity to keep warm. She began to quilt again as an adult for a very different reason: as a way to process and channel her grief after two of her sons were murdered, one in 1995 and the other in 2002. "The guild brought me out of my shell to be able to share my artwork," Ora says. "It comes from a dark but good place and is spiritually motivating for a lot of people." Ora is politically active and regularly attends national antiviolence conferences and local rallies to exhibit and talk about her quilts and sometimes to give workshops to help others, including survivors of violent crime, victim advocates, first responders, and those mourning loved ones. "I teach them nine-block piecing to help redirect their inner pain. They tell me it helps them relax and manage their stress. Now I realize why the adults kept us busy quilting as kids, because of all the pain and suffering they experienced on the plantations; doing something tangible and useful was a mind keeper."

Before we break for lunch, we go outside together to open Ora's quilt to its full length. The guild members stand tall, holding the fabric in front of their bodies, proud of the creativity, strength, culture, families, and history they represent. They support one another in good times and bad. They teach and inspire. They laugh. And they open their arms and their hearts to welcome me—and anyone else who cares to come into their embrace. Together, we are a patchwork, a quilt, a community.

BOTTOM

Detail from *Hope for the Future*, a quilt Ora Knowell made as part of the guild's annual Black History Month exhibition at the West Oakland public library. According to Ora, the marchers at the top recognize the struggles of the past (depicted along the bottom) but march forward in order to effect positive change for the future.

Sole Mates in the City

ON A FALL day back in 2003, Keiko Hirosue mentioned to her boyfriend that when she retired, she wanted to learn how to make her own shoes. She was twenty-three at the time, living in Brooklyn, working as a program assistant for an artist residency organization, and preparing to apply to law school. He wondered why she thought she needed to wait forty years. Why not start now?

The question inspired Keiko to rethink her timetable, and soon after, she enrolled in an evening class at the midtown YWCA taught by Emily Putterman, an experienced shoe designer and maker and the only local teacher outside of the formal degree programs in the city's fashion schools. From the start, Keiko knew she had tapped into a passion and, possibly, a new career path. Her first pair of shoes—made over the course of ten three-hour sessions—were metallic orange sandals with fiery feathers up the back. Then came navy blue knee-high boots with a side zipper, followed by black pointy-toed pumps with an ankle strap. "When I made my first design, and they fit my feet, it felt great," Keiko explains while sitting on a stool at a large worktable at the Brooklyn Shoe Space (BKSS), a communal studio and learning center that she now owns in Williamsburg. "Right away, people started asking me where I got my shoes. I realized that I could do something with this."

Over the next few years, "something" evolved into more classes and lots of practice at home—plus a few jobs in the fashion industry, getting married to that astute boyfriend, and giving birth to a baby boy—and, ultimately, designing a line of shoes manufactured in China, a process she found unsatisfying. "I realized that making shoes was my passion, not sending a design overseas," she recalls. She rented a 500-square-foot studio on Bedford Avenue in Williamsburg, Brooklyn, and bought some secondhand equipment so she could make shoes better and more efficiently herself. When other shoe and leather accessories makers began asking her if she would share her setup, she knew it made sense: She needed a way to offset her expenses and liked the idea of building a community, a place where makers could network and support one another. Keiko had emigrated to New York from Japan after college, and she still felt like an outsider. "When I started this, I didn't have a core network of friends. It's been nice to build that," she says.

What Keiko began gradually grew, and in 2015—at a new, larger location on Roebling Street—she formalized the business/collective under the name Brooklyn Shoe Space. Member Jessi Katz, founder of the Larry shoe brand, recalls meeting Keiko in the early days: "I remember her saying that she wanted to start a shoemaker collective,"

LEFT

Keiko, here in front of the Brooklyn Shoe Space's wall of lasts, grew up in a suburb of Tokyo, in a family and a culture where making was commonplace. She remembers doing a lot of different crafts—at home, in school, and at Girl Scouts—including knitting, sewing, woodworking, and origami.

RIGHT

The entrance to BKSS on Roebling Street.

"It's wonderful to meet shoemakers who come to visit us from all over the world."

—Ritika Bhattacharya

Sewing machines suitable for leatherwork are set up at the back of BKSS while communal worktables are situated at the front of the first floor and in the basement.

BKSS member Ritika Bhattacharya made these child's chukka boots with nontoxic distressed leather (for the upper) and recycled rubber (for the soles).

Ritika designs and makes eco-friendly kids' shoes under the brand name Brooklyn Bebe Company. One day, she hopes to find a way to collaborate directly with artisans in India to make textiles that can be incorporated into her shoes and accessories. "I would love to be part of the preservation and continuation of my cultural heritage," she explains.

Jessi explains. "And then she did it—and incredibly well—because she's wonderful at seeing how people can help each other, and she's very generous with her time." Like Keiko, Jessi began studying shoemaking with Emily Putterman, then went on to earn a master's in footwear design from the Polimoda fashion school in Florence, Italy, and a pedorthics (orthopedic foot care) certificate from St. Petersburg College in Florida. After finishing the degree in Florence, she moved back to New York and became a BKSS member. "The space is amazing because we shoemakers can share big equipment that nobody has room for at home," Jessi says. "Keiko always keeps materials on hand, and everybody is open and happy to help when you're having difficulty with something."

Member Lorna Nixon agrees. Lorna earned a degree in fashion accessories design from the London College of Fashion in 2010 and immediately flew to Manhattan to take a position as a handbag designer for a fashion conglomerate. Over the next few years, she became disillusioned by corporate culture, which she found lacked artistry and innovation and operated with questionable ethics when dealing with labor forces overseas. Rather than making use of what she saw as her greatest assets— "I have these hands. I have these skills," she says—she was spending most of her time on a computer designing trend-driven bags, then preparing instructions for factory workers in Asia to follow. By 2016, she felt unfulfilled and frustrated that she was not utilizing the skills that had brought her to New York in the first place. A colleague who knew she was a maker at heart introduced her to BKSS and, she recalls, "The instant I walked in, I felt at home."

Soon Lorna began to spend nearly every hour she wasn't working or sleeping at the space making bags. "I'd be late to my job during the week, but on Saturday and Sunday I would be at BKSS by seven a.m." Within five months, she had gathered the courage to break out on her own—though she was not really on her own, thanks to her new family of BKSS friends. "Everyone at BKSS has each other's backs," she says. "We're constantly learning from one another."

Now Lorna designs, produces, and sells a line of leather bags as well as one-of-a-

Handmade shoes modeled by makers (from left to right) Bonnie Andrus, Emily Boksenbaum, and Keiko. "Shoes are so essential," says Keiko. "They have to be comfortable or they can ruin your whole day and affect your health." The fashion footwear industry's primary focus is on business, she explains. "They don't care about feet."

Assorted projects on a BKSS worktable, including Emily's mermaid boots. She tooled the leather with mermaids on the front and "Live, Create, Make Waves" on the back to celebrate her new skill after completing an apprenticeship with a bootmaker in Albuquerque.

Keiko sources leather from distributors and manufacturers in New York's Fashion District and from shoe companies that donate their leftovers. This means that students who take classes at BKSS have an abundance of options from which to choose.

kind pieces directly to consumers and runs a company called I Made That Bag, which hosts bag-making parties and sells DIY bag-making kits. "Teaching at BKSS and seeing people who have never touched a sewing machine or cut leather, which is a skill in and of itself, make something for the first time and feel proud that they used their own hands gave me the idea for the company," she explains.

Lorna's story is a familiar one at BKSS. Member Ritika Bhattacharya also left a career in corporate fashion to do her own thing here. In Ritika's case, the decision followed an apprenticeship with a master shoemaker in Budapest and coincided with having a baby. "I was hesitant about returning to the corporate fashion world, which meant long, unpredictable hours but, of course, a great salary and benefits," she explains. "The other option was to forgo that safety net and try to forge my own path and stay closer to my son." Ritika was one of the first to join the original studio on Bedford Avenue, and she thinks back fondly to those early days when she and Keiko were both figuring out how to juggle marriage, motherhood, and their new business ventures. Ritika makes custom shoes, mostly for children, and is developing a line free of toxic chemicals and adhesives.

Over the years, Brooklyn Shoe Space has expanded from its quiet beginnings as a shared workroom to become an educational center and meeting place for the devoted and the curious alike. Here, the general public can learn what goes into making a pair of shoes and why buying them directly from a local, independent maker—if they don't want to make them themselves—is a good choice. BKSS is also a hub for all levels of leather workers, from absolute beginners to experienced cordwainers, to develop skills and support one another. "It's wonderful to meet shoemakers who come to visit us from all over the world," Ritika comments. They come from as far away as Indonesia and New Zealand to take courses that range from a six-hour espadrille session to a six-day shoe-, boot-, or sneaker-making intensive to a monthlong deep-dive into hand-welting, the traditional (now rare) practice of hand-stitching, rather than cementing, the upper to the sole of the shoe.

Emily Boksenbaum has been an instructor here for nearly as long as she has been a member. She signed up for the beginner shoemaking intensive a month after she moved to New York from Chicago, and Keiko promptly asked her to teach tooling (which she had learned after graduating from the Art Institute of Chicago, while working with a tooling specialist on furniture and wall panels). Teaching helped Emily finance her membership, and her fellow makers helped her develop her skills and acclimate to life

> "BKSS reminds you of the part of shoemaking you love most—the feeling of the materials in your hands."
>
> —Emily Boksenbaum

BOTTOM

In the basement work area, Emily sands the outsole edges of a black oxford for a client. "Making shoes with seasoned shoemakers around me—doing it wrong and getting help from the person sitting next to me—is what has taught me the most," she says.

"Everyone at BKSS has each other's backs. We're constantly learning from one another."

—Lorna Nixon

in New York. "It was automatic community. They just invited me into their world," she says. Members also encouraged her when a renowned footwear company, after seeing shoes she created at BKSS on Instagram, offered her a job in their innovation lab in New England. She's giving it a try, putting her BKSS membership on pause only because she is not currently living in the city. "I miss my friends there so much. BKSS reminds you of the part of shoemaking you love most—the feeling of the materials in your hands," she says.

Behind the scenes, Keiko is cheering on Emily and everyone else in her BKSS orbit and, simultaneously, pursuing her own evolving dreams. Recognizing that a lack of infrastructure for small-scale shoe manufacturing is a major stumbling block for independent designers who want to have shoes made in the United States, in 2017, she and BKSS member Rebecca Heykes founded the Brooklyn Shoe Factory (originally in Williamsburg and now in nearby Hoboken, New Jersey) to fill that niche. A year later, the Factory launched its own line of shoes, Loyal Footwear, designed by Rebecca and made on-site.

One day, Keiko hopes, they will have a showroom where they can display and sell Loyal Footwear as well as other members' brands. She also dreams of satellite locations of the Brooklyn Shoe Space, where she and her team can share the excitement of shoemaking and the pleasure of wearing fashionable shoes that fit properly with even more people. For now, Keiko teaches classes in other cities a few times a year and also travels to take classes herself.

"What we are doing is gratifying in so many ways," Keiko explains. "We are a catalyst and gateway for educating people. We are supporting artists and the local economy. And we are helping people reconnect with the natural human instinct to make with their own hands."

Although Keiko admits that balancing the finances can be stressful, and that she is still putting most of what she earns back into the business, she is excited about the life she is making for herself and the opportunities she is facilitating for others. "The more time you spend at BKSS, the more you get out of it," she says. "The more you contribute to the community, the more the community supports you in return."

Kindred Spirits

IN THE SMALL village of Auty in southwestern France, in a terra-cotta-pink château built in the 1700s, I felt more relaxed and at home, more present in the moment and comfortable in my skin, than I had in a while. Only a few months earlier, I had walked away from a full-time job of over a dozen years, and I was just starting to write this book, still trying to build up the courage and confidence I would need to actualize the expectations I had set for myself. I spent my time there in workshops with fifteen to twenty like-minded women, one week each of shibori and fabric collage, interrupted only by homemade meals made with fresh local ingredients and a few optional outings.

We were at Chateau Dumas together to learn and create, and in that protected space, free from the usual distractions of home, we all seemed to be able to let go of our worries and shed our inhibitions and, in turn, ignite our senses and our imaginations, about both what we were making and who we could be. There was a feeling of community, almost sisterhood, among us, as though we were girls back at summer camp discovering our strength, both individually and collectively. At this camp, we were fully devoted to our craft "den," a bright, airy studio in what was once the château's carriage house, and to the "fairy ring," a clearing in the woods where an outdoor dye studio was set up for us.

Each day during shibori class, we moved back and forth between the carriage house and the fairy ring, where we could dunk our cloth—strategically stitched, folded, rubber-banded, and clamped—into large vats of indigo without worrying about messes, then hang our work to dry on clotheslines strung between towering trees (later, we would rinse and unbind our cloths to reveal the patterns that our pre-dyeing manipulations had made possible). During fabric collage class, we spent only one day at the fairy ring, dyeing not with indigo but with woad, another natural blue plant dye, one that was widely cultivated and a source of great wealth in this region of France during the Renaissance. It was in that grassy circle that a sense of playful freedom, an almost primeval joy, seemed to spread among us. We gently lowered our materials into the oxygen-free vats, then pulled them out slowly with long poles, and watched as they emerged green and then gradually turned blue as the oxygen in the air penetrated them. It was impossible not to think of a witch's brew and to feel as though we were facilitating a kind of alchemy rooted in ancient wisdom.

The foundations of Chateau Dumas date back to the thirteenth century, and the current neoclassical structures—the main home, the L-shaped carriage house, and the small well house—to the late 1700s, but Chateau Dumas as a maker experience

"We'd sit and sew, then we'd stroll, talk, loiter about the property. We bonded over the joy we felt."

—Kay Gardiner

TOP
___

The château's courtyard and front façade.

BOTTOM
___

Lizzie (third from left) and guests gather at the courtyard table. Lizzie always has beautiful books related to the workshop themes on hand for research and inspiration.

was born in 2005, when Lizzie Hulme, an Englishwoman with familial roots in France, purchased the idyllic twenty-two-acre estate to create what she had dreamed of for herself: a special place to visit for high-quality creative workshops, delicious meals, comfortable accommodations, and warm pampering. For many years prior, she was a stay-at-home mom, but as she prepared to see her twin sons off to secondary school, she knew she was ready to take on a new challenge. "I left school at sixteen, so I didn't have a formal profession to fall back on," she says. "But I had traveled and lived abroad in France, Germany, and Greece, and I had done some event management and interior design. And I could speak French. So the château seemed like something I

could manage. And in a funny way, this feels like what I was always meant to do."

Lizzie inaugurated her retreat program just a few years later—after furnishing the interior and updating the plumbing—when she welcomed a group of millinery enthusiasts drawn to the area because of its history as a hatmaking center. Since then, she has gradually expanded her offerings to include a wide variety of subjects, including block- and silkscreen printing, etching, dressmaking, flower arranging, beading, natural dyeing, painting, quilting, basket making, cooking, and more. Each fall, she posts a menu of options for the following June through October, giving guests plenty of advance notice to reserve the time in their schedules and also to save up to pay for the blissful, sometimes once-in-a-lifetime experience.

"Most important is the quality of the teaching," says Lizzie, who spends months researching and corresponding with potential instructors, deciding whom to invite, she says, mostly by following her intuition and listening to her guests'

feedback. She also receives lots of recommendations, including from the editors of *Selvedge* magazine, who have been sharing ideas with her and helping her promote her retreats since 2013. Workshop guests are mostly female, range from young adults to senior citizens, from passionate amateurs to professional artists and designers, and travel to the château from all over the world. What they all share is a passion for making with their hands and a desire to immerse themselves in their creative pursuits.

"It is a completely protected environment. You can forget about almost everything else," says Caroline Nixon, a retired ob-gyn from England and four-time Dumasienne. "I felt like I was with my people; we were on the same wavelength. I lost track of time," adds Jan Quarles, a global journalism professor from Tennessee. For Kay Gardiner, a small-business owner in New York who coordinated her travels with four friends and was at the château a week before I arrived, it was like a weeklong slumber party: "We'd sit and sew, then we'd stroll, talk, loiter about the property. We bonded over the joy we felt," she remembers.

There is a magic about Chateau Dumas that is hard to describe. "If there were a recipe for it, it wouldn't be magic," Lizzie comments when I ask her about this elusive quality that makes time spent there so enchanting. "I sensed the château's specialness the very first time I visited,"

says Lizzie, who takes credit only for the "practical bits": making sure the instructors are top-notch, meals are well made with locally sourced ingredients, accommodations are comfortable, and the staff is friendly and hospitable. "I put certain things in place," she says. "But there is something else. The château itself radiates a positive energy that everyone who stays here feels."

Late one morning while taking a break from stitching, I followed the steps from the main courtyard down a winding path to the pool, where I sat quietly in the shade and wrote in my journal: "Women are often doing what they feel they *should* do, taking care of others, but here we are focused on what we want to do for ourselves. We are expressing who we really are, even touching upon who we might have been centuries ago. The sky is perfectly clear—not a single cloud. The leaves on the trees are twittering in the breeze."

At that moment, I felt as though the clarity of the sky were mimicking my life. I was completely grounded, alive, and awake; happy and satisfied; profoundly alert to even the subtlest of changes in the angle of the sun, the gentleness of the breeze, the sound and shadows of the leaves around me—and to the joy I felt spending my days among kindred spirits. I heard the village's church bells clanging, so I knew it was noon and that lunch would be served shortly. I closed my eyes. Then and there, nothing else mattered.

A view from the gardens up to the château.

My shibori classmate Jane Thompson stitching by the window on the château's second floor.

During fabric collage week, our projects were small and it was easy to move around the grounds to stitch. "This is heaven," Lynne Earle announced while working quietly on a swing in the shade.

Our shibori instructor, Jane "Cally" Callender, in the studio with Clodagh Kelly, a recent art school graduate from Ireland who came to the château, she explained, to slow down, get away from screens and keyboards, and reconnect with nature.

Lizzie and me chatting during afternoon tea.

"I felt like I was with my people,
we were on the same wavelength.
I lost track of time."

—Jan Quarles

Dyeing at Chateau Dumas takes place in the "fairy ring," a grassy clearing in the woods beyond the formal clipped box hedges and just a short walk from the carriage house. For shibori class, we spent the week traveling between the studio where we prepared our fabrics and the indigo vats at the ring that Cally taught us how to set up and tend. On woad-dyeing day (which happens midweek during most workshops), local expert Denise Lambert (shown below in overalls with Jan Quarles) tended the vats. Many of us began by dyeing vintage dresses and cloth we'd picked up at the village flea market and in nearby Saint-Antonin-Noble-Val; then, as "woad fever" overcame us, we hurried back to our rooms to pull clothing, even shoes, from our travel wardrobes to dye.

Integrity, Simplicity, and Grace

ON TOP OF a small bookcase in Peter Korn's office at the Center for Furniture Craftsmanship in Rockport, Maine, is a sign that reads You Can't Bullshit a Chisel. It was made for Peter by a fan who attended a lecture he gave as part of a tour for his 2013 book, *Why We Make Things and Why It Matters*. I'm in Peter's office, interviewing him after spending two weeks in his Basic Woodworking course at the school—of which he is the founder and director. The course was a unique challenge for me, as I had never before done even the smallest woodworking task beyond sanding some boards and, with the help of a friend, sawing them. Yet in just the first few days in Rockport, I was tasked with milling a piece of poplar four-square (meaning to the point where the faces and edges are straight, square, and parallel to one another) and hand-cutting both a dovetail and a mortise and tenon, the most essential forms of joinery for fine furniture making, with chisels I sharpened myself.

Peter coined the phrase on the sign, a sage shorthand, while traveling to promote his book. When I ask him to elaborate, he does so thoughtfully, relying on the same methodical logic and underlying philosophical nuance with which he writes and with which he instructed me and my eleven classmates throughout our workshop. "In some areas of life, mistakes or skipped steps are acceptable as long as the final result *looks* good. But in woodworking, the quality of the result depends entirely on the excellence with which you accomplish every little step along the way. You can't leapfrog; you can't pretend. Woodworking repays close intention. It repays integrity."

For Peter, integrity is key in every aspect of his life, a priority he traces back to his secondary education at a Quaker school in Philadelphia, where he also developed an unequivocal commitment to community. Although he went on to the University of Pennsylvania and studied history (as a precursor, perhaps, to becoming a lawyer like his father), he segued into woodworking and found his way in life first as a carpenter in the early 1970s, then as a full-time fine furniture designer and maker, and, ultimately, as the teacher, administrator, and author (as well as sailor and sourdough bread maker) he is today.

Peter founded the Center for Furniture Craftsmanship in 1993, following a six-year stint as program director at the Anderson Ranch Arts Center in the Colorado Rockies. Although the school has grown and developed significantly since then (from two rooms in a converted barn that could accommodate only six students at a time to a vibrant nonprofit with three large workshops, a gallery, an endowment, a scholarship fund, and a visiting artists

Our class spent the first two days of the program learning to bevel our chisels to the proper angle and then sharpen them. The back of the chisel must be perfectly flat, and the front must be angled at twenty-five to thirty degrees, the edge even and razor sharp. Our leaders—Peter (here demonstrating how to grind a uniform hollow bevel), Bobby Sukrachand, and Eddie Orellana—are infinitely patient but show no forgiveness if a step is incorrectly executed. They know that what Peter says is true— "You can't bullshit a chisel." If it's not beveled and sharpened properly, we will never make effective joinery.

TOP

Using a back-and-forth rocking motion on a sharpening stone, without applying pressure, I hone the blade on my chisel to create the sharpest edge possible. Without a sharp edge, I will not be able to cut and fit my joinery with the required precision.

CENTER LEFT, ABOVE

As I practice grinding a uniform hollow bevel, I am developing trust in my own hands, eyes, and instincts.

CENTER LEFT, BELOW

Each task in hand joinery requires a razor-sharp chisel in a particular size.

CENTER RIGHT & BOTTOM RIGHT

Once our chisels are properly prepared, we will begin to learn how to execute a mortise and tenon (center right) and then a dovetail (bottom right), the most essential forms of joinery for fine furniture making. Before nails and screws became commonplace, these types of joints were standard. When clean and tight, they remain sturdy for centuries.

BOTTOM LEFT

Bobby kindly explains why my chisel needs further refinement to be work ready. Bobby is based in Brooklyn, where he says there are thousands of young people trying to figure out how to make it as designer-woodworkers. He hypothesizes that many of them grew up like him, on a college-preparatory path that ignored the value of hands-on work.

"There is a
certain type
of emotional
or spiritual
hunger we
have that isn't
answered
by anything
but making
physical
objects."

program), its mission, according to Peter, has been constant: "To teach woodworking from the point of view that designing and creating beautiful, useful things is just as much an exploration of what is important in life—what it is to be a human being, and how we should live—as any other art form, including the fine arts." In fact, that mission parallels Peter's lived experience, the benefits of which he shares with the approximately four hundred students and fellows who make use of the school's facilities each year.

During the summer and fall seasons, CFC runs a full curriculum of thirty different one- and two-week courses for beginning and experienced woodworkers, most of whom are hobbyists ranging from about seventeen to eighty-something years old. Throughout the year, the school offers longer-term and more intensive eight-week, twelve-week, and nine-month courses, plus fellowships, generally undertaken by younger students who seek to develop their skills for professional purposes.

My class consists of nine men and three women, hailing from all over the country. Rex is an economist with the World Bank who has been trying to teach himself woodworking by watching YouTube videos. William, an internist from Mississippi whose wife and baby have come to Maine with him, wants to make furniture for their

home, starting with a kitchen table. Ian is a Massachusetts-based quality engineer for the aerospace and semiconductor industries who also studied theology and ethics at Harvard Divinity School and is residing in a tent in the woods on the school's grounds for the length of the course (the rest of us have secured more conventional housing nearby). As a child, he dreamed of pursuing a career in the arts, an aspiration his father didn't support.

One day, as we eat lunch at the picnic tables outside our studio, Ian says something that catches my attention: "I wonder how different my life would have been if I had worked with my hands. Most of what I have done has been intellectual stuff, and I don't have much to show for it." Instructor Eddie Orellana, who completed the CFC's twelve-week Furniture Intensive a few months ago and is an assistant for our class, is acting upon a similar curiosity and a hunch that he is meant for something different—he worked in the tech industry in Texas, but, as of recently, he is seeking a career in woodworking because he wants to "make something where you can see the result."

These stories are familiar to Peter, who hears similar ones every session. "There is a certain type of emotional or spiritual hunger we have that isn't answered by anything but making physical objects," he explains. "There is something that most people don't get nearly enough of—and get even less of now than they have historically—because more and more of our lives are at keyboards and computer screens and more and more fabrication is done by pushing buttons and watching output than by taking a tool in our hands and understanding how to use it."

While our group spends one week practicing the basics of hand joinery and one week designing and building a bench with those newly acquired skills, in the bench room next to ours, more-experienced woodworkers are taking classes in precision with hand tools and veneering. Across the yard, around which all the red clapboard buildings sit, are two additional workshops where students in the twelve-week Furniture Intensive and fellows are intently focused on their individual projects.

Jesslyn Stanley and I share our brown-bag lunches on the steps outside her studio at the beginning of my second week. She traveled here from Georgia for a twelve-week course—following an apprenticeship with a woodworker back in Atlanta—and would like to grow her business, Lluu Evelyn Furniture (named in memory of her grandmothers), when she returns home. "A lot of my motivation comes from the influence of people in my family who gave me their care and unconditional love. I can put that back into furniture I make and give it to someone else," she tells me. "Woodworking is connected to my well-

being, to how I want to be seen in the world, and to the mark I leave."

The next day, Yuri Kobayashi and I eat our lunch in the library, which is adjacent to the school's gallery. Yuri trained as an architect then as a woodworker in Japan; she came to the United States on an exchange program and decided to stay in part because she feels she is able to express her creativity more freely here. She teaches every other semester at the Rhode Island School of Design and spends much of the rest of the year at CFC as a senior fellow. Her focus is sculpture, with which, she explains, she is able to transcend language barriers and express her identity, experiences, and thoughts. At CFC, she says, she has found a second family, a home.

Although no one actually lives on campus (unless, like Ian, they decide to pitch a tent

for a while), there is a sense of camaraderie, especially among those who study here long term or come back to teach regularly. "The school is a node where people, many of whom work in isolation, build peer relationships all over the world. It has enriched so many people's professional and personal lives," Peter explains.

During the summer season, the community gathers on Monday nights for a slide show led by an instructor or fellow, and on Thursday nights, everyone on campus (plus friends of the school who are visiting or live nearby) partakes in a lobster boil/potluck dinner followed by a croquet match. The game is a fun tradition that Peter started back in the early days of the school, when a friend sent him a croquet set as a gift. "It brings people together in way that doesn't happen in the workshop. It is one

of the tools for making the school run well," he says. It's true. There's lots of laughter and friendly banter during the game, and when we reconvene the next morning, we all seem to feel a bit closer, more at ease moving from bench to bench to look at one another's progress, ask for advice, and, inevitably, share stories about our quest for perfect joints and the challenges we are facing along the way.

At the workbench across from mine is Beth, a software developer from Colorado who has come here, she says, because though she is pretty good at a lot of crafts, she wants to focus on one and develop some mastery around it. In my view, she is a woodworking wunderkind, able to grasp concepts quickly and possessing the emotional and physical stamina necessary to achieve excellence. She is also warm and

OPPOSITE

Senior fellow Yuri Kobayashi at the band saw.

TOP LEFT & RIGHT

Yuri's workstation, with a close-up of her experiments bending wood, studies for her sculptural work.

BOTTOM LEFT

Yuri assists two students in the twelve-week Furniture Intensive with clamping and gluing.

supportive of my ongoing struggle with this new world. Even operating the vise at my bench is a challenge for me, let alone paring down the sides of my mortise so they are perfectly straight and square, allowing the tenon to slide into it securely. But Beth's encouragement is unwavering, as is that of Peter and the other instructors. That mood of commitment to excellence and positivity is ingrained in every aspect of how the school is run—"If you don't work that way, you don't stay here long," Peter says—and is naturally absorbed by the students.

Although Peter, at seventy, is planning his retirement in a few years, he is not slowing down. Instead, he is gearing up to make sure the school he founded has a rich future. The goal is not growth but to make it *better*, which means increasing its social contribution. He is spearheading an endowment campaign to fund more of the fellowship positions as well as a new scholarship program called Teaching the Teachers. With excitement, he tells me: "We are going to partner with institutions around the country that teach woodworking to benefit disadvantaged communities, primarily secondary schools, community colleges, and vocational schools. The idea is for them to send one of their teachers here to take a course, to have the experience of our learning environment, curriculum,

equipment, and facility. We hope that the experience will enrich their own teaching for a lifetime."

As I prepare to say a grateful good-bye to Peter and return to the bench room one last time to clean up, I mention how reflective his goals today are of his early Quaker schooling. "I completely carry it with me," he says. "I'm not a Quaker, but what I absorbed there is that what matters is the spiritual dimension of your life, which expresses itself not by becoming rich and famous but by what you contribute to the well-being of the world as it is, or what you do to tidy up your little corner. Independent thought and service to community are parts of that Quaker ideal."

Early on in his career as a fine furniture maker, Peter reflected on his personal values and identified integrity, simplicity, and grace as the qualities he was aiming to achieve in his work. Years later, he realized that the reason he became a furniture maker was, in fact, to try to cultivate those very same qualities in himself. This realization led him to write *Why We Make Things and Why It Matters* as a way to share his ideas. It also guides the way he runs the CFC and the way he is working with his team to prepare the school for his retirement so that it will live on far into the future. No bullshit ever.

TOP

Each morning, I entered our workshop through this welcoming, flower-lined pathway. Lunches and the Thursday-night potluck/lobster boil are enjoyed at the picnic tables to the left.

BOTTOM

At the end of our two weeks at CFC, our class stands proud and happy in front of finished benches.

Art Is a Way

THE FIRST TIME I met Elsa Mora, I was taking a paper-cutting workshop she was teaching as part of a weekend Makerie event on the sprawling first floor of Urban Outfitters corporate headquarters in the Philadelphia Navy Yard. We were about fifteen women seated around a large table in a sunlight-splashed atrium, each of us with a small cutting mat, an X-acto blade, and a practice worksheet in front of us. In the center of the table were stacks of art paper in a spectrum of colors, some simple paper-cut illustrations that Elsa had prepared, and templates we could use if we wanted, after practicing, to copy her work rather than design our own (a sure way to feel successful in such a short period of learning). To begin, Elsa asked us, in her warm, Cuban-accented English, to set an intention. She was sure that we all had a lot on our minds. But, she said, "For the next two hours, the only thing that matters is that we're here and we're going to do this and we're going to put our heart into it and do it well." Elsa was a generous and humble teacher. Her prompt seemed to cast a spell over our group, all of us grateful for the reminder to let go of any worries that might be distracting us, at least for a couple of hours.

In the years that have followed, Elsa has captivated me with similar clarity and wisdom every time I have been in her presence. She is an accomplished artist who is as intent on using her art and hands to communicate her own experiences, ideas, and feelings as she is on empowering others to develop their own fulfilling forms of creative expression. She is a founding member and one of the driving forces behind ArtYard, a contemporary arts center in Frenchtown, New Jersey, that is equally dedicated to exhibiting powerful art and engaging the community in its many participatory events, from film screenings to poetry writing workshops to costume- and instrument-making events for their musical parades. On the wall in front of Elsa's worktable at home is a hand-lettered sign that reads Art Is a Way—amid her paintings, paper-cuttings, and a silver necklace she made to wear to the 2008 Academy Awards, which she was attending with her husband, film producer Bill Horberg.

While today she lives comfortably with Bill and their two children in a 1917 farmhouse on what was once a maple tree farm in rural Mount Tremper, New York (just a couple of hours north of New York City), her roots are in Holguín, Cuba, where she grew up in poverty in a family plagued by dysfunction and mental illness. It is her own life experience that makes her believe so passionately in the transformative power of art.

"I like to serve, so I want to use whatever skills I have to help people experience the transformational power of art and creativity."

"I always felt like an outsider, like I came from another planet. I would think this is like an experiment: Let's put this girl in the middle of this crazy family and let's give her a touch of art and creativity and see what happens. And that basically saved my life."

One of eight children of divorced parents, Elsa can barely remember a time during her early years when she wasn't drawing or writing or conjuring fantasy worlds in precise detail in her mind. "I always felt like an outsider, like I came from another planet. I would think this is like an experiment: Let's put this girl in the middle of this crazy family and let's give her a touch of art and creativity and see what happens. And that basically saved my life," Elsa tells me as we sit together at a low table in her home studio, with a window and a view of a yard and a wooded hillside before us. At twelve, Elsa was admitted to the local vocational art school, and in 1988, she entered the Professional School of Fine Arts in Holguín, and then one in Camagüey, where she studied sculpture and earned teaching credentials.

Her family and social life remained strained, but the school (which was free, like all education in Cuba) and a job as an art teacher after graduation provided some respite—until the fall of the Soviet Union in late 1991. At that point, the Soviets, Cuba's main economic partner, stopped sending crucial supplies. Living conditions deteriorated, eventually becoming dire for Elsa and most everyone around her. "We had nothing, and we had no infrastructure to survive," Elsa recalls of this period,

when she almost lost hope. "No food, gas, clothes, shoes." On an especially harrowing afternoon in 1992, forever forged in her memory, while sitting at her kitchen table feeling listless and desperate, Elsa spotted an advertisement for a drawing competition in the local newspaper, a chance happening for which she is eternally grateful. "Why not? I'm nearly dead; I have nothing to lose," she remembers thinking, so she decided to enter and focus on a drawing, something she "had the power to control."

That drawing—a dark, aggressive, and detailed depiction of the human suffering around her—earned her the first-place prize of one thousand pesos (a fortune to her at the time, enough to live on for a year) and now hangs in her dining room in Mount Tremper. "It's a reminder: Don't ever forget where you come from," she says. And, Elsa insists, don't ever take the power of your creativity for granted.

During the weekend event where I first met Elsa, I was giving a Sunday lunchtime presentation introducing my early work on this book to the hundred or so attendees. I told them my story and how during a period of self-exploration after leaving a stressful full-time job, I began to spend more time gardening and making small, functional objects with my hands and realized that what I was searching for was competence.

These forms are part
of a series of 101 paper
sculptures, each
representing a different
mental disorder, that
Elsa made for *Paper
Weight*, a solo show
that opened at the
Jordan Schnitzer
Museum of Art in
Eugene, Oregon. This
body of work, she
explains, "is about the
malleability of the brain
and the freedom that
you experience when
you realize that you
can actually do things
differently. You don't
have to follow patterns;
you don't have to do
what someone else
expects from you."

In this age of speed and technology and information, when the ubiquity of machines to carry out what for thousands of years required handwork is rarely questioned, I began to understand what I was missing. At the end of the presentation, I read a few lines from Anna Zilboorg's book *Knitting for Anarchists*, which I felt would resonate with this group of makers:

These days our fingers are primarily trained to push buttons. . . . To leave your fingers untrained for anything beyond pushing and perhaps twisting is like leaving a voice without singing. . . . Certainly knitting isn't the only thing that fingers can do, but it is a good thing: simple yet capable of endless complexity.

Then I asked if anyone in the audience would stand and share why making by hand is important to them personally. There was a brief silence before Elsa bounded up and took the microphone.

Elsa wanted us all to know her story and how important it is not only to believe in our own hands, our own creativity, and our own ingenuity but also to honor the time we had just spent together, two days within the warm embrace of a supportive creative community.

A couple of months later, when I visited Elsa at her home, she told me more about her journey: how her life in Cuba improved bit by bit after she won the drawing competition, to the point where she was living contentedly in an apartment in Havana and exhibiting and selling her multimedia artwork internationally; how she hadn't ever imagined emigrating from Cuba to Los Angeles until 2001, when she met and fell in love with Bill while he was in Havana attending a jazz festival; how she

planned to continue working as an artist after their children, Natalie and Diego, were born in 2003 and 2005, respectively, but then how everything changed in 2007 when Diego was diagnosed with autism. Interestingly, it was Diego's autism that led Elsa to paper-cutting and other forms of artistic expression that were, for her, less cerebral and emotionally gripping.

"Artists in general tend to be a little selfish. Not in a bad way, but you just go into your world and get lost in there. That's how you create," Elsa suggests. "I had to force myself to come out of that into real life. To be a mother, to be selfless, to be everything for this kid."

During the early days of Diego's diagnosis and her and Bill's search for information and support, Elsa found that just doing something with her hands helped quell her anxiety. She began by making drawings of vegetation and made-up animals, then, while sitting in waiting rooms during Diego's many therapy sessions, cutting the lines with an X-Acto blade on a small mat that she carried with her. "It was perfect, very repetitive, like meditation," she remembers. "Just cut, cut, cut, until I'm done." Gradually, she noticed that she was building muscles in her right arm that she never knew she had. Simultaneously, Diego was responding well to therapy, developing his own muscles.

Over the course of the next seven years, Elsa discovered a new way to nourish her creative spirit and maintain her emotional equilibrium: She focused mostly on paper-cut illustrations and sculpture and miniature limited-edition artist books that she would write about on a blog and sell on Etsy, an

Sleep Disorder
Pyromania
Oneirophrenia
Selective Mutism

experience that she says also helped her learn how to run a small business in a new country, improve her written English, and connect with other makers. Gradually, as her digital footprint grew, publishers began contacting her and proposing commissions—first for a book of characters composed of flower parts (based on a blog post she wrote about making flower characters and connecting with Diego in their garden), then for paper-cut illustrations for book covers and for periodicals like the *New York Review of Books* and *O, The Oprah Magazine*. Although some of her friends in the contemporary art world questioned her new, "less serious" route, she valued what she was doing and appreciated how it balanced with her family's needs.

The year 2014 was a period of transition, however: Wanting to slow down and simplify their lives, Elsa and Bill decided to move the family from Los Angeles to Mount Tremper. The children were doing well, and the couple agreed that this was a good time for a change. In addition, Elsa felt ready to rekindle her fine art practice, so she put her Etsy shop on indefinite hiatus, stopped accepting commissions, and started organizing an exhibition of work representing her life up to that point for the National Arts Club in New York City.

So why, then, was Elsa at the Makerie, teaching paper-cutting in the spring of 2016? That's exactly what she was wondering as she was making the three-hour drive to Philadelphia, considering all she could be accomplishing if she had stayed home. Teaching at the Makerie wasn't something she needed professionally, but when founder Ali DeJohn had extended

the invitation months earlier, the notion of spending a weekend connecting with other makers, mostly women, appealed to her. And once she arrived, she felt exhilarated by the real-life, in-the-flesh interaction and the contagious joy that was spreading, so different from the internet-based interaction she had become accustomed to. "I felt so happy making things with other people, and talking to them," Elsa remembers. The intimacy of the experience at the Makerie only served to reinforce her excitement about another community-based project she was working on but not yet daring to speak about publicly. Elsa and founder Jill Kearney would open ArtYard just five months later in September 2016.

Today Elsa divides her time between Mount Tremper and Frenchtown, and between caring for her family and working on her own art at home and facilitating the creativity of others collaboratively at ArtYard. "I like to serve, so I want to use whatever skills I have to help people experience the transformative power of art," she says. She has had what she considers the good fortune of living in two drastically different cultures, in conditions of both material poverty and material comfort, experiencing firsthand the advantages, disadvantages, and complexities of divergent social, economic, and political ideologies. Ultimately, she believes that art is a way, as she once wrote in an Instagram post, "of seeing, being, learning, understanding, connecting, searching, getting lost, finding, taking, giving, dying, surviving . . . or whatever you want/need it to be."

"When I say creativity saved my life," she tells me, "I really mean it."

OPPOSITE, LEFT

Elsa painting a papier-mâché bird head, part of a puppet for ArtYard's Hatch parade.

OPPOSITE, RIGHT

Elsa, ArtYard founder Jill Kearney, and Jill's daughter Flannery McDonnell take a puppet Flannery created for the Hatch parade for a trial run. This community event began as a way to mark the opening of ArtYard's inaugural show and has become an annual celebration. Revelers dressed in bird costumes made by community members emerge from a fourteen-foot cracked-egg sculpture in front of the current theater (once a hatchery) and parade along with puppeteers and other ArtYard enthusiasts to the center's first gallery. At ArtYard, Elsa says, "We are hatching new beginnings, creativity, community, collaborative energy, and our exciting future."

Sandlot Values

JACK SANDERS ENTHUSIASTICALLY welcomes us to Camp Heavy Metal at the Long Time, his five-acre ranch in Austin, Texas. He and his co-instructors, Parker Keyes and Dan Dyer, are eager to teach our group of five men and four women how to weld so we can spend the weekend designing and building projects out of metal and other random materials from his sprawling scrap pile. Jack is sure that what we make will be great, that something magical will happen when we collaborate. He tells us that a guitar stand/stool made at camp last year sold for over a thousand dollars at a gala auction to raise money for the Health Alliance for Austin Musicians. HAAM is a local nonprofit that provides low-income working musicians with access to affordable health care. Our projects are destined for this year's gala, and Jack is optimistic that we can at least match the previous year's record. "I'm going to feed you really well. We'll listen to some great music. You're going to learn a lot. And if we do this right, we are going to raise money for HAAM," he says. For every dollar our projects bring in, HAAM can deliver seven dollars of in-kind services. Jack calls this holistic approach "sandlot." It's about making the most of a little, innovating with the materials at hand, and having a blast and doing good (like a bunch of friends gathering on a sandlot for a quasi-organized, all-in-good-fun ball game).

Jack's inspiration for just about everything he does at the Long Time—which includes architectural design, metal fabrication, welding camps, and baseball—harkens back to his college days. He earned bachelor's and master's degrees in architecture from Auburn University in Alabama and the University of Texas, respectively, but his most formative years were spent at the Rural Studio in Newbern, Alabama. This is a satellite location of Auburn's architecture school, a place where students learn the principles and practicalities of architecture hands-on—by designing and building homes and community gathering places for some of Alabama's poorest residents, mostly out of donated, recycled, and found materials. At the Rural Studio, Jack became so engaged in his work—and its emphasis on community, sustainability, service, education, experimentation, and collaboration—that he almost forgot he was in school. "I remember thinking, 'I don't care what the degree is at the end of this,'" he says. He was, as Rural Studio founder and his mentor, architect Samuel Mockbee, liked to say, "snakebit," so completely infected with enthusiasm for and dedication to the meaningful way he was spending his time that he wanted to take the experience into everything else he did. Camp Heavy Metal is like a weekend dose of the Rural Studio's "venom."

"Some of my best experiences creatively and artistically have included a moment when somebody told me I was doing it wrong."

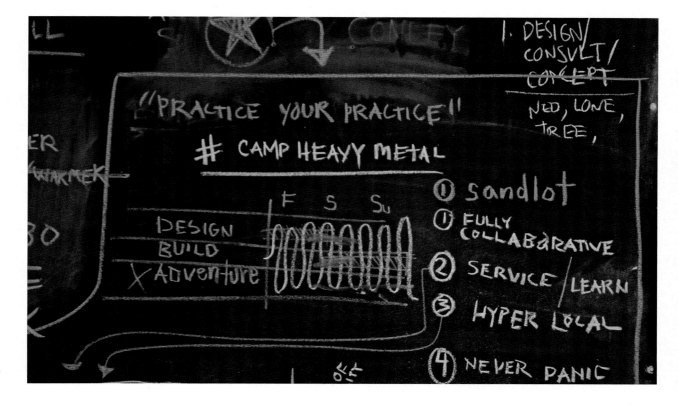

OPPOSITE, TOP & CENTER

At the Long Time and under the auspices of his company, Design Build Adventure, Jack weaves together architectural design, fabrication, project management, creative direction, and whatever else comes up along the way. The five-acre property includes a house that he uses as an office; an indoor-outdoor workshop for fabrication; and a baseball field that the Texas Playboys, the sandlot team he plays on and manages, calls home.

OPPOSITE, BOTTOM

The key concepts in Jack's practice are woven throughout our weekend experience, as Jack illustrates on the blackboard on day one.

Camp begins on a Friday afternoon with Jack's introduction, a brainstorming session, an initial scavenge through the scrap pile, and a visit to the shop to give the welding gun a first try. Then there's a happy hour on the back porch of the office and studio (once a two-bedroom house) before Jack, Dan, and Parker run off because their baseball team, the Texas Playboys, is due out on the field by seven. Although they often play right here at the Long Time, this is an away game, at a nearby park, and we're all invited.

Jack's interest in baseball is lifelong, and his passion for it today is as much about the community it can foster as it is about the pleasure of playing the game, a realization he came to during his early days at the Rural Studio, when he became a diehard fan of, and ultimately a first baseman and pitcher for, the Newbern Tigers. The Tigers are a nearly century-old African American sandlot team that draws hundreds of locals and out-of-towners to their games for friendly competition and a lively party and uses the money they collect from concessions to provide flowers for funerals; as a team, they also hand-dig the grave when a teammate's family member dies. For his undergraduate thesis project, Jack and two classmates designed and built the team a new backstop out of donated steel and chain link, an undertaking that required them to learn how to weld. It would be among three projects selected to represent Rural Studio in 2002's Whitney Biennial, a prestigious showcase of American art.

As heady as it was to have his project seen by the upper echelons of the art world, then and now Jack remains more focused on living by the values the Rural Studio and the Tigers instilled in him than on pursuing fancy honors. His practice, which he calls Design Build Adventure, is unorthodox and fluid. "Some of my best experiences creatively and artistically have included a moment when somebody told me I was doing it wrong," Jack points out. Depending on the day, his to-do list can include anything from designing, building, and welding to screen-printing T-shirts, indigo dyeing bandanas, or designing stickers for a grassroots get-out-the-vote campaign.

Jack started his welding camps first in Marfa, Texas, in 2009 (in conjunction with DBA's work on the El Cosmico hotel and campground there), then at the Long Time in 2013, as a way to weave the crucial

elements of education and service into his way of working. "Those were areas I felt like I was succeeding in at the Rural Studio," Jack says. "To drop all that and go into conventional architectural practice seemed a little odd." He was also inspired by two friends: locavore chef Jesse Griffiths of Dai Due, who was teaching butchering and hosting farm-to-table dinners, and Natalie Chanin (see page 86), who was establishing her School of Making for sewists in Florence, Alabama.

Welding, I find out during my two and a half days at the Long Time, is kind of like cake decorating (the welding gun is akin to the icing bag, which you have to move along a prescribed path at a certain angle and speed while applying just the right amount of pressure) as well as sewing (you can connect two pieces of metal with a short tack or a longer bead, or seam). When I mention the sewing metaphor to Jack, he concurs. "A tack in welding is like a pin or a basting stitch in sewing. It holds components in place while you sort out what you are doing," he says. Dan agrees. "Welding, like sewing, requires gentleness

and precision," he adds. But unlike sewing, welding involves scorching hot temperatures (over 5,000 degrees Fahrenheit), potentially damaging optical radiation, high-voltage electricity, and flying sparks and debris, so much so that we have to cover our bodies with pants and long sleeves and wear special hoods to protect our eyes. And, of course, we are not manipulating airy buttercream or malleable cloth. Instead, we are fusing pieces of hard, heavy steel to create items that we hope will generate generous bids at auction.

On Saturday morning, after breakfast tacos, a morning stretch, and a couple of hours of sketching and model building with cardboard and craft sticks, we settle on four projects—a mobile chicken coop, a sling chair, a sculpture/planter, and a combined turntable stand/record storage unit—and divide into teams to make them. Jack, Parker, and Dan circulate to help us as needed, and another helper, Austin-based singer-songwriter Amy Cook, arrives to oversee the portable band saw as we learn how to operate it.

I am on the sling chair team with Maura Ambrose (see page 76), a quilter and natural

On day one, each of us gets a chance to practice welding our first tacks and beads (a bead is a seam-like extension of a tack). When the hood is pulled down, everything goes dark except for the spot where the weld is happening and the sparks bouncing all around. Learning to stand still amid the spray of sparks is easier than it looks.

"Welding is more accessible than people think," says Jack, assisting a camper here. "You can get pretty serious and make some cool stuff quickly."

"Learning a new skill and getting out of my comfort zone was life changing, but gathering as a community and engaging in creative collaborations was my favorite part."

—Maura Ambrose

THIS PAGE

Maura Ambrose, Maxx, and I made this folding camp chair, dubbed the Sandlot Slinger. The frame is reclaimed steel square tube; the seat is salvaged fire hose. After our weekend together, Maura recounted, "Learning a new skill and getting out of my comfort zone was life changing, but gathering as a community and engaging in creative collaborations was my favorite part."

TOP LEFT & BOTTOM

Taylor, Katie, and Zach masterminded this transportable chicken coop, or tractor, made with reclaimed steel and corrugated roof metal, a salvaged mailbox, and a wheelbarrow tire. It is easily moved around the yard so the chickens can have fresh grass and bugs to feed on while spreading their nitrogen-rich waste.

TOP RIGHT

Adde made this planter/ sculpture with salvaged steel pipe and roof beam, then added succulents from her backyard and a local nursery. Once a full-time fine artist but now an art director for a publishing house, she was eager to get back to the hands-on process of making, especially with no expectation of what the result needed to be.

Once our projects are finished on Sunday, Jack and Dan let loose. Dan, once Jack's apprentice, runs his own welding business and is also a successful singer-songwriter. "My ideal is a mix of things," he says. "I like to spend six weeks touring, then six weeks making stuff."

After sharing our completed projects in a show-and-tell, we head to the porch for dinner. Jack begins with a toast: "We made new friends, had fun, and listened to great live music. We learned and raised money for local medical needs. That's a good sandlot sample: not a lot of bad for a lot of good."

Late on Saturday, Jack hosted an open house with a campfire and live music with local musicians (from right to left): our instructor Dan; our band saw supervisor, Amy Cook; and father and son John Dee Graham and William Harries Graham.

On Friday night, Jack invited us to a Texas Playboys ball game.

"We made new friends, had fun, and listened to great live music. We learned and raised money for local medical needs. That's a good sandlot sample: not a lot of bad for a lot of good."

dyer, and Maxx, a copywriter for an ad agency who is also an outfielder for the Playboys. Maxx says that as a writer, he spends a lot of time in his head, and he is looking forward to making something "real." Maura was so hyped after day one that she showed up the next morning with a model using strips of the fire hose we pulled from the scrap pile the day before. By the time we've finished our chair, made out of steel square tube and that hose, Maxx and Parker are talking about starting a business selling what we are now calling the Sandlot Slinger.

Team Chicken Coop is made up of Zach, who works for a biotech start-up in Austin and renovates and rents out Airstreams on the side ("I would like not to have to pay people to weld on my trailers," he says), and husband and wife Taylor and Katie, who own a jerky company that sources meat from farmers committed to regenerative practices; they have recently purchased a ranch, where they hope to put their welding skills to work. Adde, a lapsed fine artist turned art director in the publishing industry, is putting together the sculpture/planter on her own, but she accepts my offer to help her when I find myself with time to spare. Team Turntable Stand is composed of Jason (a software developer who wants to transition into industrial design), Alex (who works for HAAM), and Natalie (a brand manager for a hotel).

It's pretty amazing that by the end of day three, all four projects are finished and ready for a final show-and-tell before our celebratory dinner. As each group tells its story about the process and the challenges team members faced (Adde wondered for a while whether her circular oil-pipe base would ever stay balanced, and Natalie wishes she and her partners had simplified their design earlier on), alluring aromas from the smoker and grill waft through the air and Maxx's Labrador retriever, Charlie, who had been napping under the flatbed trailer that served as the stage for music making the night before, roams among us. The table is set with jars of wildflowers from the yard, and Jack is ready to turn on the twinkle lights when the sun sets. Dan picks up his guitar and begins to sing the Willie Nelson song "Yesterday's Wine." Then Parker joins in. Everyone looks relaxed and content. In the distance, beyond the campfire, we can see the baseball diamond, a field of Jack's dreams. In just three days, we did, indeed, accomplish what Jack believed in. He made it and we came. And each of us left, in our own way, snakebit, a dose of the Rural Studio, the Newbern Tigers, and Jack's passion pulsing through our hands and our hearts.

FOUR

Making a Home

Homeland

WHEN LOTTA ANDERSON was eighteen years old, after she graduated from secondary school, she took a job at the Swedish Customs office in Stockholm to start earning money. She filled out forms all day, which was, she says, a bit boring. "The fun part was I got to stamp a lot." At night, she worked as a cashier at a grocery store, which she preferred. "Talking to people, selling, pressing buttons; I loved that," she recalls—but not enough to keep her in Sweden when an American friend invited her to move to California with him. "I was trying to find my calling, had wanderlust, and needed a change, so I took that option very quickly," Lotta says.

Though she has lived in the United States ever since, Lotta returns to Scandinavia nearly every summer—to Åland, the archipelago in the Baltic Sea where she was born, as were her three brothers, her parents, and three of her four grandparents, and where she and her husband built a house on waterfront property inherited from family (virtually the only way to acquire land on Åland) in 2016. It is among these six thousand–plus isles and skerries (about sixty of which are habitable) in this autonomous Swedish-speaking province of Finland that Lotta feels the most at ease—and at home.

"Åland conditions my soul. It is in my bone marrow," Lotta tells me and nineteen other women as she welcomes us to her annual summer printing workshop on Silverskär, an idyllic Åland hideaway accessible only by small boat. This is where she learned to transport wild strawberries home from the woods by threading them onto blades of straw and discovered the pleasure of falling back against a haystack to relax. This is where she dug her first potatoes and carrots and drew her first dandelions and ferns. And it is here, to this remote region, that she invites one small group each year to join her to learn some of the stamping and stenciling techniques she uses in her work as a surface designer, author, and teacher, and to experience the ocean landscape and long-lasting daylight that inform her spare, natural aesthetic.

Lotta founded her brand, Lotta Jansdotter (which means "Lotta, the daughter of Jan" in Swedish), in 1996, with a small line of screen-printed pillows. She began by selling her goods door-to-door to a few San Francisco boutiques and in trunk shows in homes and at local bars, events that we might call pop-up shops today, at the time a new way for makers to sell directly to their customers. A couple of years later, Lotta met a Japanese entrepreneur, a friend of a friend, who helped her launch her brand in Japan, where it quickly gained a cult following, and also connected her with a linen factory in Lithuania that could produce tea towels,

OPPOSITE

Lotta returns to Åland, her birthplace in the Baltic Sea, every summer. Here she is at the pier on Silverskär, where she hosts a print workshop each July.

As much as Lotta treasures her quiet summers on Åland, she also draws energy and inspiration from the diversity and pulse of the city. On this day she was in her old Brooklyn neighborhood looking for a place to photograph some of her mini quilts (top), made with fabrics she collected during travels around the world and fragments of personal items, such as her husband's shirts, her son's baby clothing, and tea towels she inherited from her mother.

bags, and other textiles printed with her motifs for her to sell worldwide.

For a while, Lotta ran a small eponymous shop, with a work space for printing and sewing in the back, in San Francisco's Tenderloin district. Eventually, she caught the attention of companies that wanted to license her patterns and motifs to reproduce on everything from fabric yardage and bedding to rugs, luggage, and kitchenware. She also landed a deal with San Francisco–based publisher Chronicle, which launched an extensive line of Lotta Jansdotter stationery in 2003 and then a subsequent series of DIY and lifestyle books. In 2006, after Lotta and her husband moved to New York, she began hosting workshops out of her studio and accepting invitations to teach classes in other studios in the United States and overseas—for hobbyists, creative professionals, and women's cooperatives in developing countries seeking to maximize the appeal of their handwork to reach a broader international audience.

For much of her career, Lotta identified herself as a designer rather than a maker, resisting the moniker even though making with her hands was integral to her process. "I felt this stigma that being a 'maker' wasn't as prestigious," Lotta admits. Gradually, though, the DIY arm of her business came to the forefront, in part because her generous disposition and contagious enthusiasm made her a natural teacher of the techniques she specialized in, in part because the changing retail environment forced her to adapt (once Etsy launched its online marketplace in 2005, she faced competition from copycat designers willing to sell their work at a lower price point), and in part because most of the materials and techniques with which she creates her iconic patterns and projects are so easily accessible. "Now I feel more confident in myself as a maker and a designer," Lotta explains. In truth, she says, "I have always been a maker. If I'm not making something, I get antsy."

On the first morning of our Åland workshop, all twenty of us gather around as Lotta demonstrates potato-stamp printing, then we settle in at our worktables in the barn-style studio to follow Lotta's instruction: "Have fun and make a happy mess." Setting intentions is good, she explains, but so is staying attuned to the process and the exciting discoveries messes—and "mistakes"—can reveal. A couple of days later, while mixing paint colors with craft sticks for stenciling, I

look up and spot Lotta, barefoot and clad in a loose cotton dress made out of fabric from her Hemma (which means "home" in Swedish) collection, doing a dancer's cat leap as she heads out the door into the sunshine.

In the years since then, as I've gotten to know Lotta more, I've thought of that cat leap many times. Lotta's personality is effervescent (and every so often, her enthusiasm bubbles out of her in cat leaps), and she has a knack for making what she does look easy. But behind the scenes, she has sometimes struggled to balance her professional and artistic drives—how do you build a financially viable business while evolving creatively?—as well as her commitment to her family. This dilemma came to a head in the mid-2010s when she was diagnosed with a brain tumor, followed shortly thereafter by a stomach tumor. Although it took a couple of years to navigate the medical issues and subsequent emotional fallout, she is now healthy and eager to tune in to her passions and live life to the fullest, though some of her priorities have shifted so that the business and the personal are better balanced.

Lotta has been an avid designer-maker and even an entrepreneur since childhood: She vividly recalls setting up a mud cake sale for imaginary friends when she was four or five; selling candy she artfully arranged on a china plate and dispensed with sugar tongs to real-life friends when she was ten; and as a young teenager, cleaning houses and building and selling wooden birdhouses to finance a trip to England. To this day, she maintains a unique aesthetic and a knack for generating marketable ideas as well as an independent streak and a strong drive to prove herself. "I am bossy, and I like control," Lotta says. "My instinct is always to do things on my own."

When she launched her first line of pillows in 1996 after taking screen-printing classes at a community college in Santa Cruz and realizing immediately that she had found her calling, "maker movement" and "DIY" weren't even part of our lexicon. She forged her own path first as an indie designer and then as a leader in the DIY revival. Her first book, *Lotta Jansdotter's Simple Sewing*, published in 2007, sold tens of thousands of copies and was translated into six languages. As the years went by, she felt a nagging desire to explore new creative directions, but she was also busy being a mom (her son was born in 2007) and rarely felt she had time to stop and take stock, nor did she have the luxury of possibly forgoing an income while following unproven paths. The pressure she put on herself to succeed financially, she realizes now, first fueled and

TOP LEFT

Lotta sometimes refers to color chips when she is deciding on new colorways for her patterns.

TOP RIGHT

Lotta has been collecting inspiration in scrapbooks for years. "I wish creating these books could be my job," she says. She enjoys both finding imagery and incorporating it onto her pages. "I like touching the paper, feeling the glue, cutting uneven shapes. I have to fit all of them onto that piece of paper; it's a design problem I have to solve," she says. Not surprisingly, she says Pinterest, the online pin board with millions of users, is not nearly as interesting to her.

CENTER & BOTTOM RIGHT

Among the many products on which Lotta's iconic patterns have been printed are melamine plates and sewing fabric (which she used for the tunic and tote here).

Although Lotta has made pottery on and off throughout her life, she became more devoted to her practice after her brain surgery. Sitting at the wheel and centering the clay helped her feel calm at a time when, she recalls, "life felt uncentered in so many ways."

Without a specific goal in mind, Lotta made this assortment of hand-built clay objects for the pure enjoyment of the process. She glazed the plates freehand and with stencils. The black onion shape (far right) was inspired by a pair of David Bowie's pants. The small pendants and beads are meant to be put on a cord and worn as jewelry.

"When I want to take care of my home and make things for it, that means I'm in a good place. It is so satisfying. I feel so healthy."

then, ultimately, stalled her creativity. It was only during the long period of physical and emotional readjustment following her health crisis that she took the time she needed to reflect on the past and the future—and on how to more fully enjoy the present.

"I am really good at cranking stuff out in a formula," Lotta explains—a skill that is useful for licensing, when manufacturers are happy to incorporate iconic patterns in new configurations (for example, by changing colors and/or scale). "And I have always been hard on myself. That's a difficult habit to change. But now I want to be kinder to myself, more patient and less critical, and make more time to think things through creatively." Lotta is eager to make more personal work that requires her to use her own hands, like she did when she first started out. She is also interested in designing new products and working with artisans in developing countries to produce them. "I like that my ideas could help someone else make a living. That's a true collaboration," she says.

She also loves to make pottery, a medium she has explored on and off since childhood and that she turned to for solace and healing after her brain surgery. Sitting at the wheel and centering (a clay-balancing process essential to achieving a symmetrical form) helped her feel grounded at a time when she was learning to cope with vertigo and partial hearing loss.

When I look at the dishes Lotta is glazing one day at the Clayworks on Columbia studio in Brooklyn, I see swallows like the ones in the skies of Åland. Lotta is making tableware to take back to the house there. A few months later, just days before she and her family will move out of the small Brooklyn apartment they have lived in since 2006 and into a house with a yard in Montclair, New Jersey, she tells me she is working on a series of planters and bowls for her new kitchen. "I feel so happy about making a home again," she exclaims. I hear a brightness in her voice, a sparkle that was missing for a while. "I'm thinking about the curtains, the colors, what we are going to hang on the walls, what kind of cushions I am going to make," she says. "I haven't felt this way in many years, and I've missed it. When I want to take care of my home and make things for it, that means I'm in a good place. It is so satisfying. I feel so healthy."

printing on åland

Every July, Lotta hosts a group of makers on Åland for five days of stamping and stenciling, plus relaxation and rejuvenation by the sea. "I love that all these interesting, fun, creative, smart people from different parts of the world come together to spend a few precious days on this little gem of an island where I get to stay all summer," Lotta says. She typically offers instruction in the morning and after lunch, then runs open studio time for the rest of the day and evening. Participants are free to wander in and out for meals, hikes, saunas, or whatever else they might desire. The retreat happens on a small private isle, so the only other people around are a few staff members, including a chef, who arrive by boat each morning.

A Mother's Love

WHEN MEGAN FOWLER was about nine years old, her father, Bill Boling, took her to visit a favorite elementary school teacher of his whom he had stayed in contact with since childhood. The teacher, named Mildred, scrambled eggs from chickens she raised in the backyard. "They were the best eggs I'd ever eaten," Megan recalls. The next time Megan and her dad visited, they helped Mildred harvest apples and make applesauce for canning and apple butter they spread on warm-from-the-oven biscuits. "Until then, I didn't understand that you could live like that, that you could grow food and eat it and make things to eat later, too," Megan says. "It all made sense." The observant young girl, who liked to read books and write poetry in the woods, comprehended for the first time the fundamental link between other living beings and her own nourishment and pleasure, a sensitivity still at the core of her consciousness and that now informs how and where she lives and the work she creates as a letterpress artist.

In 2011, Megan printed her first limited-edition calendar—thirteen cardstock pages, one for each month plus a cover—of flora and fauna she saw during a year living out in the country. March: two hens and a cracked egg. August: heirloom tomatoes. December: rainbow chard. She has continued to create and sell at least one new calendar every year

since then, each one an ode to the natural world that surrounds her in the small rural town of Sparta, Georgia, about three hours southeast of the suburb of Rome, where she spent most of her childhood.

When I visited Megan in Sparta in the fall, she and Gaëlle Boling, her mother and business partner, had just finished printing the next year's calendar, which they titled *Backyard Garden*. Megan started doing letterpress in the art department at the University of Georgia in Athens and launched her company—Brown Parcel Press—during her junior year there. In 2011, first as a favor and then because the favor delivered rewards beyond each of their expectations, Gaëlle became an integral part of the Brown Parcel Press enterprise.

Megan handles illustration, conferring with Gaëlle on themes, colors, and fine-tuning as her ideas progress from pencil sketches to layered Adobe Illustrator files she sends to a plate maker, while Gaëlle does most of the press work. They tag-team caring for Megan's two young daughters.

"She has endurance that I don't have in the studio. She can go and go," says Megan. For Gaëlle, the long hours at the press are part of the appeal. "For some people, this type of work might be boring because it is so repetitious, but I just love it," Gaëlle explains. "It is a very Zen exercise. I love the process of starting something

Gaëlle, Megan, and Megan's daughter Gillian take a break outside the former general store on their property, once the Brown Parcel Press studio but now used for family gatherings and large art projects. The store features a vintage gas tank outside and is outfitted with 1930s-era fixtures and display cases within. Megan decided to move the studio to the house so that it would be easier to shift between working and taking care of Gillian and her sister, Emolyn.

"I have no problem making decisions for my life based on what I think is best for my family. That's how I feel happy."

–Megan Fowler

and finishing it." Then she compares the education she got from Megan to her experience training to become an obstetrics technician in the labor and delivery department of a Georgia hospital in the 1990s: "You watch someone, and you learn by observing, following instructions, and just doing, rather than sitting and thinking. Printing adds a new dimension to who I am, and a sense of accomplishment."

When Megan initially asked her mother for help, she was pregnant with her first daughter, Emolyn; managing a nearby organic farm; and doing letterpress only on the side. When she realized that Gaëlle had a knack for printing and was enjoying the challenge of learning something new, she proposed that she come on board as an apprentice. The logistics were easy since Megan and her husband, Brad Fowler, were, at the time, living in her mom and dad's weekend house, a quirky early-nineteenth-century farmhouse on thirty-one acres in Sparta, and the letterpress studio was housed in the property's original general store. In 2011, Brad and Megan bought the adjoining seventeen acres and its modest, then-derelict split-level ranch to live in, eventually moving the studio to the basement so Megan could work while Emolyn (and then Gillian, born in 2015) was sleeping. The family's combined properties are now treated as one shared compound. When there is a lot of work to be done on the press, Gaëlle will stay at the farmhouse all week, with Bill typically joining on the weekends. When the workload is lighter, Gaëlle will return to the modern loft that she and Bill share in Atlanta.

"Family is a core value. That structure is key to me," Megan explains. "One of the reasons I chose my husband is because he values his family the same way I value mine. I have no problem making decisions for my life based on what I think is best for my family. That's how I feel happy." Although Megan has always been close to both of her parents (as well as her two brothers), this new phase in her relationship with her mother has deepened their bond.

"We get along really well," says Gaëlle. "I feel like she still needs me at this stage, maybe because she is so far out in the country and she is missing peers her own age with whom she shares artistic interests." Megan agrees that living away from the cultural offerings of city life can be hard sometimes, but she regards her mother as much more than a fill-in for younger pals. "We get each other," she says. "The one regret I have is that oftentimes when we're together now, there's a purpose. I miss just getting to chill out with my mom."

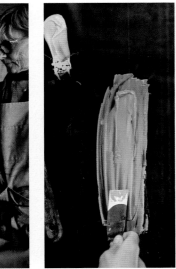

Megan and Gaëlle working together on a gingko leaf print. Megan originally created this design for her husband, Brad, for their fifth anniversary. The gingko is his favorite tree, and she made one to represent each year of their marriage thus far. Later, Megan created a small print of what she describes as "a pair of gingko leaves dancing" on handmade paper.

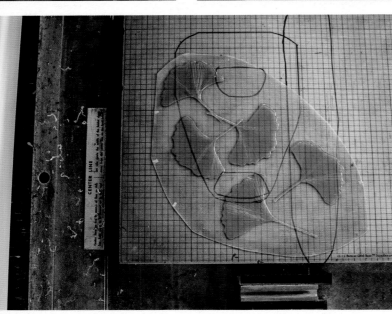

In part, Megan has Gaëlle to thank for the calendars that are now the anchor of their business (which also includes notecards, prints, and custom identity work). Her interest in them harkens back to her childhood when each year, Gaëlle would purchase a pair of Ansel Adams calendars, one to hang on the pantry door in the family kitchen, and one to send to her father, an amateur photographer. "That calendar was important. That's where we kept track of everything going on in our lives," recalls Megan. "It felt unifying because we were all seeing the same picture every day." Now Gaëlle sends a Brown Parcel Press calendar to everyone in the family, both in France, her homeland, and the United States. "They all want one every year," Gaëlle explains. "It's a way to be connected," she adds, echoing Megan's memory of why the Ansel Adams calendar mattered to her when she was growing up.

"When you choose to bring art that feels meaningful into your home, even if it is an ordinary thing, and you put it in a prominent place, it becomes part of the rest of your life," says Megan, who vividly recalls the posters she looked at every day from her bed growing up: behind her, Matisse's *The Red Room*; in front, a watercolor of fish,

artist unknown. Among the other artwork, much of it original, displayed around the house was a large painting of buttons on a sidewalk that her father had made as a nineteen-year-old art student. He ended up getting a law degree and working in health care, but he continued his artistic expression through photography and writing (which he found easier to meld with parenting than painting); he also founded and still runs a small art book publishing house in Atlanta for which Megan does design work.

Megan describes Bill as an artist through and through. "He is definitely the idea guy," adds Gaëlle. "He introduced the kids to a way of looking at life that is outside the box and fun." He was the one who originally inspired Megan to explore poetry—as his father, a poet, had encouraged him—and to take photographs. He was also the one who discovered the rambling farmhouse, with its seven fireplaces and twelve barns and outbuildings amid fields, woods, and creeks. And he is the one who conjured the idea for a favorite family tradition, a craft day followed by a festive meal for extended family and friends every Christmas.

"I was doing a lot of photography at the time," Bill explains of his original inspiration for the tradition. "Photography is

LEFT

"When I was little, I absorbed all my mom's love and patience. I want my kids to feel how she made me feel," says Megan as she sits and draws with Gillian on the dogtrot at the farmhouse.

RIGHT

Gillian, Megan, Gaëlle, and their poodle, Lucky, walking on the path that links their two houses.

kind of cerebral, and I was itching to use my hands. I didn't have a grand plan, but it was really fun, so we continued it." The project that first year was baskets woven out of kudzu (an invasive vine that grows rampant in Georgia). For subsequent Christmases, they have made everything from papier-mâché ornaments to soap, stained glass, and Bauhaus-inspired gingerbread houses.

About that itch to use his hands, Bill philosophizes, "Let's say 360 degrees is a completely alive person. When you're just thinking with your head, you may be at 180 or 200. When you pick up something, say a stick or a pocketknife, and begin to interact with it, it is instructing you as you are instructing it, and your brain suddenly jumps out of the groove of only ideas and thoughts. If you let that pocketknife slip and you cut

your finger or if you whittle the stick down to a point so you can use it to stake your plant, you've done something real. I think we're at a time in social evolution, in human evolution, when we're really starved to get to that 360-degree way of living."

Three hundred and sixty degrees—that's a circle, a cycle, a beginning and an end, like a calendar, like the roller on the letterpress, like Mildred growing food and harvesting it to eat and planting again. Like Gaëlle and Megan, a mother and a daughter working together, like families always used to do, sharing lunches, wiping away little girls' tears, and bandaging scraped knees in the process, one teaching the other, back and forth, around and around.

"They make such a great team," Bill comments warmly.

TOP

Megan and Gaëlle produced these notecards in collaboration with the Ace & Jig fashion enterprise. They drew their inspiration from Ace & Jig's custom-woven fabrics from India. Megan tries to arrange at least one special collaboration with someone outside of her field each year.

CENTER

The May 2018 calendar page: Dominique hen and chick.

BOTTOM LEFT

Kettle's Whistle, *The Plant on the Dresser*, and *Stacked Baskets*: three of six prints in a series called Inside/Outside on a mantel at the farmhouse.

BOTTOM RIGHT

Another collaboration: notecards inspired by the quilt patterns and naturally dyed textiles of Jessica Lewis Stevens of Sugarhouse Workshop.

TOP

Each calendar page
is like a visual haiku,
a snapshot of nature
and also a feeling,
something tactile
you can hold in your
hand that touches an
eternal sensitivity in
your soul. Brown Parcel
Press calendar themes
tend to reflect what is
happening in Megan's
life: Growth Spurt
(2012) commemorated
the year Emolyn was
born (the following
year, Megan produced
a second edition
for West Elm); From
Scratch (2013) marked
the period when
Megan says she was
first learning how to
be a mom; Take Root
(2014) portrayed the
growing certainty she
felt in her identity as a
mother and wife; and
Sunny Side (2019) was
a reminder that there
is always grace and
beauty to be found,
even during hard times.

BOTTOM

Assembling the printed
calendar pages is
a family affair that
happens around the
kitchen island every
autumn. Here young
Emolyn happily helps.
Gillian will certainly join
the work circle once she
is tall enough to reach.

ANN LADSON

Curiosity as Wayfinder

"MY PARENTS TOLD me I could do whatever I wanted. I took that to heart." So says Ann Ladson, a full-time metalsmith since 2013. While Ann's specialty is tabletop items, especially cutlery, plus some jewelry, that hasn't stopped her from making a brass curtain rod when she spotted one that she coveted but couldn't afford. Or obliging when the hotel down the block from her home in Charleston, South Carolina, asked her to make custom hooks for hanging ceiling installations and then jewelry displays and magazine racks. Or fabricating wooden serving boards for herself and family when she needed a break from metalwork.

"Now I mostly make flatware and follow whatever whim I'm feeling," Ann tells me when I visit her studio in her Craftsman bungalow–style home. "I don't know how to *not* work with my hands," she adds. What she makes with them is determined by her needs and curiosity as well as an ongoing quest for natural beauty. "I want my work to show signs of the hand, that it was made by a person and not a machine. And I like the opportunity to elevate or just create exactly what I'm looking for. I could pour potato chips into a plastic bowl from Target or I could make a beautiful one, small at the bottom and fluted, out of brass or copper."

Ann's journey to this studio was indirect, with many disparate adventures along the

way. As a child, she excelled at math and science and enjoyed art classes—painting, drawing, pottery—as well as tearing around the neighborhood with a pack of boys, riding bikes, building forts, and playing in the mud. Her mom, who ran a catering business from home, insisted that she sit down for high tea every afternoon during middle school, which Ann remembers hating. But today, she says, "I miss it."

After graduating from high school in 1994, Ann bounced around, from the University of Tennessee, where she thought she'd study engineering (she left in the middle of her second semester), to a nine-month audio engineering program at the Conservatory of Recording Arts and Sciences in Arizona, then to a two-year job at a recording studio in Oregon. Disheartened by the ego-driven audio engineering scene, she began taking classes at a community college in Eugene—painting, baking, and set design. Then, in the summer of 1997, intending to enroll in a vegan cooking school in New York City, she packed her Honda with all her belongings, her futon and bike on the roof, and headed cross-country. But during a pit stop in Charleston to visit her parents, she bumped into a former boyfriend who invited her to take a detour. "A bunch of us are moving to Puerto Rico to go surfing," he said. "Do you want to come?" And Ann made a snap decision to join them.

OPPOSITE

Ann likes having the right tool for the job, and because she is often experimenting with new techniques, sometimes she even has to craft her own tools. "I'm just a maker. I like tools in all areas of my life. I've always taken things apart and put them back together," she says.

"Becoming a metalsmith and business owner has given me the confidence that I can accomplish anything I set my mind to. If I can't figure something out on my own, I will find the resources I need."

A trio of Ann's explorations (from left to right): tiny taper candlesticks in brass, a three-legged vessel in bronze, and a cylindrical vase. Ann made the vessel in the center while taking a class in gravity casting at the Penland School of Craft.

Ann made this rack specifically to hold the very fine organic cotton table runner her sister, weaver Adele Stafford of Voices of Industry, wove for her. Although the two sisters work in media that could hardly be more different, Ann says they are similar in that they are both motivated to shoot for the highest level of technical and aesthetic achievement.

Ann's jewelry on display in her studio. Ann likes that making even small, delicate jewelry requires the power of fire.

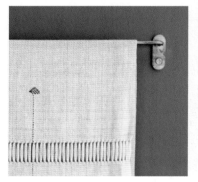

Although surfing didn't last long, Ann stayed in the Caribbean, mostly in the Virgin Islands, for eight years, working in restaurants and as a cook and first mate on catamarans. In 2003, she left for nine months to complete an intensive baking and pastry course at the Culinary Institute of America in California. Then, in 2005, she returned to the States for good, first living in New York, then in South Carolina, working as a pastry chef at a series of award-winning restaurants in both places. In 2006, needing a creative outlet outside of work, Ann decided to enroll in a jewelry-making class at the Appalachian Center for Craft in Smithville, Tennessee. "I had always been interested in jewelry, and I knew I had the dexterity," she remembers. By the end of the week, she had completed a set of sterling silver rings, and she was hooked. She went home and immediately purchased a bench and torch, plus some hand tools,

and transformed a guest bedroom into a metalsmithing studio.

But it wasn't until seven years later that she committed to this new practice full-time. Less impulsive than when she moved to Puerto Rico, Ann thought long and hard before giving up the security of a regular paycheck to pursue something risky and new. "I was feeling lost and stuck," Ann remembers of her decision to abandon the professional cooking world and the subsequent couple of years she spent searching for an alternative. "All my friends had college degrees and were well into their careers, and I was trying to reinvent myself with only an audio engineering degree and a baking and pastry degree to fall back on, knowing that I didn't want to work in either of those fields."

First, she got an admin job at a pathology lab, then began assisting a florist. But one night, after returning late from a wedding gig, Ann knew she had to make a definitive change. Breaking down and tossing out masses of faded blooms from the event had magnified her feelings of fatigue and confusion. The very next day, her sister suggested a solution. "She said, 'It's pretty obvious you should be doing jewelry,'" Ann recalls—and that's when she decided to take a chance. In the years since the class in Tennessee, she had been teaching herself through books and experimentation on nights and weekends and had begun selling jewelry on Etsy. Her sister, an accomplished weaver as well as a marketing

"I want my work to show signs of the hand, that it was made by a person and not a machine."

executive, made sure that Ann approached her new endeavor seriously, assigning exercises for Ann to complete to refine her vision and goals, and helping her write a mission statement and bio, establish a visual identity, and set up a professional website. Ann was excited—and just a little wary: "I didn't want working with metal to stop being fun," she says.

Although Ann imagined she'd be making a lot of jewelry, shortly after she launched the business, a local shop owner asked for a spoon to pair with a handmade ceramic saltcellar she stocked. "I sat down to carve that spoon out of wax, and something clicked," Ann recalls. She knew she had found her niche, a way to marry her passion for cooking and fine dining with metalsmithing. She created a bronze spoon to her client's specifications, then seven more spoons in bronze and sterling silver, each one an exploration of a different idea. "I stayed up until midnight three nights in a row, figuring out the designs and carving them in wax, and then sent them out to be cast," Ann remembers. In the years since, she has gone on to specialize in silver and bronze flatware collections plus specialty chef's utensils, work that she sells from her website as well as through retailers—and that has been recognized in publications like *T*, *Saveur*, *Food & Wine*, and *Martha Stewart Living*, and by the *Garden & Gun* Made in the South Awards, for which she was a finalist. "I'm interested in everything that goes on the table, that contributes to preparing and sharing a delicious meal," Ann explains.

Ann is not motivated to make the same pieces over and over, nor is she inclined to rest on her laurels, so nearly every year, she takes a class in a subject that is new to her or with an artist whose work she admires, often at the Penland School of Craft in North Carolina or the Haystack Mountain School of Crafts in Maine. The rest of the time, she is content to figure things out on her own. "I like setting challenging parameters for myself," she says. "Becoming a metalsmith and business owner has given me the confidence that I can accomplish anything I set my mind to. If I can't figure something out on my own, I will find the resources I need." Then Ann recalls a Christmas long ago when her parents gifted her with a new boom box, which she immediately disassembled, eager to figure out how it worked. That morning and on many occasions since, Ann's curiosity has led her on an idiosyncratic path, one that, at times, has left her feeling unsure but more often than not has been the wayfinder that has helped her move forward on her unique and fluid journey.

LEFT

A three-piece place setting of Ann's bronze Farmers flatware. The fork design is loosely based on the shape of a pitchfork.

RIGHT

Ann began pondering this collection of bronze flatware—called Barnacles—while she was in Deer Isle, Maine, taking a class at the Haystack Mountain School of Craft. Looking out at the sea, she became fascinated by the patterns barnacles formed on the rocks and boats to which they clung. Ironically, years earlier while living in the Caribbean, she spent hours in the water trying to scrape these corrosive crustaceans off the hulls of the boats she worked on.

making a bar spoon

A fine silver bar spoon begins as a narrow, approximately four-inch-long ingot (which Ann makes by melting silver casting grain in a mold). Creating the spoon is a slow process involving a series of repeated steps—heating (to soften and relax the molecules), hammering (to stretch and harden), then filing the edges so they curve, and buffing to a shine. "I like the challenge of sticking with something that requires so much time and commitment," says Ann.

NIKKI McCLURE AND JAY T SCOTT

Day by Day

AFTER NIKKI McCLURE gets up most mornings, and once her son, Finn, leaves for school, she takes a walk with her husband, Jay T Scott. Depending on whether the tide is on its way in or out, they will walk either along the beach or into the woods. Then she heads to her studio, which is on the lower level of the house she and Jay T built with the help of friends a few years ago. There she starts to sketch—a warm-up for her day's work. She sits at a long desk facing a picture window, with a birdfeeder, the rocky beach, and Budd Inlet, the southernmost arm of Puget Sound, in front of her. If she's lacking inspiration, she has a backup plan: She reaches for a broom and sweeps. Through this ritual action of hands and body, she clears her mind and connects to what she calls a "deep, genetic memory." "Ten thousand years ago, someone I am related to by blood was sweeping the floor," Nikki explained to students during a lecture at Evergreen State College, her alma mater here in Olympia, Washington (a video of the lecture appears on YouTube). Nikki is an illustrator and writer who draws, tells stories, and expresses her social ideals by cutting images out of single sheets of black paper with an X-Acto blade. There are nearly always black paper bits to be swept up from the floor.

While Nikki spends the morning in her studio, Jay T is likely to be found up the hill in his shop, where he designs and builds fine furniture. Jay T learned the basics of woodworking as a child growing up in Ohio, from an uncle who taught him and also introduced him to the seminal books of cabinetmaker James Krenov. Jay T was immediately drawn to Krenov's philosophical writings about the importance of feeling passion for one's path, whether that path is to become a woodworker or to do something else. In fact, those ideas resonated with him so strongly that when, in 1988, he visited Evergreen State College and heard about the school's independent learning contracts that allow students to create a curriculum based on their individual interests, he was sure it was the right place for him. At Evergreen, he earned a bachelor of arts degree following what he calls a generalist path, pursuing threads of interest as diverse as winter twig identification, alternative energy forms, and felting, covering most of his expenses by working for a contractor building houses. "I knew I wanted to be a woodworker, but I didn't want to be one who thought only about furniture. I wanted a broader perspective on the world," he tells me as we sit together at a dining table he built using exotic bubinga wood left over from a commission. "I meet people who have worked their entire lives in bureaucratic jobs or who work mostly in front of a

OPPOSITE, LEFT

Nikki at her desk, with a view of the rocky beach and Budd Inlet in front of her. Nikki tried paper-cutting for the first time in the late 1990s, at the suggestion of a friend, as a way to achieve the clean, graphic aesthetic she was looking for in her work. She loved it right away. The image she is working on here, paired with the word *Renew*, became February in her next calendar (see pages 206–207).

OPPOSITE, RIGHT

Nikki and Jay T walk on the beach or in these woods near the house every morning and afternoon.

"I don't think we're going to be happy as a species just interacting with computers and having robots do our work for us. I don't think that's a future that will be satisfying."

—Jay T Scott

Jay T built the boathouse by, according to Nikki, "dumpster diving in the Sound"—that is to say, he used rope to pull huge (about sixty-foot-long) logs drifting past the beach in front of their house ashore during a high tide, then cut them into manageable lengths and sent them back downstream to Olympia for milling. The milled lumber was then returned by boat to the beach in front of their house so that Jay T could build the boathouse (the easy part, for him). The next summer, he and the couple's son, Finn, started building a rowing dinghy for Finn there.

computer screen, who are wanting more, who miss the hands-on meditation of creating a physical object, of seeing a tangible result from their labor. I don't think we're going to be happy as a species just interacting with computers and having robots do our work for us. I don't think that's a future that will be satisfying," he says.

It is with this deep passion for their work and for the value of using their hands—as well as a commitment to being as present for Finn as possible—that Nikki and Jay T have designed their lives. Jay T works year-round, but when he can, he avoids taking on projects with hard deadlines in order to keep his schedule flexible. Nikki must meet a lot of deadlines, but she focuses on projects that meld with her values and preferred schedule, which includes taking summers off, at which time she says, "I become a swimmer, berry picker, and Band-Aid provider."

Perhaps best known for her wall calendars, which she has been self-publishing since 1998 and for which she has a following that is both devoted and devout, Nikki is also a popular children's book author and illustrator. Among the many books she has worked on are the Washington State Book Award–winner *To Market, to Market*, which she both wrote and illustrated, and *All in a Day*, which was written by Newbery Medal–winning author Cynthia Rylant and illustrated by Nikki. While I was visiting, she was thinking about

her forthcoming book *What Will These Hands Make?*, which she hopes will encourage adults to stop asking children what they want to be when they grow up and instead begin asking them what they will make.

"Will these hands make a stack of firewood, a fiddle to play fast, a sword for a play, a lantern to guide the way back home? Will these hands make a safe place to be, will these hands make a community?" Nikki recites from her manuscript.

When I ask her about artistic influences, Nikki mentions children's book authors Robert McCloskey, Maurice Sendak, and Tove Jansson. She recalls reading that Hans Christian Andersen would do paper-cutting while he was entertaining children with stories. "He'd unfold this thing, and it would depict a different story than the one he had just told," she explains with amazement. About other artists, she says, "I like the art my friends make." Her favorite gallery is the world outside her window. She is quick to point out that she doesn't have a formal art education. From Evergreen State College, she earned both a bachelor of arts and a bachelor of science, but she never took any art classes (though in her last quarter, she did write and illustrate a children's book called *Wetlands*, for which she learned how to carve and print linoleum plates). Nikki credits an entomology professor for helping her develop an artist's sensitivity. "He taught me how to open my eyes so I could see what is really going on."

When Nikki arrived at Evergreen in 1986 from her hometown of Kirkland, Washington, she thought she would become a marine biologist. As a young child, she would often "play artist," sometimes dressing up in her grandmother's faux leopard coat and red high heels to suit her idea of the role, and in grade school and high school, she excelled at art, but she never imagined that it could be a viable career choice. "I didn't know any artists. It seemed like a fantastical, unreal life, like a fairy tale," Nikki recalls.

At Evergreen, Nikki was studious (she spent a lot of time at the library, one of the reasons why the less bookish Jay T says they didn't meet until after college) and also quickly immersed herself in the burgeoning Olympia punk rock scene. She was a regular at concerts and became known around town for her raw, expressive style, sometimes dancing onstage with her friend and neighbor Kurt Cobain and his band, Nirvana.

After graduating, Nikki interned at the Washington State Department of Ecology and, in the process, realized that she was more drawn to the lifestyle and work of her artist friends from Evergreen than to the office scene. Her friend Megan Kelso, a budding writer and artist, was self-publishing her Girlhero comics; her friend Kathleen Hanna, lead singer of the band Bikini Kill and pioneer of the Riot Grrrl movement, had a zine; and her friend Stella Marrs was establishing herself as an interdisciplinary artist and running a successful indie postcard company after traveling around the world, making postcards out of discarded *National Geographic* magazines and selling them on the street. Nikki liked how her friends were using their creative work as a tool to share their social values and foster community, thereby constructing their own economies on their own terms. Nikki realized that she might be able to make pretty pictures "to make a better world," an idea that is, like her work, both gentle and subversive.

Not quite ready to abandon the music scene, Nikki spent the first half of the 1990s engaged in both music and art. She started writing and performing her own songs and toured with several bands, simultaneously creating T-shirts, event flyers, and album art for those bands and others. To make money on the road, she sold aprons she bought at thrift stores and chain-stitched with her song lyrics as well as mittens she sewed using scrap polar fleece from a mill in Seattle. "I am a craft survivalist," she says now. "If I want to make something, I learn how to do it. I like solving problems, and one of the problems back then was being poor and being down to my last hundred dollars and needing to figure out what to do."

"Protect Your Hands"–themed wall art in Nikki's studio (left) and Jay T's shop (right).

CENTER LEFT

The dictionary has been one of Nikki's favorite books since childhood. Jay T made this cherrywood stand with rosewood accents to give it a place of honor in her studio.

CENTER RIGHT

While composing a new calendar, Nikki put out a call on Instagram for followers to send her their favorite words, a running list of which she posted in her studio.

BOTTOM

Above the family's living room is a loft-like library of children's books. Downstairs is the adult section. "I love a night when we're all sitting around reading," Nikki says.

It was 1996 when Nikki decided to stop performing and focus on her art full-time. "I was never very good at music," she claims. "I had a lot of enthusiasm. What I was expressing was so raw; eventually making pictures became a safer place to exist from and a place where I could still be very personal."

Nikki's paper-cuttings are, like her songs, personal, raw, and imperfect. "It's very spontaneous. I make a cut, and that decision has been made. There's not a lot of time between the thought and the creation of it, really." When she is finished with the cutting, the paper is delicate and lacelike, but the message is strong and durable. If the paper-cut is going to be printed (as most are), she scans it and sends it to a friend to convert into a vector file—then the original art can be stored, exhibited, or sold. Each year for the calendar, Nikki creates twelve images (which she likens to songs on an album), one for each month, and pairs each with a word or phrase: *Breathe* (a parent and young child cuddling in a tent in the woods); *Return* (a swimmer diving into a body of water in the moonlight); *Outside* (a child lying in the grass reading a book); *Vote! Vote! Vote!* (many hands in different skin tones raised); *Defend* (two hands holding wooly bear caterpillars); *Repair* (a group of women mending textiles).

With her images, Nikki prods us to pause and contemplate, coaxes us into action, reminds us of what is important. It is the dailiness of a life well lived that interests her, being conscious of the impact our choices have on ourselves, others, and the planet. On the occasion of a retrospective of Nikki's work at the Museum of Contemporary Craft in Portland, Oregon, in 2011, her friend Carrie Brownstein wrote:

I spent many an afternoon in that studio . . . I watched her work, the images appearing like strings, like smoke; they were stories told in streamers, in a most deliberate unraveling. I felt like the figures in her work already existed in the black expanse of paper, like she was merely letting the rest of us in on what she could already see: life from deep within the void. There were scenes of promise, of hope and sustainability, of nature, of family and friends. Nikki's work conjured up the quotidian acts of ritual, the repetitions that form an eventual and spiritual connection to people and to places. Somehow, Nikki captured permanence in the most delicate of mediums.

Nikki has reached a point in her career where she is offered more work than she wants to make time for. She resists jobs that don't excite her in order to leave time for the unexpected ones that push her outside her comfort zone, among them a sixty-foot-long mural for the Mystic Seaport Museum in Mystic, Connecticut, and a thirty-five-foot-long plasma-cut metal gate for a food bank in Seattle. Nikki is happy to take on modest assignments for causes she cares about and barter with friends and neighbors who need art for their small businesses. For a nearby farm, she regularly trades paper-cut depictions of fruits and vegetables for a weekly share of their harvest. She has also been paid for her work in knitting yarn; persimmons; maple syrup; sheepskins; a big box of her favorite, no-longer-manufactured X-Acto blades; and a blackberry pie. It was a barter arrangement that first brought Nikki and Jay T together, in 1998. He needed a logo for the sawmill business he was running at the time. In exchange, he made her a lamp with paper-cut images laminated onto the inside of the veneer shade. A couple of years later, upon his return from studying at the College of the Redwoods in Mendocino, California (the school James Krenov ran for many years), the two of them became a couple.

To this day, their relationship is symbiotic. During their morning walk, they discuss their plans for the day; after lunch they walk again and help each other troubleshoot any challenges they faced earlier. Nikki is inspired by Jay T's work ethic—"Even when he's not making a piece of furniture, he's always making something," she reveals. Jay T, in turn, is energized by Nikki's courage—"Her boldness, her willingness to take action and not wait for someone to ask her to do things, has been a great model," he says. But beyond the work, there is, of course, their love for each other and their son, who is already an accomplished sailor and a maker in his own right. When his

parents refused to buy him plastic toys, Jay T tells me, he carved Japanese wooden swords and sold them at Olympia's Art Walk (a biannual event in town) so he could buy them himself. While I was there, Finn was carving fids, pegs used to splice rope for sailing. And when I spoke to Nikki on the phone after her summer break, she told me that the family had spent much of the season sailing around the San Juan Islands. But she was ready to get back to work in her studio. From that first day she tried paper-cutting, at the suggestion of a friend, she has experienced the same sensation each time her hand pulls the blade through paper. "Everything is humming and peaceful," she says.

OPPOSITE, LEFT

Ariston men hudor, or
Water Heals All, is the
McClure-Scott family
motto, and Nikki includes
an image of water in all
her calendars and much
of her other work. Here
she is holding a piece
called *Forward*.

OPPOSITE, RIGHT

Nikki on the beach
outside her home.

THIS PAGE

Finn sets sail.

february:
renew

To create artwork for her calendars, Nikki takes a photo (or has one taken, if she wants to be in it), then sketches and cuts. Shown here is the making of February 2018: *Renew*.

An Art of One's Own

FRANCES PALMER LIKES to work alone. She wakes early, around five in the morning, and after drinking her coffee, quietly heads out to her ceramics studio or gardens, all of which are just a few steps from her nineteenth-century Colonial Revival home in Weston, Connecticut. She appreciates the freshness and calm of these first few hours but will happily work all day and into the evening—making pots, often filling them with dahlias and other flowers she grows by the thousands, then photographing and posting them in her online shop and on Instagram. She will also pack and ship orders and respond to emails from customers and a steady stream of editors wanting to feature her work in their publications. A few days a week, she will interrupt the flow to take a barre class because, she says, "I want to stay strong and healthy so I never have to retire."

When she needs a change of pace, she'll hop on the train and make the eighty-minute commute to New York City to see exhibitions at the Metropolitan Museum of Art, MoMA, or one of the city's many galleries. When she takes vacations, she plans her itineraries around the art and gardens she wants to visit in person: the Moderna Museet in Stockholm, the moss gardens of Saihōji in Kyoto, the Temple of Hephaestus (ancient Greece's patron god of metalworking, craftsmanship, and fire) in Athens, and so on.

Frances started throwing pots in 1987. Every day since, she says, she has learned something new. This is a function of both the process, which is always a little different when partnering with a natural material like clay, and also the curiosity, rigor, and passion with which she approaches her medium—and her life in general. "I am a very disciplined person," she says. "I love academics and research," both of which served her well when she was studying for her bachelor's degree in art history at Barnard and her master's in contemporary printmaking at Columbia. She also loves gardening and photography and cooking and entertaining. And she has found a way to intertwine all her enthusiasms into a successful career, though "career" feels like too cold and confining a word for what is, for Frances, the luckiest way to live. "I feel so fortunate to be able to set my own schedule and do what I love to do every day of my life," she tells me one morning during a video chat—I'm sitting at my desk taking notes and she is sitting at her wheel coaxing a piece of earthenware into a bowl for an order. As long as she can work at her wheel, she says, she's happy to talk to me for as much time as I need.

Frances began making pottery in a circuitous way, at her husband Wallace's suggestion. Suffering from what she now recognizes as undiagnosed postpartum

OPPOSITE

Frances Palmer begins each day during the growing season with a walk through her gardens to tend to the plants and choose blooms to photograph in her pots. Here she is arranging the morning's haul for photographing.

TOP LEFT

The west side of Frances's two-story, light-filled studio overlooks an orchard and the tennis court she transformed into a garden. In 2007, she and her husband arranged for the circa-1790s structure to be moved from another location nearby and rebuilt on their property. Originally it was going to be a family gathering place, but their three children—teenagers at the time—weren't particularly interested, and it quickly became Frances's domain.

depression after the birth of the first of her three children and after moving from a home in New York City to one in rural Connecticut, she was struggling for equilibrium. Out of a combination of what she remembers as thoughtfulness and desperation, Wallace asked her, "What is something that you have always wanted to do but haven't had time for?" Her response: "Pottery."

Frances had been reading about Charleston, the home in East Sussex, England, of artists Vanessa Bell and Duncan Grant and a gathering place for the early twentieth-century artists, writers, and intellectuals known as the Bloomsbury Group. At Charleston, a run-down farmhouse, Bell, Grant, and their eclectic circle of friends (including Bell's sister Virginia Woolf) embraced a bohemian lifestyle well outside of the constrained social norms of the times—as well as a DIY ethos, which included painting fanciful, colorful imagery directly onto the walls and furniture, designing fabrics for their furnishings and clothing, composing their gardens, and throwing pots. Perhaps, Frances thought, she could, like the artists of Bloomsbury, imbue her home with her own artistic spirit by making the family's tableware.

It was love at first touch. Frances liked working with clay and making something that, when finished, could be put to use. In some ways, it reminded her of the printmaking she had done in high school and again in graduate school, as well as cooking, baking, and gardening: all these, like pottery, progress in distinct stages, each one requiring its own painstaking process. For inspiration, she thought about the foods and flowers her vessels might hold and how to marry them both functionally and aesthetically. She also referenced her vast collection of art books, trawling through thousands of years of history for ideas. From the beginning, she photographed each piece she made. After a year and a half of weekly classes at a local art guild, she set out on her own with a secondhand wheel, wedging table, and kiln, confident in her ability to learn by trial and error, as well as through reading and observation.

For Frances, making pottery from home balanced well with child-rearing, and as her daughter and two sons grew, she gradually began to sell her one-of-a-kind pieces, first to a few small shops near where she lived, then to some of Manhattan's most sophisticated outlets, including department stores like Bergdorf Goodman and Takashimaya. Her practice of photographing the pots with flowers in them seemed to help sales, and she was happy to expand her own gardening habit to grow more of the blooms she loved most. It was the late 1990s, when dahlias were out of fashion, but Frances didn't care. She was fascinated by their geometry, their suffused coloration—really everything about them. "It's an obsession," Frances says. "Every year, I plant more." They now grow both in a fenced plot on one side of the studio and in raised beds within a repurposed 1930s tennis court on another.

Around the same time that Frances was reaching out to retailers to introduce her work, she started opening her studio, housed in an eighteenth-century barn, to the public, a practice she continues to this day. Each year, on the first Sunday in November, cars line up bumper to bumper on the circular gravel driveway in front of the house and on nearby streets. For many of those who show up, it is an annual pilgrimage.

The first floor, where Frances throws and photographs her pots, is locked for the day—visitors can only peer through the glass door to get a glimpse of what resides inside: a wall of windows casting natural light, three Japanese-made wheels (one each for earthenware, terra-cotta, and porcelain), two electric kilns (a gas-powered

one is in an outbuilding around back), and racks and tables chock-full of books, tools, and works in different stages of progress. Instead, visitors are directed upstairs to the high-ceilinged second floor with its exposed wooden beams, a space that functions for the day as a shop and during the rest of the year as a holding area for finished pieces as well as a packing station, an office, and a library. On a series of vintage farm tables, some set upon worn Middle Eastern kilims, Frances lays out her wares: vases, plates and platters, cake stands, and bowls, organized loosely based on the type of clay and glaze and the style. While everything in sight is clearly from the same maker's hand, it also reflects the broad range of her interests, from antiquities to modernist sculpture. There might be white earthenware vases with small round handles that give them a classical feeling, then more playful pieces with fluted surfaces or ruffled, beaded, or scalloped edges; small porcelain vases may be glazed with cobalt blue, oxblood, or celadon, while some terra-cotta urns remain unglazed and stamped with Frances's simple pot chop, a classical vessel she carved into a potato many years ago and has been using as her logo ever since.

OPPOSITE

An assortment of pots ready for Frances to pack and ship on the second floor of the studio. "I like wrapping a pot and conceptualizing the box it will fit in," Frances explains. "I've gone to so much trouble to make it, I like to see the process through to the end and make sure it's packed and shipped well, too."

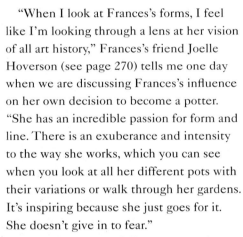

"When I look at Frances's forms, I feel like I'm looking through a lens at her vision of all art history," Frances's friend Joelle Hoverson (see page 270) tells me one day when we are discussing Frances's influence on her own decision to become a potter. "She has an incredible passion for form and line. There is an exuberance and intensity to the way she works, which you can see when you look at all her different pots with their variations or walk through her gardens. It's inspiring because she just goes for it. She doesn't give in to fear."

"I just forge ahead," Frances says about her work. Each morning when she enters the studio, she sets her priorities for the day, always trying to carve out some time for exploring new ideas. In her online shop, there is a section called In the Studio, and this is where she introduces experimental work. In the Journal section, she announces any gallery shows or pop-up shops she is participating in, but for the most part, she tries to avoid outside commitments. "I have always liked the freedom of going in and out of things without being beholden to anyone else's schedule or ideas," Frances explains. That is why she has opted to remain independent rather than seek gallery representation, even in the early days before the internet made it easier for artists to market their work directly to consumers. "On my own, I can basically be very fluid and make work as I like," she says.

There is both a seriousness and a whimsicality in Frances's creations, much as there is in Frances herself. While she is gracious and seems flattered by and grateful for the attention she garners for her pottery as well as her gardens, she is reserved and guards her time and privacy with care. It is through her work that Frances is most comfortable showing us who she is. Like the artists of Bloomsbury, she defies convention and makes her art and leads her life in her own way. She credits her success in large part to her willingness to start at the beginning and give every step of the process the attention it needs. There's no rushing, and there are no shortcuts; mistakes happen and pots break. To the many who ask for her advice, she shares what pottery has taught her: "It's okay to start doing something that you don't know anything about. Just find what you love. Take your time, have patience, and see it through to the end." For Frances, of course, there is no end in sight. Pottery is for her an ongoing and never-ending exploration.

Frances retrofitted the 1930s tennis court on the property with twenty-six raised garden beds. Though she spends long hours planting and staking carefully, she enjoys a bit of chaos, allowing volunteer plants to grow in the cracks in the court and leaving weeds be as long as they're not choking out other plants. Her passion for dahlias began in the late 1990s, after she saw a display at the San Francisco Botanical Garden. She now grows over a hundred different kinds, from the smallest pompons to the massive dinner-plate varieties shown here.

Frances maintains a corner in her studio for photography so she can document her work for her website, Instagram, and her own records, but most important, she says, for the pleasure of playing with color and form to create an artful composition. "I choose the flowers I grow based on how they work with the pots," she explains. Below, she is building arrangements in three vases (from left to right): a hand-built Napoleon (named after the Napoleonic period it reminds her of), Sam (named after a client), and Morandi (inspired by a vase in a painting by twentieth-century Italian painter and printmaker Giorgio Morandi).

Thinking a World into Being

KATIE STARTZMAN AND Laura Poulette are identical twins, born a few minutes apart in 1977—Katie, who was expected, first, followed by Laura, a surprise. They spent their first eight years living in a battered old farmhouse in the Finger Lakes region of New York that their parents were slowly renovating themselves, one room at a time, as funds allowed. Then when the twins were eleven, the family (including a younger brother and sister) moved to a parsonage in northeastern Pennsylvania, where their dad would be a pastor and their mother eventually would become a teacher and school administrator. Although Katie and Laura maintained separate friendships and interests, especially in high school, they have always felt connected, in sync. Without much money as they were growing up, they learned how to make fun with what they could find. They both have vivid memories of constant DIY projects, including woodworking, sewing, making dollhouses and their furnishings, building forts—and, for school, taking on such over-the-top escapades as constructing a six-foot-tall bejeweled King Tut sarcophagus for a world cultures fair and a similarly sized chicken-wire-reinforced papier-mâché clown head for a Carnival parade.

Today Katie and Laura live with their husbands and children (they each have two sons) in Berea, Kentucky—Katie on a residential street in town and Laura off a dirt road on the rural outskirts. Their parents retired and joined them in this small Appalachian city, a liberal pocket in a famously conservative state, in 2012.

When I started working on this book, Katie and Laura were among the first two people I asked to participate. They quickly agreed, each confiding in me separately that she could hardly believe I wanted to include her, a reflection of their shared humility and modesty. I look to Katie and Laura as role models. While they have enjoyed riding the wave of the DIY renaissance, for them a life based in creative self-sufficiency is the norm rather than a new awakening.

My admiration began when I was editing Katie's book, *The Knitted Slipper Book*, in 2013. As an author, Katie was conscientious, full of ideas, and always willing to go the extra mile when asked (even if that meant long hours of revision). Once she had submitted her manuscript (plus high-quality how-to photos she learned to take at my behest) and we began discussing how to promote the book, she took it upon herself to create a stop-motion animation trailer: a delightful tale depicting a woman (that she knitted out of wool) in her living room knitting a pair of slippers and sending them off in a gift box to a yeti friend, set to carefully selected, open-source piano music. Katie had never attempted stop-

OPPOSITE

Katie (left) and Laura (right) in Laura's living room, sewing straps onto tote bags (see pages 228–229). Katie is wearing a sweater she knitted. She taught herself to knit from a how-to pamphlet during college. Laura is wearing a blouse she sewed. "I aspire to have a closet full of clothes I made myself and love, what I need, and no more than that," she says.

motion animation before, but with the help of online tutorials as well as Laura, who constructed miniature furnishings for the mostly cardboard set ("It was like making stuff for our dollhouses as a kid," Laura remembers), and Katie's husband, Michael, who took photos while she animated the figures and then edited the frames, she created a delightful ninety-five-second spot. When Katie agreed to attend book signings at the New York Sheep and Wool Festival in Rhinebeck, Laura stepped in again and designed a collapsible cardboard tree with branches on which the slippers could be delightfully displayed—so much better than laying them out on the standard-issue folding table the festival provides. Then Laura and their mom, Jude, joined Katie for the weekend, the three of them making the eight-hundred-mile drive from Kentucky and camping in a cabin at a nearby park. "I was so proud to see Katie's book project go from sketches and swatches to contacting you and getting a contract and doing all that work," recalls Laura. "It motivated me to be ambitious myself and to do big projects."

I visited Katie and Laura for two days a few years later. This was eleven months after Laura and her husband, Strider, completed building their house on twenty acres of land gifted to them by Strider's mother, a studio potter who lives nearby. At the same time, Katie was on the verge of expanding her fledgling bagel business from a food cart (which she constructed herself) at the farmers' market into a bricks-and-mortar café (which she renovated with the help of her family) in Berea's small downtown, not far from the campus of Berea College, where she, Michael, Laura, and Strider all earned their undergraduate degrees. Berea College, founded in 1855 to serve academically promising students with limited economic resources, offers a tuition-free education to its entire student body as long as they are in good academic standing and successfully participate in the school's Labor Program. That means they have to work for the college a minimum of ten hours each week—jobs range from washing dishes in the cafeteria (Katie's freshman-year assignment, which she says solidified her determination to finish college; she earned a degree in English) and cashiering at the campus store (Laura's first gig; her degree is in studio art/fibers) to working in the craft department, where positions include broom making, pottery, woodworking, and weaving; the products made by the students are sold to the public

TOP

Laura's dining room. For many of their design decisions, she and Strider referred to the book *A Pattern Language* (which they borrowed from Katie). For the actual construction, they relied on their subscription to *Fine Homebuilding* magazine.

CENTER LEFT

When Katie started carving spoons, her husband gifted her a set of high-quality tools, including the hook knife shown here, used to hollow out the bowl of the spoon. "They're such a pleasure to use," says Katie. "When I was younger, I would try to make things as cheaply as possible. Now I understand and appreciate the value of investing in better tools."

CENTER RIGHT

After she finished writing *The Knitted Slipper Book*, Katie began to explore leatherwork. She made belts, bracelets, clutches, sandals, and the wallet shown here.

BOTTOM

An assortment of wooden bowls made by Laura, Strider, and other local woodworkers, plus cutting boards Strider made after he, Laura, Katie, and Michael took an evening hand-woodworking class at Berea College together. The class was part of a long-standing program open to students, faculty, staff, and townspeople who want to learn skills that will make them more self-sufficient and better informed consumers.

"I want to make necessary things that will last a long time and can be repaired, things that I handle every day."

—Laura Poulette

lower," explains Laura of her three-bedroom modern farmhouse. "I always have to have a project going," adds Katie.

There's nothing these women seem unable to figure out through research, a habit they both developed as children visiting their local public library. After outgrowing their beloved Little House and Anne of Green Gables series, Katie remembers checking out piles of cooking and homesteading titles. Laura focused on the art stacks. Today they share books back and forth, except for a few that they each feel are important to keep within reach at all times, among them the full set of titles by Natalie Chanin (see page 86) about hand-sewing and embellishing cotton jersey clothing and accessories. For Laura's first project from those books, she created two identical indigo-dyed, reverse-appliqué T-shirts, one for each sister. "We have a tradition of giving each other handmade things," explains Katie. She knit Laura a cabled cardigan for their thirtieth birthday; Laura reciprocated with a set of stenciled canvas totes.

There was a time when Katie and Laura got together regularly to work on their projects, especially when they were both homeschooling their sons and cowriting a blog called Duo Fiberworks. These days they tend to work separately and confer when they meet up for lunch or to run errands in Lexington, the closest large city. "We are each other's biggest fans. One of the best things about our relationship is that I never have to bring her up to speed. I never have to give her background on what I'm thinking because we have such a shared frame of reference. When she gives me feedback, I know that it's valuable," Katie says.

to raise funds for the school and used to furnish campus properties.

For our visit, we convened in Laura's studio, known as the "tiny house," a 384-square-foot cabin that Laura and Strider built in the summer of 2011 and where the family of four lived for more than three and a half years while they built the "big house" up the hill. We were to make waxed canvas bags like one I coveted when I saw Katie carrying it back at the Sheep and Wool Festival. Prior to my arrival, Laura pulled cotton canvas from her fabric stash and Katie cut a pattern template for the bag body out of newsprint and retrieved leather left over from a different bag-making project for the handles. We would create three totes, one for each of us, and we would split up some of the tasks for efficiency. It was a fun assembly line, an energizing and inspiring afternoon of DIYing among friends.

Making things from scratch, finding their way through trial and error: These are habits Katie and Laura live by, sometimes because of economic necessity and sometimes because that's just the way they prefer to do it, often a combination of the two. "I could never live in a house like this if we hadn't built it ourselves here, where the costs are

Katie is the natural entrepreneur of the duo; buoyed by the success of her Native Bagel Company, she is eager to expand. Laura tends to stay closer to home, where she strives to make a living as an artist. In 2011, when she and Strider moved the family into the tiny house, Laura began exploring the woods and fields on their property, first photographing then painting bits of nature she picked up along the way. "Getting to know the geography of this place and the stuff that grows here is so amazing," Laura gushes. "Twenty acres is not that much land, but I can't get over how diverse it is. I especially love the challenge in winter when it looks like there is nothing to paint because everything is so gray, but there is still so much out there." To generate income, she sells original and reproduction artwork derived from this exploration—on her website, at art fairs, and at shops in the region. As much as she loves painting, though, she can't imagine not making more-functional work, too. "Painting doesn't scratch that itch," she says. "So much of what we consume comes from an exploitive or disposable place. I want to make necessary things that will last a long time and can be repaired, things that I handle every day."

To further her point, Laura references a quote from the book *Why We Make Things*

and Why It Matters by Peter Korn (see page 142): "What I have come to see is that creative effort is a process of challenging embedded narratives of belief in order to think the world into being for oneself, and that the work involved in doing so provides a wellspring of spiritual fulfillment." Laura continues, "It feels more like spiritual practice than spiritual fulfillment for me; what I can relate to most is the idea of 'thinking the world into being.'" And that is, it seems, these sisters' shared strength. They think about the world they want to live in, then they figure out how to create it for themselves. Wisely, they both chose husbands who are up for the adventure.

When I ask them about their goals for the future—what they are "thinking into being," Laura admits, "Sometimes Strider and I are super-busy, and just keeping the house tidy and dinner made is all we can manage." Then she can't help but begin describing a few of the projects she is excited about: a fire pit on the porch, a mudroom, maybe a teahouse in the woods. She also mentions auditing a field botany class at the college to learn how to identify plants in the wilderness and taking some printmaking courses. Far into the future, when carrying in firewood and tending large gardens are too much for them, she can imagine moving into town. "I see the

OPPOSITE

A display of some of the sisters' favorite books; Laura's are on the left and Katie's are on the right, though there's lots of crossover. For example, Laura borrowed Katie's copy of *A Pattern Language* for several years while she and Strider were designing and building their house.

LEFT

Laura takes regular walks on her twenty-acre property to find her painting subjects, here mosses and lichens, showstoppers from the winter woods. The grayish plant with red on top of the watercolored "O" is called British soldiers, which grows all over one particular rotting log along an old logging road that crosses the property. On the horizontal stem at the bottom of the painting and in the dish is reindeer moss from a little cedar glade on the property's south side.

RIGHT

Laura refers to her field guides to identify the plants she spots and the specimens she picks up during her walks.

A FIELD GUIDE to WILDFLOWERS

A FIELD GUIDE to the BIRDS

rees & Shrubs of Kentucky   KENTUCKY

advantage of being able to walk to the library," she says, then adds, "It would be cool to have a mobile art studio/camper you drive to national parks and to different art fairs to sell work." Strider, it turns out, is already talking about putting a reliable engine in a Volkswagen bus.

Katie, meanwhile, is helping her older son convert an old school bus purchased at a government surplus auction into a camper so that he can travel around the country in it. "It's such a fun project," she comments. Then there's a shanty boat for which she has already purchased plans. The entrepreneur in her is thinking about opening a microbrewery in town. For the first time, she has all her bills on autopay, confident that she has enough income flowing to cover them, and she wants to keep it that way. Although writing her book brought in only modest funds, Katie says that it was an important stepping-stone: It gave her the confidence to think bigger. "That was the largest project I had ever done on my own, and it helped me realize that I can do hard things." Making a slipper or shoe, writing a book, opening a bagel business—they are all, she says, puzzles, projects to be researched and solved.

When I reiterate to both sisters how impressed I am by their confidence and grit, they both say something about the reality of their situation—they live in a place where self-sufficiency is required. "Berea feels like a frontier in a way," suggests Katie, referring to its untapped potential. Lest I misunderstand and overromanticize how they live or exaggerate their accomplishments, Katie points out that she and Michael are so preoccupied with the bagel business that they haven't done laundry or cooked a family meal in

weeks. But when I press them to give themselves some credit, Katie says, "I keep going back to when we were kids and had a little work space in the basement where we were allowed to do whatever we wanted, scrounging materials and making a mess. When I finally had the motor skills and coordination to actualize my ideas, I felt capable, even if I was just doing a small woodworking project or putting wallpaper on the dollhouse walls or gluing fake shingles onto the roof."

"That definitely built confidence," Laura agrees. There was the model of their parents, who (taking cues from their own hardscrabble families) DIYed their home before it was fashionable. "My mom and dad renovated a farmhouse and had a big garden and canned tomatoes out of necessity when it wasn't cool, not as part of a wider movement," Laura explains. And there was also their much-admired maternal grandmother, who pursued everything from knitting, stained glass, and tole painting to furniture making and building projects not typical of women of her day. "Now she's living in this tiny retirement apartment, but she has a little making area in her bedroom because that's important to her," says Katie.

Laura compares success, or leading a good life, to her yoga practice and "finding balance between effort and ease in each pose." Katie is less philosophical: "To have the time and financial and other resources to pursue the kinds of projects I'm interested in. I would like to have a beautiful home with generous gardens that are well tended and time to enjoy them. I would like to have a place to eat outside with my family, to have people over. Laura and I were talking about building a sauna." Together they can surely think anything into being.

Katie and Laura take a spin in two of four small boats Katie built for their four boys. She followed open-source plans she downloaded from the internet. Laura's hat is an Alabama Chanin design that she hand-sewed and -embellished.

DIYing among friends

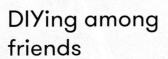

To make our bags, Katie, Laura, and I overdyed canvas previously dyed with walnut hulls in Laura's organic indigo vat, then applied melted beeswax to it and heated it in the oven. Next we cut out the canvas and a linen lining fabric from Laura's stash according to a paper pattern Katie drew, and then sewed the bags' bodies. Finally, we cut leather left over from another project to use as straps and sewed them to the bags with strong pink thread.

FIVE

Finding a Voice

Learning a New Language

FOR WINDY CHIEN, 2016 was the Year of Knots. That January, she challenged herself to learn one new knot each day for 366 days (it was a leap year) and post her progress in real time on Instagram. Thirty-six months prior, she had made a dramatic change in her life: She had left her secure (and coveted!) job at Apple to forge a new path for herself, not knowing exactly what that path might be. She was employed by the global tech giant from 2005 to 2012, first as a product manager, producer, and curator for a fledgling iTunes, then as a managing editor for the App Store. Before that, she worked at and then owned San Francisco's influential independent music shop Aquarius Records for fourteen years. But in December 2012, no longer fulfilled by curating and promoting the work of others, Windy decided to invest in herself and nurture her own creativity. Letting go of the security of her full-time position at Apple—not to mention the prestige and family approval that came with it—took some serious thought. But on that last day, after she had handed in her company-issued, state-of-the-art laptop and shared a champagne toast with colleagues, she drove from the company's Cupertino headquarters to her home in San Francisco's Mission District feeling elated. "When you first leave your job and are embarking on something new,

anything seems possible," she recalls. "It is such a delicious place to be."

Windy had prepared for this moment with characteristic practicality, setting aside enough savings to cover her basic living expenses for at least a year and positioning herself to take on a few part-time consulting gigs with app developers. Her next move was to sign up for a series of classes—in anything that even slightly interested her, and with teachers whose work she admired. This led to explorations in stone carving, LED lighting, block printing, ceramics, weaving, interior design, and—the two media of the more than a dozen she tried that resonated—spoon carving and macramé. Her father, a career military officer who took the family to live at West Point, New York, and then on bases in Hawaii while Windy was growing up, was a weekend woodworker and carpenter. Her mother, who stayed at home to raise Windy and her younger brother, had taught her macramé in the 1970s. But Windy was still surprised that these two forms of creative expression, neither of which stuck with her as a child, were so appealing to her now that she was in her forties. Her interest in them, she surmises, must have been lying dormant, waiting.

Windy delved into woodworking first, taking bowl-turning and spoon-carving classes at the Crucible, a maker space

OPPOSITE, LEFT

Windy in her studio, in front of her Year of Knots installation. The process of making it, one knot a day for the 366 days of 2016, taught her, she says, about the elemental building blocks of art: line, form, shape, space, texture, color, and value. In 2017, Facebook asked her to re-create the wall as a permanent installation at their campus in Menlo Park, California.

"When you first leave your job and are embarking on something new, anything seems possible. It is such a delicious place to be."

TOP RIGHT

Windy working a series of classic square knots, called Solomon's bar.

BOTTOM RIGHT

Cotton rope lashed with gold thread. Lashing is a technique for binding together two or more objects. Sailors lash with heavy twine or waxed floss. Windy elevates the technique by lashing with vintage 24-karat gold thread.

An assortment of Windy's wooden spoons, including three with her signature squared-off corner.

Windy removed the doors to her backyard storage shed when she transformed it into her woodworking studio. "It's empowering to have a space dedicated to you, where you get to determine what happens, a safe place where no one is going to judge you, because you're the mistress of the domain."

Helix Lights hang above the worktable in Windy's backyard studio.

in Oakland, in the summer of 2013. She didn't care for the machinery or the flying wood chips inherent in turning, but she immediately loved everything about carving spoons, from the satisfaction of digging into and gliding through wood with a sharp spoon gauge or rasp and shaping it to her will, to the sanding and polishing of the wood to a velvety smooth finish, to the functionality of the finished product. Almost right away, she transformed a backyard storage space into a woodworking cottage, and within six months, she was selling her wares, including a unique cooking spoon with a squared-off corner that reaches into the curves and flat surface of a pan in a more efficient way than a conventional spoon.

While deep into spoon carving, Windy began exploring macramé. "Within five minutes, I remembered how much I loved it as a kid," Windy recalls of the Saturday-morning refresher class she took with well-known instructor Emily Katz. As with spoon carving, she enjoyed the process, but she felt an even deeper kinship with the material. "Very quickly, all the expressive possibilities of the cord became apparent to me," she says. "I loved how I could take what is essentially a line—one of the basic building blocks of art—and make it into something three-dimensional that has heft and weight and volume." One of Windy's early ideas was to create lighting for the bay window at the front of her Victorian house by combining macramé-covered wiring with utilitarian bulbs. When neighbors began knocking on her door to inquire about the cascading lighting system and friends asked her if she would make lights for them, Windy realized that she had created a viable retail product. She named her design the Helix Light since the macraméd square knots spiral like strands of DNA around the wires, and her work immediately caught the attention of consumers.

Windy saw macramé as a new language, each knot a new word, but she didn't feel fluent in her usage of it yet. She needed to learn more knots to express her ideas and achieve a new aesthetic, distinct from traditional macramé, which relies on just a couple of knots repeated in different sequences, all tending to have a similar retro-bohemian look. And thus began the Year of Knots, an idea that came to her in a flash while she was sweeping her studio floor. Looking back now, she recounts, "When you're a woodworker, sweeping happens at the end of a day or

Windy showed me how to make her Ringbolt Necklace, which requires working the ringbolt hitch around a wooden hoop. After designing these necklaces, one of which you can see her wearing on page 234, Windy started playing with the idea of enlarging her scale; this led to her Diamond Ring series, a group of large (about five-foot-wide and -tall) works composed of sixteen plywood rings assembled in a diamond pattern and adorned with a curvilinear pathway of knotted rope (see page 314).

Windy is pointing to a doughnut-shaped knot she named the Cruller. "This knot is significant," she says, "because it represents the growing confidence I experienced during the Year of Knots." As her understanding of knots' structure and mechanics evolved, her confidence grew and she felt able to invent a handful of her own knots, like this one, which is derived from the Heaving Line knot.

project and marks a transition between what just happened and what you're going to do next," which was exactly what was transpiring, literally and figuratively, on that January morning.

Windy's main reference for this daily exercise was the massive, six-hundred-plus-page *Ashley Book of Knots*, a guide to more than thirty-nine hundred different knots first published in 1944 and still in print today. Each morning, she would flip it open, choose a knot to puzzle through, and make it out of white cotton rope. The simplest knots she chose required one strand, the most complex over a dozen. While the basic lanyard knot that she began with on day one took just a few minutes to learn, the star knot, a five-strand two-layered knot in the button family, took her well into lunchtime and required that she augment her book learning with a few YouTube videos (a multimedia approach that Windy succumbed to only a couple of times).

From that disciplined practice came a high level of knot proficiency, as expected, as well as an unforeseen mind shift. During this morning routine, Windy found herself entering into a previously difficult-to-come-by state of creative flow. In an essay on her website, she remembers it like this: "The practice allowed me to quickly access flow, that elusive state of blissful productivity

I'd heard about and longed to experience, where one is working with extreme focus, expanding and growing one's abilities, free of cares and distractions. As I tied a new knot each day, I had the palpable sense I was connecting to a larger consciousness of creative energy."

Windy had begun 2016 defining herself as a product designer and maker, but by year's end, her mission and identity had evolved. She now self-identified as an artist. She saw the wall on which she had carefully hung each knot with a copper nail as an artwork in and of itself, marking a passage of time, a learning process, and the elevation of a quotidian material through her own intervention into a thought-provoking expression of her ideas. As she learned new knots, she developed a vocabulary for further exploration, often feeling inspired to experiment on a much larger scale. By posting her progress daily on Instagram, she had grown her following from a few hundred to over ten thousand, garnered press coverage from outlets as diverse as the *New York Times*, *Wired*, and *Martha Stewart Living*, and built up a clientele not only for the individual items—like the lighting and spoons on her website— but also for installations, many of which involved complex engineering challenges. There was a ninety-foot wraparound

Windy's beloved greyhound, Shelley Duvall, is a regular in the studio. Here she is napping in front of an assortment of Windy's supplies. Windy began this art odyssey with ordinary cotton rope. Since then she has explored many other materials, including polypropylene sailing rope, felted wool rope, and Ethernet cable. "If you think of my work as being an exploration of the line, the material could be anything," she says.

TOP LEFT & RIGHT

Windy's Victorian house in the Mission District of San Francisco. She had the front painted in stripes ranging from yellow through orange to red and the back painted in stripes ranging from yellow through green to blue, a nod to the late 1960s–early 1970s graphic style to which she is drawn.

CENTER

Windy made her first Helix Light for the bay window at the front of her home. Although the creative part was in the designing, she still finds making the lights satisfying. "I put on a podcast or audiobook, and it's heaven," she says.

BOTTOM LEFT

Windy is named after her grandmother, who was, Windy recalls, "an amazing artist." Her needlepoints hang in the entryway of Windy's home.

BOTTOM RIGHT

A prototype for *Twisted Planes* (see page 240) installed in the stairwell leading up to Windy's bedroom.

rope wall for the IBM headquarters in Cambridge, Massachusetts, and a thirty-foot-tall rope tree for a restaurant in Virginia. "I like making big things," Windy stresses. "I want to take up space."

Windy was born with a certain audaciousness, always compelled to pursue what she found most interesting and culturally vital—whether that involved music, film (which she studied in college), the maker movement, art-making, the creative potential of technology, or even having her three-story Victorian house painted in multicolored ombré stripes. Her confidence allowed her to cut short her college education when she was one math class shy of finishing her degree ("That sort of certification never felt significant to me," she explains) and to purchase the record store she started working at while in college and expand its reputation internationally by seizing on the communicative possibilities of the internet. It gave her the courage to apply for a job at Apple, one of the world's most powerful companies, and to leave that company while still at the top of her game.

Interestingly, it was Windy's yoga regimen that helped her recognize that it was time to leave Apple. Having practiced on and off since college, in 2012 she enrolled in a teacher training course in vinyasa, a modern yoga iteration in which poses flow together in energetic sequences. At the time, she thought she was seeking a disciplined exercise routine, but the benefits of the practice turned out to be deeper and subtler than she anticipated. She became more attuned to what her body and mind were trying to tell her. Through yoga, she says, "I was able to feel in my body and hear in my mind what my feelings were. I would observe what my day felt like and what my headspace was like and realized that I was living with all this negativity swimming around in my brain all the time." The negativity came, in part, from the inevitable politics that impacted office life and also from an unfulfilled longing to join in the growing maker scene. "I kept seeing other people's great work floating across my computer screen. I was in awe of the women who were making these beautiful objects," she remembers.

By leaving Apple, Windy is quick to clarify, she wasn't rejecting technology. While some makers see tech as antithetical to what they're doing, Windy embraces it. She still preorders each new version of the iPhone and looks to video game design as a new artistic frontier. "How beautiful would games be if they were made for you and me?" she wonders. And as impressed as she remains by the hand makers who influenced her decision to leave her job at Apple, she is equally awed by many of the techies she has

encountered. "It is inspiring to be around tech folks who have big eyes and big ears and are soaking it all in," she says.

At Apple, she recalls, everything had to be perfect, and she absorbed the Steve Jobs ethos, then in its heyday: Every detail must be thought through; the inside and outside and the back and front must be equally beautiful; and all inessentials must be stripped away to find the essence. When Jobs died, the company held a private ceremony for employees at which they distributed a folio of his now-famous 2005 commencement address at Stanford University, which to this day Windy keeps on a table in her bathroom. Her favorite passage reads, "Remembering that I'll be dead soon is the most important tool I've ever encountered to help me make the big choices in life. Because almost everything—all external expectations, all pride, all fear of embarrassment or failure— these things just fall away in the face of death, leaving only what is truly important. Remembering that you are going to die is

the best way I know to avoid the trap of thinking you have something to lose. You are already naked. There is no reason not to follow your heart."

Keeping Jobs's counsel in mind, Windy now embraces her life and follows her heart by staying present in and enjoying each and every possible moment. "I pretty much love every minute of what I am doing," she says. "I love cutting the rope, measuring, talking to the client, making the work, finishing it, and taking the photos and sharing them."

What lies ahead for Windy? There will be more exploration, more collaborations for interior and exterior spaces, and the publication of a book, called *The Year of Knots*. And then, the unknown. "Craft evolves one step at a time. You don't plan it out twenty-five steps ahead. You do what the material is suggesting to you. Maybe this is how we should look at our lives. Here is what I have now. What makes sense and is going to bring me some joy? Next thing, then next thing. And four years later, you're an artist."

OPPOSITE

Windy created this installation, called *Twisted Planes*, for the San Francisco headquarters of AngelList, a website for connecting start-ups. "I loved the idea of making a whole environment," Windy remembers. She used the rafters, what she calls the "bones of the space," as part of the installation. To work out the design, first she drew on photos of the space. Next she created a prototype and installed it in the stairwell leading up to her attic bedroom at home (see page 238). "It is made of straight lines and tension, but you see different curves depending the axis you view it from," she comments. "It's nice to have fiber above our heads, in spaces that are usually neglected and where we're used to seeing metal."

THIS PAGE

Windy made this installation, called *Rope Frameworks with Canopy*, out of cotton, steel, and leather for a venture capital firm in San Francisco.

ALEX DEVOL

Journey as Destination

ALEX DEVOL'S PERSPECTIVE on his work, and the way he lives, can waver, sometimes within a single conversation, between practical and philosophical, concrete and conceptual. Sometimes he wonders if he should go outside and carve spoons in the woods, turn bowls in his backyard shed, or throw pots at the pottery wheel in his art studio; if that sort of traditional, meditative work will be enough to make him happy, or at least content. More often he is committed to pushing himself further, developing novel ideas in wood and other materials—strong, ancient ones like bronze, or newer ones like epoxy—believing that in order to fulfill his destiny, he must do something innovative, never done before, modern. Along the way, he faces challenges—the need to make a living, his own ego, the tales he absorbed as a child at a traditional British prep school about striving and success.

Alex has always enjoyed being creative. In some ways, the contentment he finds now working by himself echoes the hundreds of hours he spent as a child drawing, painting, and building models on the floor of his bedroom in a suburb of Manchester, England, experimenting and figuring things out on his own. And the satisfaction he felt in art classes in school when he insisted on challenging his skills even when his teachers didn't demand it: for instance, the time he constructed a

three-dimensional chessboard out of walnut, maple, and frosted glass instead of making elementary bookends like his classmates. But to Alex's dismay, the number of art classes he could take, despite his school's well-equipped facilities, was limited. The emphasis at Arnold's in Preston, England, was on traditional academics, rigorous courses in subjects like literature, Latin, physics, and calculus that the competitive school presupposed would prepare its student body to enter esteemed universities and then engage in "important" white-collar careers. Success—and, in turn, happiness, it was understood—would be judged in direct correlation to the size of one's salary and the prestige of one's title. "Art was looked at as a hobby," Alex remembers. "We were being prepared from a very young age to get jobs that would pay us a lot of money to do very specific things. Not for a second were we encouraged to question the idea that financial success and a big title were what we wanted."

In a twist of fate that, to this day, seems to surprise Alex, he found himself running his own menswear business in his mid-twenties. Though he never intended to work in the fashion realm, his first opportunity to make a living wage—after skipping out on the university experience he was groomed for and spending eighteen months bumming around Australia—was

OPPOSITE, TOP

The cows in the pasture next to Alex's house regularly munch on his hedges. Alex left Manchester, the second-largest urban area in England, for a small, quiet village after shuttering his fashion enterprise in 2015.

OPPOSITE, BOTTOM LEFT

Alex working on the porch overlooking the Leeds and Liverpool Canal at the back of his house. Even though he rarely whittles spoons as part of his creative or commercial practice anymore, he still makes them from time to time for the sheer pleasure of it. "It's hard for me to stop once I've started," he says. "There does certainly seem to be a real joy to be had in doing practical things and creative, practical things particularly."

OPPOSITE, BOTTOM RIGHT

Two bronze spoons displayed on a cross section of warped oak that was part of an experiment Alex ran to learn more about how wood behaves under different atmospheric conditions.

illustrating graphics on men's T-shirts, which ultimately led him, via hard work and a few lucky breaks, to launching his own brand of casual streetwear. At first it was a fun and heady business, and he felt proud of the quality of his product and the positive work environment he was able to create for his employees—thirty of them at the brand's height—but ultimately, he had to move manufacturing from Europe to Asia and lower the quality of the materials to cut costs to satisfy the retailers.

Bit by bit, he became dissatisfied and disillusioned, a decline that was exacerbated during the recession of the late 2000s, when many of his smaller customers closed shop and he became more dependent on the large chains that fully embraced the intensifying fast fashion mantra of "make it cheap, quick, and trendy" (basically, make it so that it will either fall apart or go out of style so quickly that the consumer will need to come back for more soon). Alex's once-satisfying job turned into sitting at a computer designing clothing he didn't like to meet a retailer's brief for garments to be sewn by the hundreds of thousands in factories in Asia, garments he would likely never see and would definitely never wear.

And that's where this story took a turn. In the winter of 2015, believing that his only options were to either embrace the fast fashion ethos that he abhorred or quit, Alex put his business up for sale and prepared to take some time off to figure out what to do next. Demoralized and confused, he stepped away from his computer and began drawing on paper. Then he began working with green, unseasoned wood (that is, wood from recently felled trees that hasn't yet dried out and is, therefore, more malleable as well as delicate), a material he had first dabbled in at age five or six, when his grandfather gifted him a workbench and tools. He made some rudimentary furniture, carved spoons in different shapes and types of wood, then took an introductory course in wood turning and began to make bowls. "The process itself felt therapeutic," he recalls. "I was actually making things I didn't hate, with an old material that felt fresh again, and I was getting to teach myself something new and take a bit of pride in it." When he had a question or problem, he could generally figure it out by researching it on the internet and experimenting on his own, just as he had as a kid. After about a month, he began posting photos of his work on Instagram under the handle @woodwoven (the "woven" part because he initially thought he might also delve into textile design), and he enjoyed getting feedback. He gave away a few of his pieces as gifts and gradually began selling some on a Wooden & Woven website. "I started posting on Instagram as a work diary," Alex remembers. "I developed this routine where I would make things, then upload a photo and share. I felt motivated by the response." During his first year, Alex racked up nearly thirty thousand followers and collaborated and traded with

"We were being prepared from a very young age to get jobs that would pay us a lot of money to do very specific things. Not for a second were we encouraged to question the idea that financial success and a big title were what we wanted."

other creatives whom he met there and whose work he admired. Although retailers wanting to stock his product reached out to him, he sold to only a few, wary of developing a production-line mentality. To this day, Alex says, "I want to be an artist, not a machine."

Alex was enjoying his new work and making enough money to get by for a while, but he was also fielding calls about much more lucrative positions back in the fashion industry. Fearful that he might succumb to an offer, tempted by a salary or a promise of creative freedom that probably couldn't be kept, he took out an insurance policy of sorts: He enrolled in a master's degree program at the University of Central Lancashire. With credit for life experience allowing him to leapfrog over an undergraduate degree, he intended to study design by way of making. "I wanted to make a commitment to myself and learn more about wood and elaborate upon that. I didn't want to sit in front of a computer and have to plan something out in CAD before I started on it. I wanted to be hands-on, to be able to correct my mistakes because I'd physically experienced why what I'd tried to do didn't work instead of drawing it up and giving it to a factory and never

knowing that they had to fix my mess," he explains.

Alex spent two years at the university, first studying the properties and behavior of green wood, working with as many varieties as possible (from maple, cherry, and olive to sycamore, zebrawood, and silver birch), then investigating other materials, including clay and metal. He began throwing his own pots at a pottery wheel. He came up with the idea of creating a vessel in wood, then using that to make a mold with which he could cast the same form in other materials, such as porcelain, bronze, and iron. He experimented with glazes for his porcelain pieces that he concocted by burning the wooden masters from which he made the molds and combining the ash with clay and water. He investigated different methods for creating patinas on his metal pieces, including burying them in wood shavings and blowtorching them with liquid chemical solutions. Gradually, his work became larger and more conceptual; his forms, though often originating in function, became more abstract. For his thesis, he wrote about perceived value in art and design and, in particular, how it pertains to issues like material choice, handwork, reputation, and narrative. His graduation show in spring

OPPOSITE, LEFT

Alex says that every horizontal surface in his home eventually ends up serving as storage space. "In the beginning, I was precious about everything I made, even if I didn't like it, because I wasn't sure I could make it again," Alex remembers. Now he is eager to move work out of the house but admits that he sometimes procrastinates before posting it online to sell because he dreads the next step: the tedium of boxing and shipping.

OPPOSITE, TOP RIGHT

A bronze bowl cast from a sand mold, from a bark-edged wooden master.

OPPOSITE, BOTTOM RIGHT

Alex burned scraps from logs he used to make the bowls on the top two shelves to use in glazes for the hand-cast porcelain bowls on the bottom shelf. He likes his work to communicate a sense of origin and the process that went into making it.

CENTER

Alex generally composts his wood shavings or burns them to use in the glazes he applies to his ceramics. He remembers how much he resented taking science classes in high school and now admits, "I would love to get another chance to have my kid brain and just be like a sponge and learn about physics and chemistry. That would seriously help me with what I am doing today."

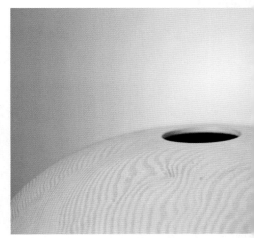

2017 led to invitations to participate in a few group shows in museums; representation by a gallery in London; and inquiries about commissions from interior designers and architectural firms.

I reached out to Alex for the first time when he was about halfway through his graduate school experience, and I followed along as his work and perspective evolved. When I visited him at his home in the village of—not joking—Whittle-le-Woods, he was happy to show me what he was making and share his story. Still recalling his early school years with some resentment because of the stress and confusion they caused him—"I was made to feel that my life would end if I didn't get A's," he remembers—he also recognizes that the discipline, patience, and willingness to work hard that serve him well today were ingrained in him there.

A few months later, after he completed his degree, we talked again, and he shared that success is still a concept with which he grapples. "For me, it is partly about recognition and people, not just individuals but big organizations or galleries that have accrued credibility, saying, 'Well done,'" he explains. "I'm still pursuing that, and yet I know that it doesn't really give you anything when you get it. It doesn't make you happy at all. Instead of just acknowledging that and being like, 'I should go and make pots, then, because I like making pots,' instead of doing the logical thing, you say, 'I have to do something bigger next time, get into an even better gallery.' It goes around in circles."

When I suggest to Alex that he consider an ancient Greek definition of happiness—the joy we feel from striving toward our potential—he pauses, then responds, "I really like that." Success, he acknowledges, is a target that can move in the space of a single conversation as well as over the course of a lifetime. Naturally, the people who surround us, especially in childhood, influence what we believe to be true, but ultimately, we must find our own way. "I really enjoy what I'm doing now," Alex adds. "I'm constantly learning. I'm constantly getting to experiment. I'm constantly getting to play. I'd love to keep doing it. But now that school is over, there is no finish line. I don't know what tomorrow looks like."

And so the journey—the joy of striving toward one's potential—continues.

turning a bowl

As a piece of cherry spins on the lathe, Alex uses a gouge to shape the exterior and then hollow out the interior into a bowl form. All the while, wood shavings are shooting out and piling up around him.

Although Alex watches what is happening closely, he says that what he hears gives him the most information. "I have to listen for the hiss of the tool," he explains. "The sound is telling me whether I'm cutting the wood cleanly or ripping the grain."

Living with a Big Brush

FROM EARLY CHILDHOOD, Charles "Chip" Dort dreamed of becoming an artist. Most of the boys he grew up around in Ipswich, Massachusetts, in the late 1950s and early 1960s wanted to be astronauts or pilots, as he recalls. Chip was much more interested in creating cool stuff with his hands than in any kind of air travel. His mother recounts stories about how, as a toddler, he would pick through the trash in search of materials for art making. "I remember being thrilled because she had thrown away a cylindrical oatmeal container and thinking, 'I can do something great with this,'" he says. He also reminisces about making scrolls with pretend Japanese writing, engineering a mazelike contraption for delivering water colored pink with cake-decorating crystals through a tunnel into a teapot, and carving heraldic crowns into carrots and potatoes for stamping. During elementary school, he painted a mural of a scene from the Revolutionary War on a wall in his classroom, and all the students in the school were paraded through to see his work. Chip was embarrassed by the attention but says, "That teacher was proactive in helping each one of us figure out what turned us on."

Then there was Sister Vincent de Paul and her art classes at the new novitiate in town, off the main road and up a hill. Chip attended the sister's Saturday-morning workshops for two years while in junior high and immersed himself in many types of media, including gouache, oil paints, pastels, and enameling. "I can still hear her voice," Chip recounts. "She said, 'Little brushes are for painting a mouse's eyebrows. Get a big brush. Get in there.' I loved going there. It was the only place or time of the week where I felt like what I thought and felt was important and there was someone to listen to me."

Chip was the eldest of four. His father was a high school biology teacher; his mother stayed at home until all the kids were school-aged and then went back to school herself and became an occupational therapist. Chip was the only family member interested in art and aesthetics. His father built the house they lived in, but not because of any creative urge. Chip explains: "We didn't have money. If we were going to have a house, he would have to build it, so he taught himself how to do it."

This is the same modest, ranch-style home overlooking Ipswich Bay where I meet Chip on a late-summer day and where he shows me the block-printed fabrics he began producing and selling under the brand name Drusus Tabor in 2015, forty-three years after he graduated from high school and left Ipswich for the first time. Chip headed to London to attend the Ravensbourne College of

OPPOSITE, TOP

Chip at Clark Beach, located just down the hill from his house—a favorite place to take walks when he was a moody teenager in the 1960s, as well as today.

OPPOSITE, BOTTOM

A close-up of the block Chip uses to make his Indian Sun fabric. Chip limits the size of his blocks to about eight inches square to ensure that he can print with them comfortably and consistently. He glues flanges onto the backs of his blocks to make them easier to flip and print.

"The feeling I get when I make something I'm pleased with is like no other feeling I experience in my life. It's a calm, quiet sort of jubilation. Other people can think what they want, but that doesn't matter to me if I think it's good and if I'm happy. Now I'm free to move on and make something else."

TOP

An assortment of Chip's pillows and fabrics arranged together on his back deck. Though the patterns Chip makes reflect a lifetime of studying art history, he says, "I don't really care that someone understands that these patterns have a foot in ancient Rome or Egypt or China. If people can understand that there is a historical antecedent to the patterns, great, but that's not first and foremost with me. I just get a kick out of them really loving it."

BOTTOM LEFT

Chip sketches, designs, and carves blocks in the house or, as shown here, on the back deck. He heads to a spare room at his sister's place a few streets away to print them on linen, then ships the fabric to an expert upholsterer to make pillows.

BOTTOM RIGHT

Chip pushes his lino cutting tool through the negative space of the design as precisely as possible in order to ensure that the positive space will print cleanly.

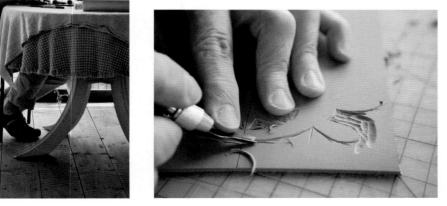

Art and Design, to become, he thought, a painter. Ravensbourne was the first of the five schools he studied at before earning his undergraduate degree in painting from Montserrat College of Art in 1992 and his master's degree in painting and printmaking from Yale University in 1996. Being the eldest as well as single, Chip wasn't all that surprised when, in 2015, it was determined that his elderly parents would need full-time care that he was the family member tasked with tending to them. He is, however, surprised that after so many years of artistic struggle, he has found his creative stride back in Ipswich, carving blocks for printing on his back porch and printing them in a makeshift studio down the road at his sister's place.

On the wall in his parents' living room is a large painting from Chip's thesis show at Yale. The canvas is a remnant of 1950s upholstery cotton with a linear floral print he found in a fabric-store sale bin, on which he layered paint—depicting what looks like Japanese cherry blossoms at the top and gold baroque forms at the bottom. "I was playing with the juxtaposition of different decorative cultures," Chip explains.

Decorative art has always been Chip's passion, and he credits years of studying auction catalogs, from the time he was a teenager on, for much of his knowledge. "I find decorative art—the chairs people sat on, the utensils they used daily—to be a more immediate way of understanding the flavor of a time than the 'important' paintings and sculpture," he says. But this lifelong passion has also made him feel like an outsider in the fine-art world. When one of his first college professors in London told him that his work wasn't serious enough and he had

"too much dash" to be a painter, he took that to mean that he didn't have enough talent and dropped out. At Yale, he says, the faculty—despite admitting him into their MFA program—couldn't comprehend what he was doing and criticized his work for being too decorative (which he interpreted as superficial), not, in their estimation, soul-searching, important, or relevant enough. "I kept casting about, searching for something I could sink my hooks into as a significant cultural, social message," Chip remembers. Without that "imperative" message, he lacked the confidence to exhibit or try to sell his paintings and, in the meantime, found other ways to make a living. This included everything from managing a gourmet store to doing faux-finish paintwork, designing glassware, working with color expert Eve Ashcraft (whom he met while freelancing as a production assistant at *Martha Stewart Living*), and doing sales and research with renowned decorators and antiques dealers Amy Perlin, John Rosselli, and Bunny Williams.

When Chip moved out of his apartment and art studio in New York City in 2015 to return to Massachusetts, he knew he would have to give up painting for a while—he would have neither the time nor the space for it while caring for his parents—but he also knew that he had to find something else to make with his hands. ("Otherwise I would lose my mind," he says.) So he turned to block printing, a medium he had dabbled in over the years, and nearly right away, shapes and patterns began spilling out of him as they never had before. It was as though all the previous decades of searching and struggle had led him to this moment when, with time and space so severely limited, everything he had taken in about the art of other eras and cultures was coming together. He was discovering his artistic voice—and a confidence that had, until then, eluded him.

Within the patterns he cuts into linoleum and then prints on linen, one can see hints of classical Greek vases, medieval shields, chinoiserie, African *kuba* cloth, and 1960s Marimekko prints, plus, of course, the idiosyncrasies produced by his own hands. His color combinations are bold, sometimes surprising, vibrating. At last, he is having fun—and feeling sure enough about his work to show it to the world. "The feeling I get when I make something I'm pleased with is like no other feeling I experience in my life," says Chip. "It's a calm, quiet sort of jubilation. Other people can think what they want, but that doesn't matter to me if I think it's good and if I'm happy. Now I'm free to move on and make something else." The pillows he has made from his fabrics are for sale at Andrew Spindler Antiques & Design, a shop in the nearby town of Essex, where he also works one day a week, and on DrususTabor.com, where he shares his and the brand's point of view: "We believe in the ineffable beauty and grace of handmade things. In today's digitized, mechanized world, true luxury resides in those things made in real time, by a real person, using real materials."

While there are those in the fine-art, and particularly the painting, community who may always see decorative art as lesser, Chip no longer feels that he needs to convince them otherwise or strive to satisfy them. "I was stubborn. I was sabotaging myself," Chip understands now. He had set out to be a painter and felt as though straying from that course would be an admission of defeat, of unacceptable failure, so he kept trying to prove himself to a group of people whose ideas he didn't actually agree with. But now he realizes that he was allowing their belief system to diffuse his own creative expression and, subsequently, holding himself back from full engagement with and enjoyment of his own life.

When we look at his pillows and fabrics arranged beautifully on his deck, near the table where he sits and carves his blocks, he says, "There they are in this big pile, all these ideas and colors and decisions, brought together. This makes me happy because it's very lighthearted and positive."

"It brings home the idea that you have found your voice," I tell him, to which he adds, "Yup. I have. For me, there were times when it seemed like it was never going to happen, like I would drift for the rest of my life from one thing to the next trying to figure out what I am supposed to be doing. *This* is what I'm supposed to be doing."

Chip expects that he will paint again, too, but it will be different from before. "It will be freer, more of an exercise in joy," he says.

Chip will paint with a big brush as Sister Vincent de Paul, clad in her full dark habit and wimple, advised. "She was telling me to cut loose, not to be afraid; to try it, to get in there and muck about. Go for it." And so he shall—on his own terms, in his own way.

LEFT

A display of Chip's pillows alongside a Frances Elkins chair at Andrew Spindler Antiques & Design in Essex.

RIGHT

Chip chose the brand name Drusus Tabor, shown here on his label, to convey an illusion of history and grandeur. Drusus is an ancient Roman name. Tabor was on a wall of names, carved over decades, in an old British boarding school (a photo of which he spotted in *World of Interiors* magazine). He tried out every name on the wall with "Drusus" before making a final decision.

printing day

As Chip block-prints his Gilded Star design at the long table he built for this purpose, he speaks about the allure of the medium: "There's a natural progression that I find satisfying. You can count on it. You have to do this before you do that. There are no shortcuts. It's due diligence." And then there is the suspense and surprise. "You work very hard to carve this thing; you think it is going to print a certain way. Then you get to print it, but you don't see what's happening until you lift the block away. And that's when you find out if you've achieved what you have been hoping for. Is it even better than you thought it would be?"

Work in Progress

AS I ENTER Tif Fussell's mock Tudor home in Sammamish, Washington, among the first sights to catch my eye are the objects hanging on (or otherwise adhered to) the walls of her studio, which occupies about half of the family room. Not only are these objects intriguing in and of themselves, they are also displayed in curious and imaginative ways: A densely embroidered heart in multiple colors, on a swatch of brown knitted wool, is bound within a slightly oversize thrift-store picture frame; the frame, which is wooden and glassless, is nailed on top of a yet bigger sheet of yellowed paper, torn from an old-fashioned order book that is tacked to the wall. A photo of narcissi, swiped from a magazine, with the phrase "Simplify your life" running along the bottom, is taped to the wall, with a narrower rectangular frame (also wooden and without glass) nailed off-center on top of it. There are dioramas with metallic beetles inside of cigar boxes. There are fantastical fabric creatures, dried leaves, and vintage scissors.

That wall—and much of the house— serves as a canvas for Tif's evolving creative interests and moods. For a long period, the aesthetic was bohemian granny-chic: bark cloth–upholstered footstools, aprons stitched from vintage pillowcases, crocheted afghans, and the like. That was the style of "Dottie Angel," a sort of alter ego Tif had created to help her navigate life as an expat British stay-at-home mother of four in a Seattle suburb and in whose voice she blogged for eight years starting in 2007, at the height of the craft blog phenomenon.

Tif explained Dottie Angel in the introduction to her first book, published in 2011, as follows:

dottie angel lives in a rundown cottage overlooking the sea. She has two Airstream trailers in the yard, one is her studio and the other stores her vast collection of vintage notions. Her eight children are homeschooled and spend the day outside running barefoot and their evenings sitting by the fireplace, learning ancient crafting techniques. They never talk back to their mother and always smile. She has several chickens, seven rescued greyhounds and a bearded dragon named Stig. dottie spends most days dressed in an old vintage slip that belonged to her grandmother, which she customized. She thinks to herself, surely everyone dreams of living this life, or at least dressing like they do . . .

dottie, in all her bohemian glory, was all I wished to be at the time but sadly was not. She quickly got under my skin and into my waking thoughts, having a say in everything I crafted. When I went to make an item, there she would be, lurking in the depths of my imagination, encouraging me to be her and to see the world through her eyes. It appeared that with dottie by my side, my rose-coloured spectacles firmly upon my nose and a vintage slip peeking out from under my skirt, I could be who I really wanted to be.

Tif in her studio, an ever-evolving tableau of her creativity, with her dog, Little Olive. She embellished the sweater she is wearing with one of her "woolly tattoos," motifs stitched with wool yarn onto parts of clothing where a flesh tattoo would typically be inked.

Dottie Angel's appeal was international and exuberant—at its height, the blog attracted tens of thousands of readers daily—and it led to Tif's opening an Etsy site where she sold her creations, many repurposed from thrift-store finds, as quickly as she could make them; a line of Simplicity sewing patterns; and two books—first the Dottie Angel "diary" (part of the *Uppercase* magazine Suitcase Series) and then *Granny Chic*, a collection of recipes and projects. For a long time, Dottie Angel elevated Tif's confidence and connected her to an enthusiastic online community with which she would share her photos, projects, and stories. But by 2014, Tif was beginning to feel weighed down by expectations, some real and some admittedly imagined, and the blurring of public and private boundaries. In fact, she felt like her blog persona, and the attention it evoked, had begun to constrain her. She wanted to step back and move on, but she was frightened, not knowing what would come next. And thus began a gradual shedding of an old skin.

By the time I arrived at Tif's house, she was deep into an exploration of a more independent and spiritual side of herself. Metamorphosis—in herself and in the natural world around her—was occupying her thoughts. Though the walls of her studio were still studded with creative manifestations of her ideas, much of the house was spare, and three of her four children had already moved away for college and other pursuits (the fourth was to depart just a few months later).

Sending her children off to explore new worlds was exciting but challenging for Tif, as she had married at twenty-one and began having babies soon after (all four were born within six years); she became a wife and mother, she says, before she even understood who she was as an individual. While Dottie Angel helped her carve out space for her imagination within a busy family life, now she was in virgin territory. Her newfound freedom was enticing in theory, but it left her feeling lost and confused. Ultimately, she found refuge in a yarn shop. After she posted a photo on Instagram of a pair of embroidered, brown leather clog boots she had picked up at a local thrift shop, her friend Jennette messaged to tell her she recognized them: They had originally belonged to another friend, Anna Dianich, who was getting ready to open Tolt Yarn and Wool in the nearby town of Carnation. Jennette felt Tif really should meet her.

"I needed to get out of the house and do something because I was becoming a hermit," Tif recalls. After the two first met, Anna, whom Tif took me to meet at Tolt, remembers thinking, "I want this person in my shop and in my life." Anna hired her to work on the shop floor, then to style the window displays and to teach. And once Tif started working, Anna recalls, "She brought her spark and magic to the shop. She made everyone feel welcome; she put colors together in a way I never would have imagined. Tolt would be totally different if she weren't involved."

In return, the way Tif tells it, Anna and the Tolt community saved her. "It is an extraordinary place," says Tif. "No matter who you are or where you come from,

Tif and I embroidered on our jeans in her studio.

Tif had this floral motif tattooed on her forearm as a good-bye gesture to Dottie Angel, the blog persona in whose voice she wrote while in the throes of raising her four children.

Tif sought out a job at Tolt Yarn and Wool in nearby Carnation, Washington, as way to get out of a funk after she stopped blogging as Dottie Angel and her children began moving away from home.

Tif's passion for knitting and embroidery was rekindled at Tolt.

LEFT

Tif rediscovered the glory of yarn when she started working at Tolt Yarn and Wool. At home, she keeps her well-edited yarn stash in this vintage cabinet.

TOP RIGHT

Along one wall in Tif's bedroom is a rack of Dottie Angel dresses, plus sweaters Tif has embellished with embroidered "woolly tattoos." The Dottie Angel dresses, now available as Simplicity patterns for sewists, began when Tif wanted a dress without fastenings. She cut out the shape from a piece of vintage wallpaper, then cut fabric from yardage in her stash and stitched it together with French seams and bias binding, which she had learned in home economics class as a child. "For me, it was the traditional way to make a garment, with the intention that it would last. I like that the inside is as beautiful as the outside," Tif explains.

you're accepted. The knitting and other stuff is almost secondary." Secondary, but significant: At Tolt, Tif discovered the most alluring array of yarns she had ever encountered, which in turn renewed her interests in knitting and, most of all, embroidery.

Back in the 1980s, in order to complete secondary school in her hometown of Cambridge, England, Tif was required to retake a math course. To fill out her schedule during the extra term, she also enrolled in two electives—embroidery and religious studies—both of which she enjoyed much more than math. While working at Tolt, Tif came up with the idea of embroidering what she calls "woolly tattoos," motifs she stitched with wool yarn onto parts of clothing where a flesh tattoo would typically be inked. One of her first woolly tattoos was her take on a sacred heart, which she placed on the center front of a sweater. For Roman Catholics, the sacred heart is a symbol of Christ's divine love; for Tif—who isn't religious in a typical way, though she has always been attracted to religious paraphernalia and seeks out churches for calming respites—it is a symbol of faith. The idea quickly caught on, and Tif began teaching her unique take on embroidery at Tolt and then farther afield, including at the much-loved Squam retreat,

a twice-yearly getaway for creatives on Squam Lake in New Hampshire.

Tif was no stranger to inked tattoos, having gotten her first ones—a tiny heart on her chest and a couple of butterflies on her lower back—when she was in her mid-twenties. "A small act of rebellion against the traditional mainstream life I was leading," Tif says. Today much of her upper body is covered, with each piece of art representing a different period in her adulthood. On her right forearm is a vintage floral motif (a good-bye gesture to Dottie Angel), and on that upper arm are dogwoods, a remembrance for a beloved pup. On her chest, she's got two swans facing each other with the space between them creating an open-heart center. Swans, Tif explains, are her soul animal. "They look like they are gliding along, but under the surface they're paddling like hell to stay afloat." She is in the process of adding flying insect specimens to her upper back and foresees a composition reminiscent of a vintage bookplate. So far she's got beetles, a cicada, a dragonfly, and, most significant, a moth. "To go into a cocoon and come back out is incredible," Tif says, comparing the moth's metamorphosis to her own: first shutting herself down when her Dottie Angel period concluded and her children started leaving home, then shedding

OPPOSITE, BOTTOM RIGHT

Tif wears one of her "leap of faith" medals every day. She also sells them and teaches classes on how to make them. "I never got a big tick and gold star back in school," Tif says. "All anybody wants sometimes is to be recognized, noted, and seen."

Dottie Angel completely and beginning to reemerge and fly (literally, in some cases, as she has begun accepting teaching opportunities in far-flung locations). "Moths are also attracted to the light," Tif adds. The script on her left forearm reads: "You stand in your own light. Make it shine," a quote from a fortune cookie.

Tif's natural inclination to dress up her body, her language, and her home in a manner that transforms it from ordinary to extraordinary goes back as far as she can remember. However, the imagination that such transformation requires was not validated for her as a child. "I saw myself as a person who failed in school and lacked stick-to-itiveness," Tif says. An avid reader from a young age, she lovingly recalls the quirky characters of fiction that entranced her and kept her company growing up: She wanted to be Pippi Longstocking, living a wild life on her own, riding a horse through the house. She adored the My Naughty Little Sister books as well as the Mrs. Pepperpot series—"I almost dress like Mrs. Pepperpot now, with my bun on top of my head, my apron, and my glasses," she comments while looking at a copy of *Mrs. Pepperpot in the Magic Wood* that she saved from all those years ago. "Those books, and all those little quirky characters not leading the lives they were supposed to lead, transported me to another world," she explains.

I can't help but make the connection to Dottie Angel, a quirky character whom Tif created to help her navigate her personal journey through motherhood, a character she ultimately outgrew just like those books. Tif leaves dottieangel.blogspot.com intact online and continues to receive correspondence from people who discover it. She responds, "I'm delighted she's found you and she's doing for you exactly what she did for me."

After my visit, Tif and I remain in contact by phone, and each time we talk, she reports on her ongoing metamorphosis. In 2017, she and her youngest child, Marlon, launched curious.and.coe, a website and online shop (Coe is Tif's maiden name and the middle name of all her children). In 2019, they expanded with a brick-and-mortar retail space in Carnation called The Fabricated & the Found Atelier. Curious. and.coe began as a way for Tif to tiptoe back into the online world without too much pressure—though there is a place for her to write, in the voice of Milo the cat, Milo contributes only sporadically; in fact, sometimes the site opens with an announcement explaining that it is closed for a while. It was also a way for mother and son to share their first creative collaboration: beetles that Marlon output to Tif's specifications on a 3-D printer and that they embellished together, plus Tif's leap of faith medals and T-shirts with illustrations by Meg, the eldest of the four children. The first T-shirt showcased Meg's depiction of Tif's sacred heart woolly tattoo with the words "I am a w.i.p." in the center. "That is what I am, what we all are," Tif says. "A work in progress."

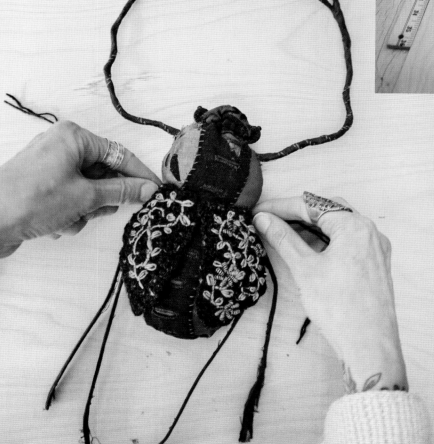

Tif calls this work "Billy Beetle and His Cape of Kindness." To make him, she created a wire form, wrapped it in wadding and tape, then built up the body by patching and piecing vintage cloth. She crocheted, then embroidered, the wings, or "cape of kindness," that she is tying around his body here.

Together Tif and her younger son, Marlon, now run the curious. and.coe website as well as a brick-and-mortar retail boutique/ maker space called The Fabricated & the Found Atelier, in Carnation, Washington. Here they are each wearing a T-shirt with an illustration by Tif's daughter/Marlon's sister Meg.

The Fabricated & the Found Atelier, a five-room, 560-square-foot retail cottage and maker space, is a different kind of stage on which Tif and Marlon can present their ideas. There's a large front yard, dotted with red lanterns and geraniums in season, where knitter friends gather to stitch together; there's the main room and a small lean-to attached to it for sales of Tif's continuously evolving creations, as well as treasures from other sources and fresh flowers; plus a storage area/photo studio for curious.and.coe business and a private studio for Tif.

Tif's husband, Mark, grew up traveling the world, and he and Tif talk about leading a more transient life once he retires from his job at a tech firm, but, for now, Tif says, "I'll find a little bit of happy right where I am." She and Marlon love their work together (Marlon mostly behind the scenes from his home base two hours away and Tif on-site as chief creator, curator, and host). Meg has taken over the management of Squam in New Hampshire from its founder. Daughter Esme is in South America teaching English,

and son Levi is in Europe studying artificial intelligence. A birthday card from Levi is adhered to the refrigerator.

Mum, Mum, Mum . . . You are like the electrons from the sun released as solar waves that get caught in the Earth's magnetic fields. Because sometimes they are overlooked as simple particles, but through miraculous feats, they create the northern lights—wonderful and shining, no matter how hard they work or how many obstacles they have to get to the Arctic! Keep shining! Love, Levi

Ultimately, Tif says she enjoys the freedom she has now that her children are grown, but she is happiest when the whole family—or as she likes to call them, her clan—is together. Her children, she says, are her best teachers and her cheerleaders. "Without a doubt, they have shown me how to be braver and how to grow. I wouldn't be traveling and teaching and opening a new business if they hadn't done that. I've seen the world through their eyes. It's okay to be scared. It's okay to take that step. Anything is possible."

Tif and Marlon collaborated on making these beetles, the first products they sold on their curious. and.coe site. Marlon outputted the insects to Tif's specification on a 3-D printer, Tif painted them, and together they artfully arranged them in cigar boxes, small drawers, and other receptacles they sourced from thrift stores.

An Internal Imperative

WHILE WALKING IN the SoHo neighborhood of Manhattan in early spring 2001, Joelle Hoverson started daydreaming about opening a yarn shop there. As she moved between Houston, Spring, and Canal Streets, amid old-fashioned bakeries, small independent boutiques, and a few of the luxury flagships that were just beginning to move into this downtown district at the time, the daydreaming evolved and became more like a vision—a charming store was beginning to form in her mind's eye.

That vision became Purl Soho, which Joelle opened to the public in August 2002 on a warm, sunny morning forever cast in her memory. "I was nervous and excited. I didn't know if it was going to work," she remembers thinking as she inserted her key in the lock and entered. But this jewel box of a shop, with its old-fashioned aqua facade, checkered tile floor, tin ceiling, and walls lined with a rainbow spectrum of yarns, all in natural fibers, almost instantly caught the attention of devout knitters and curious newcomers alike—as well as of the media. This was, indeed, the height of the turn-of the-millennium knitting boom (and the early days of the modern-day DIY renaissance), and the exquisite Purl became one of its young stars.

Joelle had learned to knit a few years earlier along with colleagues at *Martha Stewart Living* magazine, where she was

an editor. She immediately took to it and spent many months making just scarves, immersed in the simple splendors of color and texture. When she left *MSL* in 2000 to return to a fine-art painting practice and to freelance as a photo stylist, knitting found its way into her life more and more with each passing day. At the painting studio, she fantasized about going home to her apartment to knit; during downtime at photo shoots, she knitted; and when shopping for props for shoots, as she was on that fateful day in 2001, she kept an eye out for special yarns. But there weren't any yarn shops in SoHo at the time. And, in what she describes as "a lightbulb moment," Joelle realized that she could manifest one.

Over the course of the next year, she researched the market, drafted a business plan, secured a loan, and found an affordable space on Sullivan Street, all of which required her to cultivate new skills. In contrast, when it came to designing the store interior, she was firmly within her comfort zone—she had spent four years in the style department at *Martha Stewart Living* learning how to make beautiful things and to stage alluring photographs, and prior to that she had earned an MFA in painting from Yale. Color and high-quality natural fibers were her passion, and she knew she wanted to see an expansive palette of yarn, and nothing but yarn, lining

OPPOSITE

After so many years in the business, Joelle still loves to knit, especially simple, useful things that allow her mind to meld into the soothing rhythm of the stitches. Here she is, with her dogs, Harper and Betty, in her home office in Connecticut, working on a baby towel in linen stitch. "A piece of knitting has all these moments of time in it," Joelle says. "This stitch is a little tighter, that one is a little looser. Overall, the fabric looks the same, but it has this kind of human quality because it is made by hand."

Hot pink is a Purl Soho hallmark, but softer, worn-looking pinks, mauves, and apricots started to seep into Purl's palette after Joelle visited Corsica and was inspired by the sun-washed hues there. One of Joelle's gigs before opening the shop was to develop colors for a line of Martha Stewart Living paint. She went to Stewart's house in Connecticut and mixed pigments and painted swatches based on references she found there, everything from dishes to wall colors to plants. Here she is debating colors for her own company's wares.

TOP

A close-up of the linen-stitch baby towel Joelle was knitting during my visit. The yarn is Purl Soho's Cotton Pure.

BOTTOM LEFT

The facade of Purl Soho on Broome Street. When Joelle opened the original storefront on Sullivan Street, she thought she would manage the shop on her own and spend a lot of time interacting with customers, maybe even sitting with them and knitting. Today she wishes she could do more of just that, but she is usually behind the scenes with her business partners, Page and Jennifer, keeping the enterprise running—and making it beautiful.

"A piece of knitting has all these moments of time in it. This stitch is a little tighter, that one is a little looser. Overall, the fabric looks the same, but it has this kind of human quality because it is made by hand."

the walls (no tags dangling, no distracting sweaters on view—even the shelving was meant to disappear). A charming window display, a central wooden worktable, and a cash register in the rear: those were the only accoutrements included in the small storefront on day one.

While much has changed in the years since—Joelle brought on two partners (her sister Jennifer Hoverson Jahnke and fellow *MSL* alum Page Marchese Norman), moved the store into a larger space a few blocks farther downtown on Broome Street, established a considerable online presence, and expanded into other areas of textile creation—it is color, natural fibers, and the joy of making with her own hands and sharing what she loves with others that still inspire her. Although for a long time she thought that all she wanted to do was paint, she has come to realize that her raison d'être, the mission that makes her feel whole, is not limited to painting (though it is related to her painting practice). Her motivation is celebrating color and form and creating beauty, and working with her hands is integral to that. "It's the point of my whole life," she tells me as we sit and talk at her kitchen table in Easton, Connecticut.

It was the conceptual part of painting—the constant quest for higher meaning, which seemed so crucial at Yale—that tripped her up and led her to give it up for a long time. "I am passionate about painting, not art as a vehicle to express something else. I want to do color and make space out of a two-dimensional surface," she explains. With knitting, the intention is more straightforward. "I've never had to deal with that layer of 'What does this mean? What am I trying to say?' that snagged me as an art student," she says. "I'm knitting this because it's beautiful and warm and I want the experience of making it, then wearing it or giving it away."

Joelle now divides her time between an apartment she shares with her husband and stepdaughter on the Upper West Side of Manhattan and the house in Easton, where she spends most weekends on her own with her dogs, gardening, making pottery, and—after a sixteen-year hiatus—painting again. When she's in the city during the week, she meets with the Purl Soho team to collaborate on the many facets of the constantly growing business, including their website, which reaches thousands of customers daily, new craft projects (which they design, write instructions for, and photograph to post on their website), and the new products they are continually developing, including a full range of Purl Soho–branded yarns and knitting, sewing, quilting, and embroidery kits. Like her early employer Martha Stewart, Joelle and her team have cultivated a brand with a strong and distinctive point of view: sophisticated, fresh color palettes; classic, unfussy styling; and the most straightforward of techniques.

A collection of white objects plus a nautilus shell in Joelle's home office. She made the cylinders on the middle shelf and the bowl on the left on the bottom shelf.

When Joelle arrives in Connecticut, she checks on her plants and picks flowers to bring inside. "I love weedy, crazy flowers," she says about the overgrown asparagus, California poppies, and Queen Anne's lace shown here.

A few of Joelle's porcelain bowls, plus a handmade brass spoon.

Co-owning and comanaging the Purl Soho enterprise, which also includes a warehouse run by her sister in California, can be stressful, Joelle admits. She has had to exercise discipline to maintain balance in her life, much of which comes from her commitment to spending time in the country every week. While the interior of her small nineteenth-century Federal-style house was once quite colorful, it is now a study in mostly white and gray, providing her with a serene reprieve from the multihued Purl Soho universe and the hustle of city life. She took up pottery in 2015; she attends a class at a nearby art center on Saturdays and contentedly creates pots at her wheel in her attic studio on Sundays. "It is meditative and a pure exploration of form and materials," Joelle tells me as her hands transform a mound of smooth porcelain clay into a cylindrical vessel with a narrow opening at the top. This is a form that Joelle has been practicing for a while, and it recently struck her as an upside-down version of the bowls she made when she first began to throw: Though shaped very differently on the wheel, they are the same in their essence.

At Yale, Joelle struggled to connect with what one of her professors called her internal imperative: that is, the work that would flow from her naturally when her creativity was unhindered. But with her pottery, she began to recognize it, which, in turn, led her to pick up her paints and brushes again and set up an easel in her attic. "Your hand and your mind go together, and you get what you get based on that internal imperative. The voice that comes out is who you are as an artist. The forms that come out are your forms," she says. It is what makes an artist's work recognizable, part of the reason we can differentiate a painting by Renoir from one by Monet even without seeing the artist's signature.

Though Joelle would surely demur if I were to compare what she does to the great Impressionists, I do, in fact, recognize her internal imperative in all of it. There is a clarity and honesty to the porcelain vessel Joelle brought forth before my eyes, just as there is in the baby towel she knit in squishy cotton while we talked during our photo shoot and in the paintings she began making just a few months later.

Pottery, she believes, was the gateway that allowed her to come full circle, from turning away from painting to eventually re-embracing it. Totally separate from her work in the knitting world and from any expectations of "success," or even of functionality, it brought her back to the pure joy of exploring color and form with her hands. "Ideally," she says, "I would like to weave or knit some cloth, put a bowl on it, paint it or photograph and print it, make the whole world of it."

An Artful Life

BRITTANY WATSON JEPSEN started her blog, The House That Lars Built, in 2008. She was a graduate student in Washington, DC, studying interior design at the Corcoran School of the Arts & Design. For an assignment in one of her first classes, she was tasked with designing the interior of a family home. Whereas all the other students went the conventional route—creating physical client books—Brittany developed a blog to present her ideas as well as her progress to her fictitious clients: a family seeking a home that reflected their artful life, born in her imagination. Lars, the father, was a fashion designer; Imogen, the mother, was a fine-art painter; and children April Showers and Abraham pursued their interests in crafts and music. The previous summer, Brittany had discovered the burgeoning world of design blogs while interning for designers Jonathan Adler and Celerie Kemble and was intrigued by the platform, then in its infancy. Her first postings on The House That Lars Built included floor plans, furniture specs, digital renderings, design inspiration, and mood boards for each room.

Today The House That Lars Built blog has grown into a full-fledged online business, with Brittany as the creative director and master influencer at the helm. It is positioned around the same "artful life" theme she used for her fictitious

family's home, but with an added emphasis on DIY projects. The DIY part is thanks to Brittany's natural affinity for making things—and her love for making them beautiful—as well as a series of seemingly random events.

During the summer of 2009, between her first and second years at the Corcoran School, Brittany enrolled in a six-week textile design course at the Danish Design School in Copenhagen. Before setting off, she wrote to over two dozen blogs to offer her services as an intern-correspondent in Scandinavia. The only one to respond was Design*Sponge, a trailblazer of that era. In classes in Copenhagen, Brittany learned about color and repeat patterns as well as screen- and digital printing, and she visited the studios of prominent designers and factories where textiles were produced, including the famed Marimekko headquarters in Helsinki, Finland. During downtime, she traveled throughout Scandinavia to interview interior, product, and stationery designers and photograph their homes and studios for Design*Sponge. In the midst of all that activity, she met Paul Jepsen, whom she would marry a year later. While Brittany's work for Design*Sponge helped her draw readers to her own site, which was still very small, the attention her wedding photos generated turned out to be the game

Brittany standing in front of *What Are You Waiting For?*, a mural she art directed as part of a marketing campaign for Dove chocolate. The bold theme is in keeping with her perspective on life, and even the way she dresses. "When I returned home from my mission to Brazil, I had tons of confidence," she explains. "I decided that life was too short to dress boring, and I've been going with that motto ever since."

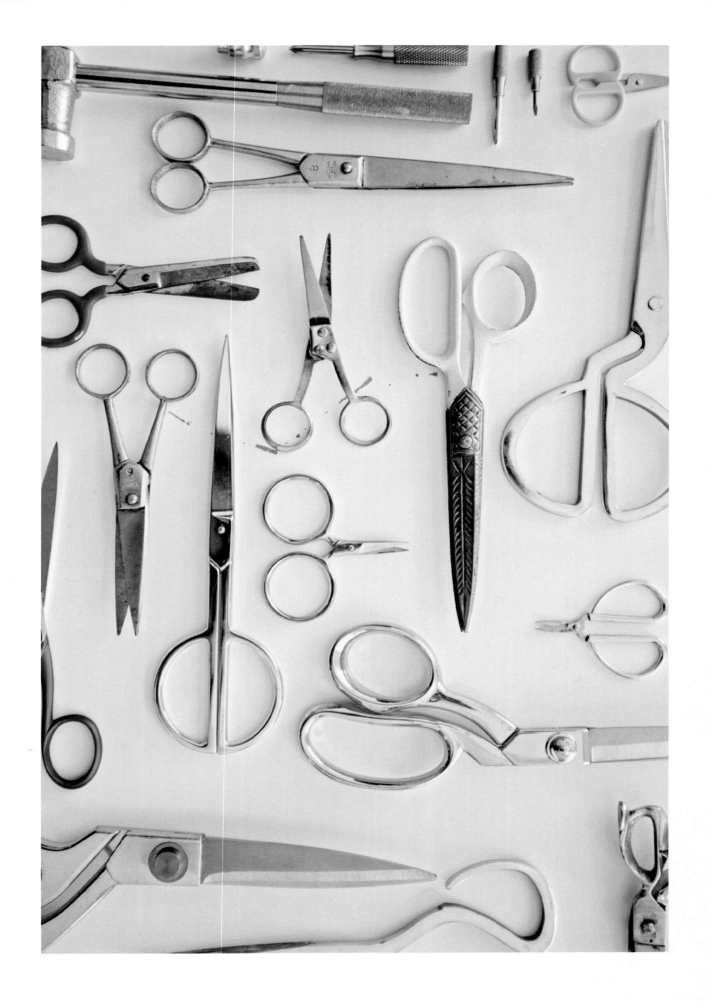

changer that drew in the most followers and put her on the design blog map.

For the fun of it, Brittany had decided to treat her wedding in Southern California, where she grew up, like a full-on art and design project. Her outdoor garden reception was, for her, a chance to create a fantastical wonderland that reflected her love of crafting, flowers, and fashion, as well as the story of her courtship with Paul in Denmark and her own Danish heritage. There were carefully curated mood boards and palettes, letter-pressed invitations addressed with calligraphy, hand-painted banners and table aprons, and bow ties sewn out of Liberty of London florals. But, probably more than anything, it was the paper flowers that set the mood. For the centerpieces, walkways, and stairs, Brittany and her mom and sister transformed art paper into gigantic (eighteen-inch-wide) poppies inspired by the landscape in the story *Thumbelina* by Hans Christian Andersen, arguably Denmark's most famous writer. Her bouquet was a humongous paper poppy, watercolored in blush tones on a three-foot stem. The overall effect evoked a cross between an enchanted fairy-tale garden and the set of a high-fashion photo shoot.

Brittany posted photos from the wedding on her private Facebook page after the reception, and right away, a colleague from her internship at Jonathan Adler linked her to a friend at the 100 Layer Cake blog who asked her to produce a paper-flower tutorial. Next came requests from other wedding and craft blogs for DIY projects, then from new fans around the world who wanted to buy finished flowers. The couple had returned to Copenhagen to live, but Brittany didn't have her Danish working papers yet, so she was relieved to find this small stream of income. She opened an Etsy shop, began posting on Pinterest and Instagram, and amped up her own blog, where readership was continuing to grow thanks to the traffic her contributions to other sites was generating. Among the customers who found her via social media platforms were fashion designer Vivienne Westwood, who was considering using the mega-size flowers for displays, and the retailer Terrain, which ordered five hundred miniature poppy, ranunculus, and rose gift toppers to sell in their shops.

By 2011, Brittany had been granted her working papers but had not yet found a formal job, so she kept on chugging along as one idea led to another, including a decision to travel to London for the wedding of Prince William and Kate Middleton and to design and sell royal wedding memorabilia. While the memorabilia—a plate, mug, tote

"I feel you appreciate your belongings more if you have some hand in making them."

bag, and print—was meant to be the focus and sold well from her station on Portobello Road, at some English boutiques, and from her Etsy shop, it was Brittany's hat, festooned with one of her huge pink paper roses, that garnered the most attention, landing a photo of her on *Vogue UK*'s website and on CNN's homepage.

This full-on, no-holds-barred approach to the royal nuptials—not to mention her graduate school assignment and her wedding design—reflects her bold, goal-oriented attitude toward life in general. "I have always thought of myself as coming from this great heritage, from people who did really cool things, and that has fueled me and made me want to do cool things myself," Brittany explained to me as we sat together in her office in the House That Lars Built headquarters, which were, at the time, in Springville, Utah, at the base of the Wasatch Mountains. For starters, her mother and aunt both danced for George Balanchine at the New York City Ballet in the 1960s; another aunt was a successful television actress; her paternal great-grandfather was the president of the American Dental Association. Many of Brittany's ancestors were Mormons who made the arduous crossing of the plains from the Midwest to Utah by foot and in

covered wagons in the mid-1800s, including Patty Sessions, her fifth great-grandmother, a midwife whose prized journals provide historians with a firsthand account of daily life at the time and a record of thousands of births.

During her childhood, Brittany, her three younger siblings, and her parents lived in Dana Point in Orange County, California, and she vividly recalls visits to her grandmother Dorothy's house about an hour and a half north in Bel Air (back then a small, cozy Los Angeles neighborhood). "Her sewing room was legendary to me," Brittany says. From there, Dorothy made all her own clothing and taught Brittany and her sister to sew. "She had a cabinet full of fabric. We would sew clothing for a Shirley Temple doll and for ourselves," Brittany remembers. "And I would sew things at home and gift them to her for Christmas. She always expressed how grateful she was, which taught me the value of a handmade gift." Back in Dana Point, Brittany's mother was no slouch in the crafting department either. A trained interior designer, she posted a sign on the family refrigerator that read A Creative Mess Is Better Than Tidy Idleness.

"Our house was messy because we were always making things," Brittany

TOP & CENTER RIGHT

While I was visiting, the Lars team worked together to make paper-flower crowns for some of the young girls who would be in the upcoming wedding party of blog coordinator Becca Hansen (seated at left).

CENTER LEFT & BOTTOM LEFT

Inspired by a Chanel couture runway show featuring massive, mechanized blooming paper flowers in Paris's Grand Palais, Brittany created this charming tablescape adaptation for the blog.

BOTTOM RIGHT

Brittany and her team created this tablescape inspired by traditional blue-and-white porcelain, complete with five vases made out of painted recycled cardboard.

remembers. Painting, coloring, sewing. "My mother was super-experimental." One of Brittany's most vivid memories of her creative aspirations as a child was trying to emulate the folk-art style of her hero Mary Engelbreit, an illustrator who licensed her images for use on all sorts of products, from greeting cards to housewares, and also ran her own magazine, *Mary Engelbreit's Home Companion*. In response, Brittany's mother encouraged her creative daughter to paint her Engelbreit-inspired motifs directly onto old family furniture.

Brittany fantasized about studying for an undergraduate degree in interior design at Brigham Young University in Provo, Utah, but she didn't have the portfolio required for admission to that program—having spent her high school years focused on academics, tennis, and the cello—or the confidence to figure out how to put one together. Instead, she studied art history, thinking she'd become a historian or work at a museum, but an internship during her last semester with the research department at the National Museum of Women in the Arts in Washington, DC, convinced her otherwise. In the windowless office where she was stationed, she realized that she felt more in sync with the artists visiting to study the collections than to the administrators and academics. After graduation, she managed to land a job in the interior design department of a major hotel chain, but she realized quickly that she needed more skills.

Fortunately, her undergraduate experience had imbued her with the courage she needed to finally put together a portfolio, as had an eighteen-month mission to Brazil in between her sophomore and junior years. This voluntary church program involved learning to speak Portuguese, living in remote villages, participating in service projects, setting goals, and sharing her Mormon faith. "It was," she recalls, "the hardest and one of the most rewarding things I have ever done." The experience was such a confidence booster that by the time she entered the Corcoran School graduate program in the fall of 2007, she was on her own mission: to eke every last drop of value from this opportunity, which she was taking out loans to pay for. Brittany figured out right away that her primary interest was adornment: anything to which she could apply pattern or color. And that led her to Denmark to study textile design and, eventually, to marrying and living there with Paul until the end of 2012, at which point the couple decided to move to Provo, where Paul enrolled in an English literature degree program at BYU.

Back in the States, Brittany was the main breadwinner—this time Paul was the one without working papers—so she immediately began job hunting. Simultaneously, companies who wanted to sponsor her blog content began approaching her, and she gradually realized that she had a viable business on her hands. Among her clients that first year (2013) were Microsoft, Caesarstone, and EuroLighting. Since then she has collaborated with many more companies, big and small, including True

Value, Godiva, Coca-Cola, and Netflix. Over time she has hired help, taken on a business partner with a master's in art business from Sotheby's Institute of Art, and moved the office out of her living room and into first the raw 3,000-square-foot space in an old industrial building on a dairy farm where I met her, and later into a four-bedroom nineteenth-century house about ten minutes away in Spanish Fork.

These days, Brittany and her team post on their site every weekday, mixing homegrown unsponsored content with, several times a month, paid campaigns. Although craft tutorials remain the big draw for Lars readership, the content covers many facets of interior design as well as travel, home-keeping, party planning, fashion, and art. Brittany sees clients whose products aren't obviously aligned with craft as among the most interesting. "There's always this thought that this could be super-tacky, and to some people it could look like selling out, but I like to think about what I can do with it to make it awesome and beautiful and still read House That Lars Built." Often, these turn out to be Brittany's favorite projects. For example, for Capital One, the Lars team created a floral paper swag for a wedding getaway car, and for the EcoScraps soil company, they created a Polish planter-chandelier called a *pajaki*.

While the blog landscape has changed and the format is no longer as popular as it once was, the House That Lars Built readership has remained steady in the hundreds of thousands, and Brittany and her business partner are exploring ways of growing their enterprise, including product design, retail, video, and collaborations with other artists.

Brittany's long-term intention is to become a full lifestyle brand. Interestingly, while she understands the importance of social media in her business model, she doesn't look to it for creative inspiration nearly as often as she used to. On Instagram, for example, she bemoans creative homogenization. "It's awesome that we can be in the same kind of tribe all across the world," she says. "But we need people to continue telling their own stories." She worries about skills being lost, about artists being lured by ideas that make them more popular on social media but result in a sameness in their work.

To keep her own ideas fresh, Brittany goes back to somewhat "old-school" ways: She travels, references her library of art books, and draws upon the knowledge, tools, and perspective she gained during her undergraduate and graduate school education. Then she adds her own unique flair, the seeds of which were surely planted by her ancestors "who did really cool things."

OPPOSITE

"Live Artfully" is the House that Lars Built motto. Here, the sign sits next to a wedding-day photo of Brittany and her mom, who Brittany says is the most creative person she has ever met.

TOP

Brittany dreams of running a full lifestyle brand with a handmade theme running through it. "I feel you appreciate your belongings more if you have some hand in making them," she says.

BOTTOM LEFT

These grade school reports attest to Brittany's long-standing attraction to art and flowers.

BOTTOM RIGHT

During my visit, Brittany was tracking the progress of two projects on a wall in her office: (top) photography for her first book, *Craft the Rainbow*, and (bottom) early ideas for expanding the retail side of the Lars website.

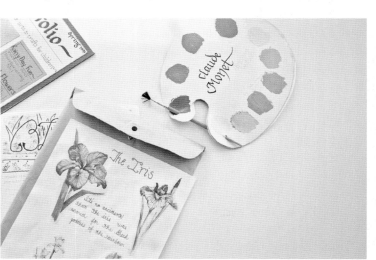

I Make, Therefore I Am

LABYRINTH, FAIRY TALE, fantasy, carnival, treasure chest, bazaar, wonderland . . . all these words come to mind when I step inside Nathalie Lété's enchanting two-level studio, housed in a former iron factory complex in Ivry-sur-Seine, a southern suburb of Paris. I hear birds chirping and at first assume they are coming from the white canary in a wire cage near a wall of windows, but the chirping is a sound track Nathalie plays because she likes to feel as though she's in the forest when she works.

Nathalie is simultaneously down-to-earth and ethereal, waiflike and modelesque—she looks as though she could be a ballerina. She is wearing a blue, paint-splattered apron over a blue dress, a hand-knitted mohair lace cardigan, cherry-red tights, blue Converse high-tops, a beaded necklace, and a silk floral scarf of her own design. The scarf is wrapped around her neck in that effortlessly chic way that seems to be in a Frenchwoman's DNA. Or maybe it just comes from spending one's life in France, since Nathalie, though a French citizen since age twelve, is the only child of a German mother and a Chinese father.

Nathalie's fascination with fairy tales began early and was nourished by her mother, who read them to her at bedtime and dressed her in a red cape that earned her the nickname le Petit Chaperon Rouge (or Little Red Riding Hood), and her

beloved grandmother, who, when Nathalie visited her in Bavaria in wintertime, would take her into the forest to fill mangers with straw for the deer. About those early walks, Nathalie wrote the following for an article in *Flow* magazine:

Cela m'a profondément marquée. Elle était habillée de façon traditionelle, tablier et foulard sur la tête. . . . Je me voyais princesse d'une forêt enchantée, entourée de biches, de nains, de champignons, de fleurs magiques et même du prince charmant. (That affected me profoundly. She was dressed in a traditional way, apron and head scarf. . . . I saw myself as a princess of an enchanted forest, surrounded by does, dwarves, mushrooms, magical flowers, and even Prince Charming.)

Her childhood wasn't easy, as her parents did not get along well (and, ultimately, divorced) and her father was involved in some precarious business dealings that put the household on edge both economically and emotionally. The art she makes today, she says, is very much like that which she created as a child, reflecting an imaginary, fairy tale–like world in which she continues to seek refuge. "When I am making my art, I feel calm. I feel with myself. I am not thinking about outside," she says. "I'm not interested in speaking about the real world. Modernity doesn't interest me. I can survive if it is terrible outside. I feel it is easier when you are a bit cut off from

OPPOSITE, LEFT

Nathalie at her painting desk, in front of the large picture window in her studio.

OPPOSITE, RIGHT

A detail of Nathalie's painting *Les Lapins* (*Rabbits*).

TOP

Hand-sewn and
-painted dolls, part of
a butchery series that
began with drawings
that evolved into dolls,
then ceramic pieces,
then meat motifs on
a variety of products,
including rugs and
plates.

BOTTOM & OPPOSITE

The two-level studio is
packed with Nathalie's
artwork as well as
samples of products
from the many
companies with which
she collaborates.

others and you do things your own way." And it is alone in her studio that Nathalie is able to spend most of her time now that her children (a son and a daughter) are young adults.

Nathalie grew up in another Parisian suburb southwest of this studio and the home, also in this complex, where she now lives with her family. "We work all the time," Nathalie tells me about herself and her husband, artist Thomas Fougeirol, whose studio neighbors Nathalie's and whose minimalist, abstract paintings exploring absence and disappearance could hardly be more different from her own multicolored, narrative expressions. What Nathalie shares with her husband, she says, is devotion to their creative purpose. "We both have complete passion for what we are doing. We understand why the other one's mind is always so self-focused because we are the same in that way."

Nathalie's propensity for making by hand—everything from drawing and painting to knitting, crochet, silkscreen, and ceramics—has been with her for as long as she can remember. As a teenager, she sold her drawings and hand-painted silk scarves to earn pocket money and to help support her family; however, upon finishing her *baccalauréat* (the French equivalent of a high-school diploma), she did not imagine pursuing a career as a maker. She thought she might become a flight attendant, which she saw, like her art, as a means of escape, but with a surer path to financial security. Before applying for an airline job, however, Nathalie went to see an astrologer who was so certain she could become a successful artist that she convinced her to change course. Nathalie went on to study fashion at Paris's École des Arts Appliqués and then lithography at the famed École des Beaux-Arts (the same school where Renoir and Matisse and so many French masters learned to paint), finishing in 1993 and never looking back. She credits the rigor of the program at the École des Arts Appliqués for helping her develop her work ethic as well as her understanding of the commercial side of creative production. At Beaux-Arts, she had a well-equipped studio at her disposal day and night, so plenty of time to refine her technique.

Today Nathalie earns a living as an independent artist by creating one-of-a-kind artwork, designing products to sell directly to customers, and licensing imagery for use on a vast array of goods around the world—from children's puzzles and lunch boxes to cosmetics and clothing to fabric and wallpaper. As when she was a child, she moves from medium to medium as her interests dictate, unfazed by distinctions and judgments others like to make about the value of art vs. craft vs. manufactured goods. "In fact, I don't care," she says. "I wouldn't like to work only with art galleries. To work with a fashion brand is as interesting to me as working with an architect or with a butcher shop." Actually, pieces from a meat-themed series Nathalie began out of her own curiosity did make it into a Parisian butcher's window, as well as into a 2015 retrospective of her work at the La Piscine museum in Roubaix in northern France, and into John Derian's boutique in New York.

Although many of the products Nathalie designs these days are ultimately produced by others, they all begin in her studio. "Making things with my hands makes me feel happy and optimistic and gives me confidence," Nathalie explains. "People say, 'I think, therefore I am.' I say, 'I make, therefore I am.'" And by extension, she is drawn to what others make by hand as well. "I am attracted to things in which I can feel the human hand—its gesture, its force, its patience, its dexterity," which is in keeping with her affection for folk art, and the desire to make the most utilitarian of objects beautiful for the enhancement of everyday life.

Nathalie's creative vision is, indeed, all-encompassing. Each product is more than a single object, she says, but part of a larger story. For her showroom in the center of Paris, about 400 square feet in a former button factory, she created a full living space—kitchen and bath included—with nearly every detail made and/or designed by her: It began with an entire ceramic wall, consisting of three hundred tiles on which she hand-painted birds amid more abstract, decorative motifs. (About painting birds, she wrote in her 2017 book, *In the Garden of My Dreams*, "When I paint them, their

CENTER

Nathalie has some of her paintings reproduced on silk scarves (like the one shown here). Although she often works with seemingly childlike imagery, the overall effect somehow transcends age. When I mention to her that there is a darkness in her work despite the seeming sweetness of many of her subjects, she says matter-of-factly, "It is like life."

BOTTOM RIGHT

Nathalie walking outside her studio with her dachshund, Spike. She can easily visit her husband's studio, which is in the same building, or head home, just a five-minute walk from here, in the same complex (a former iron factory where part of the Eiffel Tower was built).

"I am attracted to things in which I can feel the human hand—its gesture, its force, its patience, its dexterity."

OPPOSITE, TOP

In the garden (meant to look like a forest floor) in front of Nathalie's studio sits a chair upholstered with fabric she designed, plus a hand-embroidered cushion based on her artwork. The flower stool is an extra piece from the collection of custom furniture that she commissioned a local woodworker to create for her Paris showroom.

OPPOSITE, CENTER & BOTTOM

Nathalie sewing a prototype Bambi doll using fabric from the Japanese fashion and textile brand Minä Perhonen. This collaboration was organized to coincide with the release of a new edition of the Austrian author Felix Salten's original Bambi story (published by Cernunnos), which Nathalie illustrated.

free spirits embody me, and I can feel the freedom they must have when they fly in the sky.") A nest-like bed is suspended from the ceiling, its interior walls hand-painted with flowers. Nearby are a wooden tree sculpture and a table, chair, and stools sculpted to look like flowers.

Similarly, in collaboration with the French department store chain Monoprix, Nathalie has created all-immersive pop-up shops. In Tokyo, her fans can shop at Le Monde de Nathalie, a retail space stocked only with her creations. For customers who desire a similar albeit less encompassing effect, Nathalie enjoys painting display windows, something she has done many times in Japan and also at Loop in London and at Anthropologie on New York's Fifth Avenue. And for herself, she is refurbishing a hilltop nineteenth-century house on the edge of the Fontainebleau forest, a home in the country where the fantasy world of her art will merge more intimately than ever with her daily reality. There, every surface will become a canvas, no detail too small for her creative attention. "An art house," she says, "because I have to express myself."

A few months after visiting Nathalie in her studio, I see her again in New York, at a book signing for *In the Garden of My Dreams.*

When I walk in, she is seated behind a table festooned with fresh flowers, a stack of books, and some art supplies she has brought with her from France. She stands up and greets me warmly, then returns to her work, which includes composing a personal note and a special illustration with colored pencils and rubber stamps (her own owl, deer, and tree) for each book and its recipient. While guests mill around chatting and sipping wine, Nathalie sits peacefully at her table working. Dressed in jeans and a sweater with a floral-garland motif based on her artwork (a limited edition for the Japanese brand Antipast), and with butterfly clips glittering in her hair, she looks serene and safe, somehow present but separate from the hubbub of customers around her. Elegant and chic and with a childlike focus, she is absorbed in a world of her own making.

All My Life Is in That Quilt

THE FIRST TIME I meet Mandy Pattullo, I am at Chateau Dumas (see page 134) in the small village of Auty in southwestern France. She is teaching Thread and Thrift, her textile collage workshop, and I am pitching in as her assistant. Basically, this means that I will prepare materials that the twenty of us enrolled in the class will need to complete the series of projects she has planned for our busy week together. On the first morning, she asks me to cut swatches out of a vintage comforter so that each of us will have a piece to unstitch in order to access the multiple layers of fabric of which it is composed. Next I carefully wrap twenty different worn men's leather wallets, sourced from French flea markets, in navy-blue linen and place them in a basket so that each of us can then choose one "blindly" and transform it into a book of cloth pages. Later, I cut and press long lengths of vintage floral fabric, once curtains in the château, to be used as the base for accordion books that will unfold into panoramic tales.

Throughout the week, Mandy talks to us about composition, color, repurposing, and visual storytelling, and teaches us collage, appliqué, paper-piecing, embroidery, and finishing techniques. We hear about her influences (among them, French American artist Louise Bourgeois, American artist Robert Rauschenberg, and the quilters

of Gee's Bend) and her pet peeves (appliquéing with iron-on adhesive instead of hand stitches, the appropriation of Japanese *boro* textiles by Western makers, and the term "textile artist" as opposed to simply "artist"). We also enjoy her unique wit, a surprising blend of merry and offbeat epitomized in the doll that we come to call Julie, whom Mandy picked up for a few francs at the village's flea market to repurpose her dress fabric and who, in her underclothes, ultimately becomes our class mascot, mysteriously and mischievously moving around the château and into the neighboring cemetery.

Mandy designed a thorough and challenging curriculum for our time together, giving us a sense of what it might have been like to be a student of hers at Newcastle College in northern England, where she taught from 2000 to 2007. Back then, Mandy was instructing undergraduates enrolled in the school's textile program, encouraging them to push the boundaries of surface pattern techniques and media and training them to foresee commercial clothing and interior design trends, but with us she was doing something quite different: tasking us to pick apart old quilts, establish a connection to makers of the past, and create something personally resonant in response. Exiting her position as head of the department marked a turning point in her

"It is important to me to continually tell women's histories and stories and appreciate the beauty of things that were created in the domestic space."

Mandy works full-time in her studio at the Hearth in Horsley, Northumberland (about a fifteen-minute drive from her home) unless she is away teaching. "I want to be making work that is seen and is taken seriously. Having a studio that people see you working in is quite important. They take you more seriously than if you are doing lap work in front of the TV."

Mandy gathers fabrics she thinks might combine well on clipboards. Once she begins working, she rarely has a specific plan but rather lets the work evolve organically.

As we sit and talk in her attic studio at the Hearth arts center in Horsley, Mandy points out the south-facing window, and says, "The first quilts in the United Kingdom were made not very far from here in County Durham. I'd never felt at home in the northeast, but when I started buying these old quilts after leaving teaching, I suddenly felt grounded in this region. At that time, quilts were selling very cheaply and weren't particularly appreciated."

Mandy's studio brims with inspiration and in-progress and finished works.

career and the beginning of her life as an artist, Mandy explains. "The world I'd been in—training students to work in the fashion industry, taking them to fashion shows in Paris—suddenly seemed very shallow. All I wanted to do was unpick an old quilt, look at the layers of history, and reuse them in some way." Through the slow process of removing the stitches and repurposing the timeworn fabrics, Mandy began imagining the lives of the original makers, then creating work that honored them and was meaningful to her.

"The feminist movement for a while disparaged items that were made in domestic settings," Mandy remarks when we meet again nine months later in Newcastle, where she has lived since leaving her hometown in Norfolk in the 1970s. Despite the subservience—or in some cases, boredom or lack of choice—that may have led many women toward needlework,

"that doesn't mean the work they did and the stories around them weren't valuable and important," Mandy insists.

"All my life is in that quilt." This phrase, which Mandy backstitched onto a vintage cotton crazy quilt, came from one of her many books on the history of quilting and quilters (though she doesn't remember which). "I like this quote because it sums up why we do what we do. It is about using the scraps, it is about putting time into something, it is about the thoughts and discussions that have gone on while making, it is about family and societal events that have occurred in the time frame of the quilt's making. There is a feeling of pride there."

Mandy and I are sipping tea in her attic studio at the Hearth, an arts center in a restored Victorian church manse in the rural village of Horsley, about ten miles west of her home. Surrounding us is evidence of the great pleasure Mandy takes in handwork and the reverence she feels for past makers, including her own grandmother, with whom she was very close growing up and who sewed most of her and her sister's clothing—as well as their dolls' clothing. "When my first grandchild was born, I suddenly had an appreciation for what she did for us," Mandy explains. "I wanted to reflect and connect her and me by spending a lot of time hand-stitching notes from her diaries."

Mandy backstitched this simple yet powerful phrase, found in a history book, onto a vintage quilt.

Mandy often works with fabrics she unpicks from utility quilts of England's north country, dating back to the nineteenth and early twentieth century. A machine-sewn top might reveal any manner of hand-quilted layers beneath: blankets, wool, old clothes, lace curtains, even a worn-out quilt of a previous generation. "Women in the past saved every little scrap of fabric and used it in patchworks," Mandy explains. "I carry on that tradition."

17 May 1967: "Jill came up in the evening and we lengthened the children's summer frocks."

12 July 1968: "Started making Mandy's two two [sic] *at 7 o'clock P.M. Finished at 5AM Saturday morning."*

Mandy stitched these entries, carefully reproducing her grandmother's wobbly script, onto narrow lengths of cloth that she pieced together from fragments unpicked from debilitated quilts in her collection. "I put time and love into it by actually piecing tiny bits together into a linear form before I even started to embroider," Mandy elaborates. "I could have easily embroidered onto cotton tape, but I wanted to use something that I use all the time and to bring my love for north country quilts and her experience together in this work."

In 2016, that work became part of a solo exhibition called *Worn* at the Customs House in South Shields, and now it is in her studio, reeled onto thread bobbins placed on and around her grandmother's black Singer sewing machine and alongside a black-and-white photo (circa 1978) of her grandparents in their barn plucking

chickens for a local butcher. "They were very poor and always trying to make ends meet by doing extra jobs," Mandy recalls.

11 November 1968: "Plucked chickens and pheasants for Walter for 15 shillings."

Although Mandy grew up enjoying drawing and enthusiastically completed the Penelope needlepoint kit her parents gifted to her each Christmas, she was generally disinterested in needlework. Her grandmother took care of making and mending her clothes. At school, stitching lessons, which focused more on neatness than on creativity, bored Mandy. She went to a convent school and was taught by nuns whom she despised. "I was quite a truant," she recalls. It wasn't until a holiday break from Newcastle University, where she was studying library science, that Mandy's curiosity was piqued when she saw her mother paper-piecing hexagons to make a patchwork quilt. "I joined two hexagons together, and I was immediately hooked," Mandy remembers. She went on to spend every spare moment for several years making conventional quilts, many of them

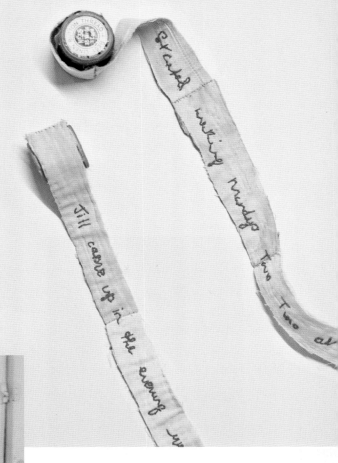

TOP RIGHT

Reflecting on memories of her beloved grandmother, Mandy decided to hand-stitch lines from her grandmother's diaries onto lengths of thin patched-together coverlet remnants. Though this work is very personal, it also speaks to Mandy's broader vision. "It is important to me to continually tell women's histories and stories and appreciate the beauty of things that were created in the domestic space," she explains.

BOTTOM

Mandy keeps elements from her 2016 art exhibition called *Worn*, including her grandmother's sewing machine and lengths of cloth stitched with entries from her diary, on display in the studio.

Mandy combines fabric collage and embroidery to create portraits, often of animals, that she sells to an avid customer base. She enjoys creating and selling these works but admits that sometimes commercial work becomes a distraction from her deeper and more personal explorations.

Mandy at her garden
allotment, which she
has been tending
for more than thirty
years and where she
goes every afternoon,
in season, before
returning home from
her studio. "It creates a
barrier between home
and work, which I want,
because otherwise I'd
leave my studio and
go home and feel a bit
resentful that I have
to leave something I'm
really involved in."

On the cloth wrapped
around the handle
of her grandmother's
worn-down gardening
fork, Mandy hand-
stitched a quote from
her grandmother's
diary on the day
she acquired it—
November 11, 1969:
"Ken went to an
auction at Watton and
brought home a fork
for the garden." About
gardening, she says,
"I like having my hands
in the soil, picking
out little seedlings
with my fingers, the
physical work of
digging, changing a
piece of bare earth
into something that
is productive and
beautiful to look at,"
all of which, she says,
she learned from her
grandmother.

out of the Laura Ashley scrap fabric that was widely available at the time, then art quilts in which she pushed the boundaries of tradition, influenced by pioneers in that field like Michael James and Nancy Crow. Ultimately, she was inspired to go back to school to earn degrees, first in education (1979) then, while raising two children—Alice, born in 1986, and Jack, born in 1988—in surface design (2000), which segued into her teaching position.

"The first quilt making in the United Kingdom was done not very far from here in County Durham," Mandy tells me as she points out the south-facing window of her studio toward the Tyne and Wear Valleys and the hills of the North Pennines. "When I started collecting local quilts after I left teaching, I started to feel grounded in this region for the first time." Rather than gathering refined showpieces, which weren't common in this part of England, Mandy was collecting utilitarian textiles, many of them patchworks filled with layers of either worn-out quilts from an earlier time or more randomly stitched-together pieces of repurposed fabric, whatever was available to create warmth—bits of old clothing, blankets, curtains.

Mandy compares her unpicking of these quilts to an archaeological dig, as the process reveals layers of clues about the makers' lives and temperaments as well as the domestic textiles of the period. "Stitching is a sort of handwriting," Mandy explains. Some quilts, she finds, are difficult to unpick because the maker, seemingly a perfectionist, made every stitch tiny and precise, even in areas that would never be seen, while others come apart easily thanks to the larger, more haphazard work of perhaps a more laid-back or just busier maker. "I like the connection I feel with the original maker, whom I actually know nothing about." Wear, tear, stains, imperfections—Mandy celebrates and contemplates the very details that compel many others to deem these pieces worthless.

Mandy's studio is brimming with finished works and works in progress. Her most commercial pieces are her textile collages, like the ones she was teaching us to make at Chateau Dumas, and her animal portraits. On the walls is clothing—skirts, a girl's dress, a boy's jacket—made out of or refashioned with remnants of old quilts or other forms of needlework, sometimes embellished with new embroidery. There are also all sorts of cloth books, bound in imaginative ways, such as with buttons, with more fabric, or into leather wallets. And there are hints of darker artistic expressions—for example, *Memento Mori*, part of a multiyear body of work and eventually a solo exhibition inspired by the epitaphs on the gravestones in the Victorian cemetery next to her garden allotment.

"I like to sell what I make, but I do put aside a period every year, usually the beginning of December to mid-February, to just develop work for myself," Mandy explains. Often, the discoveries she makes

Mandy became interested in men's wallets while working on a series of multimedia artworks about death and cemeteries. Today she uses wallets as a form of binding for cloth books. "Old-fashioned wallets are like a leather book form," Mandy explains. "I like how you can open and close them and how you have to turn the pages or open up the flaps to find things within." Often, she says, pockets of old wallets will hold a lone, long-forgotten stamp or receipt, a small hint of the original owner's life; Mandy leaves these mementos deep inside for those who handle the wallets now to discover on their own.

during those weeks, filled with drawing, reading, experimentation, and culling, lead to exhibitions or new classes. That is how the work for her *Worn* exhibition began. And it instigated, a few years later, an investigation and reinterpretation of her own mother's cross-stitch.

"My mother did cross-stitch all her life. She would sit in a chair with a magnifier around her neck and lights behind and next to her. She didn't have ideas of her own and always followed somebody else's pattern. I think I despised her a bit for that," Mandy admits. In response, Mandy's cross-stitch is freeform, void of the grids, even-weave fabric, and patterns on which her mother's cross-stitch depended. "I'm not even worried about direction," Mandy adds. "I'm seeing if I can use her patterns in a more creative way on top of my collage work. I think I may be trying to defy her." Mandy is also using cross-stitch to develop work inspired by drawings by her daughter, Alice, a professional illustrator based in London of

whom she is understandably proud and with whom she confers regularly. In an interview with the two on TextileArtist.org on the occasion of the publication of *Textile Collage* by Mandy and *An Animal ABC* by Alice, Mandy hinted, "We do critique each other's work, but neither of us takes criticism easily and so it can lead to arguments! However, we really respect each other's opinions and it hurts because it really counts what the other says."

"There are complicated relationships among the women in our family," Mandy tells me, "that I'm trying to work out through my textiles." Of course, Mandy is not the first mother or daughter to attempt to disentangle her emotions and stitch her stories into cloth. She is, in fact, carrying on an age-old tradition. Her creative expression—made with and in response to cloth work that came before hers—stands as a testament to the enduring complexity, beauty, and value of generations of women's lives.

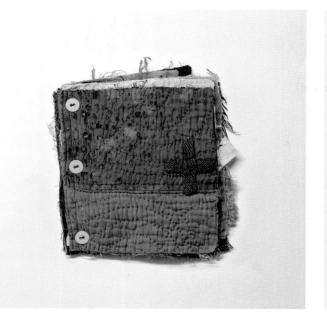

Inspired by French American artist Louise Bourgeois's fabric works, Mandy began making her own textile books. This one, called *Cross Patch*, bound with buttons, contains pieces of all eight layers of the single original quilt (the first one she ever unpicked) from which she harvested the fabric. It is paginated according to the order in which the fabrics were positioned in the quilt. Each page reveals a different small collage with its own unique composition.

DOLORES SWIFT

New Moon

IN JULY 2016, Dolores Swift signed a lease to rent a storefront and studio on Trafalgar Street, near the train station in Brighton, an artsy seaside resort town on England's south coast, an hour's train ride from London and four hours from where she grew up in Lancashire. Although eager to move in, she waited a few days before starting the transition. She loved the jewel-box space, tidily divided among three floors and a basement in a nineteenth-century building. And she was excited to do some decorating and organizing before opening to the public, but she was also occupied with a house-painting gig—and, admittedly, a bit nervous. Dolores had been designing, making, and selling her leather bags since the early 2000s, but never before had she worked and sold full-time in a dedicated venue all her own. A single mother, she'd earned a living in a variety of ways over the years—painting interiors and designing, making, and wholesaling notecards, bags, and linen breastfeeding clothing to boutiques among them. She signed the lease for her shop, called Neoma, just as her daughter, Jamela, was beginning her first year at university. *Neoma* means "new moon" in Greek—and is Jamela's middle name.

"This is my first space of my own, where I have full responsibility and full control," Dolores tells me when I visit her at Neoma on a sunny spring day. "Being here has taken feeling established to a new level."

Dolores got over her initial moving jitters quickly, and her "new moon" endeavor took off from there. She painted the first-floor woodwork and ceiling a very specific blue-black color, Farrow & Ball No. 31 Railings, to frame the lightly polished plaster walls and worn wooden floor; brought in some furnishings (mostly mix-and-match vintage pieces from her home); and collaborated with a carpenter to design, build, and install plywood shelves held in place with caramel-colored leather strapping. Although she planned to do most of the bag making in a private area on the second floor, she placed her sewing machine in front of the window of the street-level retail space, where the light is brightest and where passersby are able to witness part of her process.

"I started making bags on my living room floor," Dolores says. "And now my studio looks like my living room." This was all part of her plan to create a friendly environment where she would feel comfortable working and could easily connect with customers and others who stop by. That personal connection is an important part of the draw for Dolores. "I don't know if I'd be making bags if I didn't have somebody to make them for," she explains.

TOP

In addition to the leather bags that are a constant at the shop, Dolores sells other items she makes when she feels inspired. Here you can see hot water bottle covers sewn out of boiled wool, and some cushions she covered with vintage army blankets. "I have always been quite confident when it comes to making things with my hands," she says.

BOTTOM

Neoma is in an ideal location, just a short walk from the seaside as well as the Brighton train station.

> "I'm not saving anyone's life, but what I'm doing makes people happy, and that feels important."

The first time I see Dolores's work, I am instantly struck by her flair for blending organic forms and utilitarian function in a simple, modern way. She explains that her inspiration often comes from nature as well as everyday packaging (for example, a box or a paper lunch bag), quite ordinary items that she imagines will take on a completely different identity in leather. Her interest in packaging was piqued when she was studying graphic design in college. She never completed her degree, but that training helps her now. Her knack for sewing, and making things in general, is intrinsic. "I have always been a natural on a sewing machine," she says. "In home economics class in school, we sewed very simple things like aprons and stuffed toys. My friends would be struggling, but for me it came easily." Dolores was adopted as a toddler by her mother, a social worker, and her father, a history teacher. It was interesting but not surprising to her when she found out, at age twenty-five, that her birth mother was

a seamstress. "It must be in the genes," Dolores surmises.

On the day I visit, she decides to make a new version of her Shopper, a roll-top bag originally inspired by a potato sack. On the walls around us are similarly timeless designs, including the Neoma Classic Curve, a slender rectangular clutch with a curved top outlining a small oval opening for the hand (an adaptation of the very first bag she made back in 2000) and the Artist Bag, suggestive of a classic tool pouch: a shallower rectangle with inside pockets, a deep flap, and two narrow straps spaced about a third of the way in from each end. But Dolores's main business is custom, or bespoke, bags—sometimes new iterations of styles on display, and sometimes original ideas dreamed up in collaboration with her customers.

"I see so much lovely leather," Dolores explains—her weekly sourcing trip to London is sacred to her—"and when customers come in, I tell them they can have the bags they see in different colors or types of leather or with different straps, whatever. People love having bags made to order, and it is what I love, too, because it's so personal and creative."

It also suits Dolores's preferred workflow, which is to move fluidly from one idea to the next rather than according to a rigid schedule or prescriptive formula. Back when she was selling wholesale to boutiques, the requirement that she design six to twelve months ahead discomfited her, as did the expectation that she would

THIS PAGE

Dolores was inspired to make this rectangular Artist's Bag by her friend ceramicist Sarah Jerath (see page 48). The triangular bag is the Neoma Classic, the very first bag Dolores designed back in 2000.

OPPOSITE, TOP

When Dolores spotted this medal sitting on a shelf while moving in, she took it as a sign of good luck. Today she keeps it on the same shelf where she originally found it.

OPPOSITE, BOTTOM

Leather in Dolores's second-floor private work area, waiting to be transformed.

pay heed to fashion trends. "I don't follow fashion or want to tell my customers what they should be wearing this season," she explains. "I work very organically, and I make bags for people to keep and use for a long time." At her shop she'll even repair bags she didn't design, because it's better for the environment than tossing and replacing them—a significant contrast to some companies these days that seem to rely on changing trends or breakage or wear as a way to ensure future sales.

On one of Dolores's first days moving into the shop, she spotted a dusty coin on a shelf next to the second-floor hearth, a commemorative depicting an angelic-looking woman that Dolores took to be a sign of good luck. Upon further research, she discovered that the coin depicts the story of "La Laitière et le Pot au Lait," seventeenth-century French poet Jean de La Fontaine's retelling of an ancient fable about a milkmaid who, on her way to market, gets so lost in daydreams about how she will spend her profit that she drops her pail and spills the milk. It is a cautionary tale—believed to be the origin of the expression "Don't count your chickens before they hatch"—that seems well suited for a new business owner.

Dolores concedes that sometimes the economics of running Neoma can be stressful. "Making isn't always relaxing," she says. "I'm always thinking, 'I need this to sell so I can pay for that leather or because the rent is due.' It's unfortunate that this is the way it is, but that's business." Still, she says, "I'm very lucky to be in the position I'm in, to be a creator, and I'm happy to be able to work in a way that is true to who I am. I'm not saving anyone's life, but what I'm doing makes people happy, and that feels important. I am not going anywhere for a long time."

To start making a new iteration of her Shopper bag, Dolores laid out on her wooden worktable the silver leather she had purchased in London a few weeks earlier, inspected it carefully in order to ascertain how to use it most efficiently and take advantage of its most beautiful markings, then began following a rough sketch she'd drafted years back. "When I make a bag, I take it apart in my head, put that onto paper, and translate that into a pattern. It comes quite naturally to me." Just as Dolores finished making the silver Shopper and was happily rolling the top up and down to show me its sculptural quality and how it can be worn either way, her daughter arrived, so we asked her to model it for us.

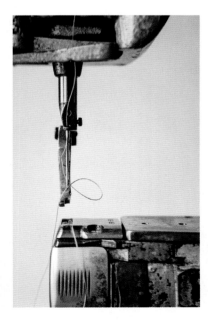

THIS PAGE

Dolores inspects a beautiful piece of rich brown leather she purchased during one of her weekly shopping trips to London. Sometimes it is the leather that dictates what the finished piece will become, and until Dolores begins working on it, she doesn't quite know how it will turn out. During my visit, she taught me how to make the very simple hand-stitched bag below.

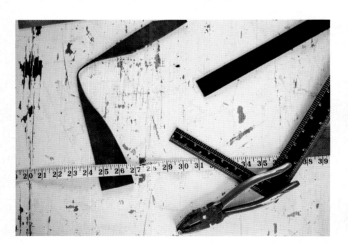

Saying
Thank You

OPPOSITE

A close-up of one of Windy Chien's works from her Diamond Ring series. Each piece is composed of plywood rings assembled in a diamond formation with a single very long rope hitched along a unique path. For me, this beautiful piece mirrors the ins and outs of my journey writing this book, a journey I never could have undertaken without the help of the many generous people who made time to assist me.

CREATING THIS BOOK has been a passion-filled, laborious, and at times overwhelming process. I could never have done it without the support of family, friends, and colleagues—or, of course, without the trust and generosity of the inspiring makers featured on these pages. I am deeply grateful to all of them.

Liana Allday, a friend and former coworker, was the first person with whom I shared my thoughts on writing a new book, and her encouragement was unwavering from start to finish. Right away, she urged me to pick up a copy of *Cooked: A Natural History of Transformation* by Michael Pollan, understanding how Pollan's ideas about cooking—and its relationship to nature, health, tradition, ritual, self-reliance, community, the rhythms of everyday life, and consumerism—directly related to my premise. Later, when I faced a bout of insecurity over the scope of the work I had taken on, Liana came through again with a pep talk and by arranging for a copy of *Big Magic: Creative Living Beyond Fear* by Elizabeth Gilbert to land on my doorstep. Thanks, Liana, for always being there for me—with kindness, wise words, and literary backup.

Artist and author Kaffe Fassett was another early supporter of my concept. I met Kaffe on a knitting retreat in the Shetland Islands in the 1990s, and many years later, I had the honor of editing some of his books, including his autobiography, *Dreaming in Color*. Kaffe recommended that I listen to Grayson Perry's Reith lectures on the BBC (Perry's commentary on how we think about and experience art and other forms of making in today's consumer-oriented culture is astute and thought-provoking), and then he kept up his cheerleading in his annual holiday cards and email correspondence in between. Kaffe, had you been at home in England rather than on the other side of the world when I was there doing research and photography for this book, I would have asked you to be part of it. You are an inspiration to me and countless others.

Suzan Mischer and I have been close friends ever since we worked together on her book, *Greetings from Knit Café*. We have spent countless hours talking, laughing, confiding in each other, and making things together. At the same time that I decided to write *Making a Life*, she began pursuing an art degree at the Rhode Island School of Design. As I type this, she is most likely in the textile lab at RISD, doing amazing work as she completes her classes. Suzan, your support has been integral to my completing this project and to my finding my way in life in general.

Throughout this process, I was reminded again and again how generous people tend to be when you simply reveal what you need.

Early on, my friend the clever, enthusiastic creator Hannah Rogge came to my home for what she thought would be a weekend reprieve from city living and helped me organize my work—and my headspace—for the challenges that lay

ahead; artist Sabrina Gschwandtner shared her perspective on the DIY renaissance and gave me lots of leads and a valuable reading list; curator, writer, and historian Glenn Adamson shared his wisdom about "art" versus "craft" in the garden of the Cooper Hewitt museum; and Abby Glassenberg of the *While She Naps* podcast and the Craft Industry Alliance encouraged me in general—and introduced me to a specific computer application that allowed me to record Skype and Facetime calls, a seemingly small detail that was a huge help and an important stepping-stone. Katharine Daugherty accepted my application for a creative residency at Drop Forge & Tool in Hudson, New York, so I could focus and dig in. Betsan Corkhill, author of *Knit for Health & Wellness*, talked to me about her research. Eric Mindling, author of *Fire and Clay: The Art of Oaxacan Pottery*, helped me process my joyous travels to the Mexican state to which I am eager to return. *Uppercase* magazine publisher Janine Vangool invited me to track my journey researching and writing in the Beginnings column of her magazine (the essays I wrote appear in Issues 30 through 40). And when I needed some support getting back into the writing groove, author, editor, and friend Betty Christiansen was there to nudge me forward.

Julie Weisenberger of Cocoknits introduced me to Lizzie Hulme, who welcomed me at Chateau Dumas; and Ali DeJohn, founder of the Makerie, invited me to attend the Sweet Paul Makerie. While there, I met Elsa Mora, the first person I asked to be a part of this book, and Michelle Kohanzo, who stunned

me with an invitation to join her on a trip to India. At the Makerie, I also met many passionate creatives who generously shared their thoughts in response to my query "Why is making by hand important to you?" Their enthusiasm and interest in what I was planning gave me the boost I needed to go forward boldly. Soon after, I posed the same question to a larger community of makers via social media, and Lauren Chang kindly offered to help me organize and analyze the many heartfelt and moving responses I received. Despite his busy schedule, master builder Bobby Convertino said yes when I asked him to teach me how to make a bed swing for my porch, then said yes again when I wanted to rewire a chandelier. Liza Prior Lucy gave me my first lessons in patchwork and quilting during a fun weekend at her house—and lent me years' worth of her *Selvedge* magazines to pore over.

Although I used to meet up with Susan Cropper many years ago at National Needlework Association conventions, we had never actually spent time together outside of a convention hall—until I contacted her to ask her for some advice about a trip to England for research. At that point, she immediately offered her help— and accommodations at her London flat.

Susan owns Loop London, which is now one of my favorite yarn shops in the world. I have included photos of Susan and Loop (opposite) because how could I not? I was so enchanted by her treasure chest of a boutique on Camden Passage in Islington that I couldn't imagine not recording it. While in London, I also had the pleasure of meeting Polly Leonard, founder of the beautiful *Selvedge*, at her office and

Susan Cropper's help organizing my trip to England—with a side trip to Paris—was invaluable. Spending time at her shop, Loop London, was creatively invigorating and relaxing at the same time. So much beauty in one place!

shop, where we talked about her mission to support makers and their work and to promote textile knowledge, and also about our cultures' reckless "love of stuff."

Photographer Rinne Allen signed on to this project early, believing in my mission before I knew exactly who, what, or where we would be photographing. We met in person for the first time on our first shoot—in Berea, Kentucky. Over the course of the next year, we spent many days and nights traveling together, getting to know each other and learning how to collaborate effectively. Her elegant, sensitive photographs are integral to this book, and I am forever grateful to her for her commitment to excellence and for her patience during the long process.

I must also thank Laurence Mouton and Tiina Tahvanainen, who took the photographs at Chateau Dumas and on Åland, respectively.

Traveling so extensively meant sleeping in a lot of different beds—in homes, hotels, and Airbnbs. I must thank Jenny Hallengren, who put me up in Stockholm in the days before I set sail for Åland; my brother, Jeff Falick, and sister-in-law, Gina Telcocci, who put Rinne and me up in Oakland; Mary Jane Mucklestone and Susan Osberg and Winston Roeth, who

welcomed me into their homes in Maine; Martha Hopkins and John Fulmer, who lent me a room (and a car!) in Austin; and Heather Ross, who invited me to escape with her to beautiful Merriewold to write.

I also wrote at the Penland School of Craft during their winter residency. Surrounded by makers in the books studio, I found a new way to approach the inevitable lulls in ideas and energy that my process involves. Whenever I felt tired or stuck, I would switch to either papercutting or painting (borrowing supplies from my generous studio mates—paper-cutter Annie Howe and multimedia artist Jon Verney), letting my mind rest and my hand follow whatever path the blade or paintbrush led me down. By allowing my creativity to flow freely and wordlessly, without any expectations of a particular result, I was able to play and, in turn, refresh myself. The discovery of this creative portal continues to serve me to this day, as does my (admittedly on-again, off-again but still meaningful and helpful) meditation practice. While writing this book, I regularly turned to Oprah Winfrey and Deepak Chopra's guided meditation series as well as to Giovanni Dienstmann's clear, powerful writings on meditation and peace of mind on LiveandDare.com.

OPPOSITE, LEFT

Photographer Rinne Allen at work during Camp Heavy Metal in Austin, Texas (see page 158).

OPPOSITE, RIGHT

Selvedge magazine founder Polly Leonard and me sharing our enthusiasm for textiles in her London office.

My first two books, *Knitting in America* and *Kids Knitting*, were published by Artisan in 1996 and 1998, respectively, and I am pleased to be back to my first home as an author.

Although Artisan has grown and changed a lot over these many years, it maintains the commitment to quality that drew me there in the first place. Publisher Lia Ronnen made me feel comfortable and valued. Editor Bridget Monroe Itkin was patient, supportive, and wise throughout all the ups and downs, decisions, researching, picture-puzzling, and wordsmithing that making a book entails. After being an editor myself for so many years, it felt good to be on the other side of the equation and in such competent hands. I was lucky enough to work with the extraordinary creative director Michelle Ishay-Cohen at another publishing house, and I was thrilled to be on a mission together again at Artisan. Graphic designer Nina Simoneaux immediately connected with the subject matter, developing, with Michelle, an elegant design language to frame the words and images and then, with great care, composing what you see on each and every page. Michelle and Nina also worked with lettering artist June Park, who found a poetic way to communicate the themes of each chapter with simple pencil strokes. Production editor Sibylle Kazeroid and her team worked with impressive rigor and precision. Production director Nancy Murray and the publicity and marketing team led by Allison McGeehon took great care every step of the way, reassuring me that the attention to detail that is so important to me and that is sometimes sacrificed in these fast-paced times lives on at Artisan.

This book is dedicated to my family because they have always believed in me and supported me, even when I have chosen uncertain and unconventional paths. While I was growing up, my father, Howard Falick, made a living teaching architecture and engineering but loved working with his hands and made doing so a priority, seemingly gifted at everything he set his mind to: drawing, painting, landscaping, gardening, sculpture, ceramics. He was also a great appreciator of the handwork of others and always encouraged my brother and me to respect fine workmanship and aesthetics. My mother, Diana Falick, sewed many of my clothes when I was very young and also altered clothing for others in our community to make extra money until she established her career as first a high school history and psychology teacher and then a psychotherapist. Since then, she has joined me in many handmaking adventures, from sewing to knitting to shoemaking, and has become a devoted oil painter. Thank you, Mom and Dad, for raising me to understand the value and pleasure of making by hand and also for encouraging me to be curious.

In a way, I started writing *Making a Life* for my son, Ben Whipple, who for years kept asking me when I was going to write another book. Here you go, Ben. Thank you for believing in my potential with the same kind of intensity with which I believe in yours.

Finally, I must thank my husband, Chris Whipple, who has supported my wanderlust and independence for the last three decades—and counting. *Je t'aime.*

MELANIE FALICK is an independent writer, editor, and creative consultant—and a lifelong maker. Formerly the publishing director of STC Craft / Melanie Falick Books, an imprint of Abrams, and the editor in chief of *Interweave Knits* magazine, she is also the author of *Knitting in America*, *Kids Knitting*, and *Weekend Knitting*, as well as several other titles. Find her on Instagram @melaniefalick and at melaniefalick.com.